Updated and Expanded

ROADSIDE
BASEBALL

The Locations of America's Baseball Landmarks
Second Edition

Chris Epting

Foreword by Joe Buck

D0925834

Published by:

Santa Monica Press LLC
P.O. Box 1076
Santa Monica, CA 90406-1076
1-800-784-9553
www.santamonicapress.com
books@santamonicapress.com

Printed in the United States

Santa Monica Press books are available at special quantity discounts when purchased in bulk by corporations, organizations, or groups. Please call our Special Sales department at 1-800-784-9553.

ISBN-13 9781595800411

LIBRARY OF CONGRESS CATALOGING-IN-PUBLICATION DATA

Epting, Chris, 1961-
  Roadside baseball : the locations of America's baseball landmarks / by Chris Epting ; foreword by Joe Buck.— 2nd ed.
    p. cm.
  ISBN 978-1-59580-041-1
  1. Basebal—United States. 2. Historic sites—United States—Guidebooks. I. Title.
  GV863.A1.E68 2009
  796.3570973—dc22

                        2009002306

Cover and interior design and production by Future Studio

PHOTO CREDITS

All photos appear courtesy of the Sporting News Archives unless noted below:

P. 9 (*bottom*): Jean Epting; pp. 7 (*top*), 8, 15, 17, 22, 25, 26, 52, 60, 61, 62, 63 (*right*), 65, 67, 70, 77, 82, 89, 92, 100, 114, 159, 177, 205, 220, 225 (*bottom*), 234 (*top*), 246, 247, 248, 250, 255, 256, 258, 259, 264, 266, 267, 286: author's collection; p. 11 (*top*): Fred Willard; p. 12, 163: Jim Lytle; p. 20: Cal Ripken Museum; pp. 34, 36, 37, 51, 69: David McAleer; p. 45 (*bottom*): Dennis LeBeau; p. 97: William Gill; p. 121: Peter McGovern Little League Museum; p. 128 (*bottom*): Virginia Sports Hall of Fame and Museum; p. 132 (*top*): Alabama Sports Hall of Fame; p. 133 (*top*), 109: David Brewer; p. 136: Arkansas Travelers; pp. 141 (*top*), 165, 173 (*bottom*): Eric and Wendy Pastore/www .digitalballparks.com.; p. 148: Charleston River Dogs; p. 150 (*top*): Linda Walden; p. 151: Ed Jackson; p. 164 (*bottom*): Tony Farlow; p. 167 (*bottom*): John Byrne/Fuquay Mineral Spring Inn & Garden; p. 169 (*bottom*): Harriet Woodard; p. 173: ©2003 by Grand Slam Enterprises, Inc., appeared in baseballparks.com website. Used by permission of photographer Joe Mock and Grand Slam Enterprises; pp. 192, 222, 276 (*top*), 281: David Stalker; p. 210: Courtesy Billy Sunday Historic Site Museum, Winona Lake, Indiana; p. 226: Stew Thornley; pp. 239, 245 (*bottom*), 246, 247: Joan M. Thomas/Barbara Sheinbein.

Back cover photograph: Charlie Epting

Contents

Dedication

The book was originally dedicated to my "home team": wife, Jean; son, Charlie; and daughter, Claire. Also to Richard "Dick" Davis of Chanute, Kansas. Dick's tremendous heart and dedication toward recognizing and establishing the historic sites in Humboldt, Kansas, for Walter Johnson and George Sweatt only begin to tell the story. His passion for the history and glory of the game is matched only by his courage and sparkling optimism, and it is because of people like Dick (and his wife, Gloria) that a book like this can exist in the first place. Thank you, my friend. The game is better for having you here.

It was also dedicated to the real MVPs, the men and women of the United States military, whose bravery and unselfish dedication during these tumultuous times make it possible for the rest of us to do simple things like go out to the ballpark for a baseball game. Their hands were full in 2003 when this book first came out, and as we know, many challenges still exist today. So thanks as always to the troops.

I'd like to add a dedication with this new edition. To my friend Anthony D'Ambrosio, a New York Mets diehard whose friendship and tireless support of books like this is much appreciated. Love from all of us "Eppys," Anthony.

Acknowledgments

Eternal thanks to my family, including my wife and children, my mom, sisters Margaret and Lee, Ciro, Luca, Billy and Linda. Also to the memory of my late grandmother, Margaret Gallo, and my dad, Lawrence Epting.

I'd especially like to thank the team at The Sporting News, who originally published this book: Joe Hoppel, Ron Smith, Bob Parajon, Christen Sager, Pam Speh, Vern Kasal, Steve Romer and Steve Meyerhoff for their interest, encouragement and consummate teamwork. You guys were simply awesome; it's a privilege to work with you.

To my friends and family who share the passion of baseball, both along the side of the road and in the ballpark: Jack Riley, Thom Sharp, Fred Willard, David McAleer, Gabe Miller, Ronnie Schell, Smitty, John Mungo, Bryant Lewis, Ed Monette, Brian Nicalek and Charlie.

To Joe Buck, Ken Burns, Joe Garagiola, Bill "Spaceman" Lee and Jim Bouton for their kind and thoughtful words that appear in this book.

To SABR (Society for American Baseball Research), Bob Bluthhardt, Joe Mock, David Burkett, and Terry Cannon (founder of The Baseball Reliquary) for their research and dedication to the game's history. To Joan M. Thomas, Barbara Sheinbein and their SABR team members for the terrific work they've done in the placement of ballpark markers.

To Gail and Dave Vize, our Angels game "neighbors."

To the entire Hampton Hotel Save-A-Landmark team.

To everyone who was so generous with their time, information, resources and stories, particularly John Outland, Henry Thomas (author of the exceptional *Walter Johnson: Baseball's Big Train*), Lee Gibbs, Stew Thornley, Joe Mock, David Brewer, Milton Babb, Terry Hembree, Virgie Ott, William Gill, David Brewer, Terry Stembridge, Boyce Cox, Chuck Foertmeyer, Dennis LeBeau and Dr. Linda Walden.

And to Jeffrey Goldman at Santa Monica Press for deciding to publish the second edition of this book. Thanks, my friend. Also, Brittany Yudkowsky at Santa Monica Press provided exceptional editorial skills, and Amy Inouye stepped up with her usual terrific design talents.

And to you, the reader, for holding this book in your hands right now. Thank you for being a part of this.

Foreword

by Joe Buck

I don't care if you consider yourself the foremost authority on the history of the game, this book can't help but put a smile on your face. It put one on mine because not only are the pages filled with information that I thought I knew but really didn't, but also stories of which I was totally unaware and now am glad I know. The real treat, however, is that each piece is short, to the point, and stated in a way that I have a chance of remembering impressive and important facts should I find myself at a cocktail party with, say, George Will or Bob Costas. I guess I am known as a baseball guy, but after reading through an advanced copy of this gem, I realize I have been living a lie. I dare even the most diehard baseball fan to pick up this book and not learn something from any random page.

What Chris Epting has done here is put together a travel guide filled with landmarks around the country and beyond, added tidbits of fascinating information about the game and those who played it, and given you a one-stop shop to read through at home or take with you as you journey far and wide learning about the game we all love. What makes this book special to me is the focus on happenings away from the famous stadiums we all know and remember. Yes, they are detailed in the book as well, but what I love are the stories that remind us all that these players were just men making a living doing what they loved. They were people who had lives away from box scores and cheering crowds, with stories that are as legendary and noteworthy as the accomplishments that you can find in an encyclopedia. Whether it's Hubert's Flea Market, where Grover Cleveland Alexander entertained after giving up baseball, or it's Dyersville, Iowa, where *Field of Dreams* was filmed, there is so much detail about what happened and happens on the periphery of the game. From hometown plaques dedicated to the birthplace of local legends to burial sites, and all the stories in between, there is information contained here that makes the game come to life in a very unique way.

Baseball is a very personal game. Because of my privileged youth growing up as Jack Buck's son, I can track the years of my childhood along the recent timeline of the St. Louis Cardinals' franchise. I was born in 1969 and missed not only a golden age in the history of the game, but specifically the Cardinals' organization. Timing is everything, and growing up in the '70s in St. Louis meant idolizing Gibson, Brock and Simmons as individuals, but as a team there wasn't much about which to cheer. If Chris Epting were to detail my travels with my father in this book, the specifics of our trips that would warm my heart would be the spots we would retreat to after the games. If we were in Los Angeles, a trip to Hollywood Park to place bets alongside Walter Matthau would make the itinerary. In San Francisco, it was always a day at Candlestick, golf at the Olympic Club, and a late dinner at Lefty O'Doul's restaurant and bar named after a San Francisco baseball legend. In Chicago, in the later years, it was Wrigley and a dinner at Harry Caray's. In New York, just about when the plane would land, there woud be tales of late nights at Toot Shore's, where press and athletes came together for food, drink, stories and other nighttime activities (to put it mildly). These stories and the people around the game who would join us from time to time would probably entertain more people than you think. Those days on the road and the different things we did all related in a way to the game of baseball. These cherished times in my childhood are exactly why I picked the profession I did. As fun as the games and the thrilling moments that come with them are, it's the life around it and the people and personalities that make it all so much fun.

The beauty here is that you don't have to be a Hall of Fame announcer's son to have baseball memories that will always be a part of you. Whether it is a recollection of the first time you walked into Crosley Field

Buck grew up idolizing Gibson and Brock (left and right ends), while his father, Jack, broadcast games involving Musial and Schoendienst.

for a Reds game, or where you were when Mazeroski hit the Series-clinching home run at Forbes Field to beat the Yanks in 1960, now you have a guide to trigger those stories and addresses to tell you exactly where they happened. Maybe more important than that is that all the stories that have been handed down from one generation to another, from grandpa to grandson, mother to daughter now can come to life a little easier with this guide to tell where these pieces of baseball and American history actually took place. I believe people in my generation would be shocked to learn how close Yankee Stadium and the Polo Grounds were to each other. Any baseball fan would be interested to see the spot in Boston where the Chicago players planned the "Black Sox" scheme of 1919. Or to know that a banyan tree that Babe Ruth planted in Hilo, Hawaii, in the 1930s is still thriving and can be visited thanks to this book. I cannot think of a better way to learn the history of this great game.

And, remember, if you do use this book as a travel guide and you are going east to west, those bugs on the grill of your car will need to be washed off. Don't worry, this book will tell you exactly where Lenny Dykstra's car wash is in Simi Valley. Just don't get the tobacco-scented air freshener; it's not a big hit on dates.

Introduction

"It breaks your heart. It is designed to break your heart. The game begins in the spring, when everything else begins again, and it blossoms in the summer, filling the afternoons and evenings, and then as soon as the chill rains come, it stops and leaves you to face the fall." —A. Bartlett Giamatti

Completing this book has satisfied a journey for me that began long ago. The history of baseball has been a wonderful tonic for me, as much then as it is now. And a lot of that pleasure has been derived from studying the old structures, the ballparks. I remember pitching in Little League, looking off at our old bleachers at the field and thinking, "This is just like playing in the old Polo Grounds . . . or League Park in Cleveland!" Taking my son to the same field years later and watching him run those bases crystallized why I love baseball so much. It's something we hand down to our juniors as readily as we do the golden rule. It's the continuum of the ages. One ball, two mitts and all of a sudden life's lessons become easier to explain. Bonds are forged, and we are so much richer for the simple act of having a catch.

Author's son, Charlie, places his hands inside Reggie Jackson's handprints at Edison International.

I think the seeds for this book were planted when I was about 11 years old. Looking through a baseball picture book, I remember seeing the famous Charles Conlon photograph of Ty Cobb sliding hard into Jimmy Austin at third base. The caption said the picture had been snapped at Hilltop Park in New York. Though we lived in New York and I was a huge baseball fan, I had never heard of the stadium. The Polo Grounds, torn down in the early '60s when I was about three, I'd heard of. Ebbets Field, where my mom and many relatives had grown up seeing ball games, I was well aware of. But not Hilltop.

After some more reading, I learned that this was the original home of the Yankees and had been torn down many years earlier. And I became intrigued. If I wanted to go stand in that spot where the picture was taken, to sense what it might have been like there so many years ago, would it be possible? If the ballpark was gone, what stood there now, if anything? I managed to uncover that Columbia Presbyterian Hospital had been built there in the stadium's place, but that was all I knew. As for where the exact site was, well, some day I knew I had to go investigate to see if I could stand where that wonderful baseball image had been captured. I got to thinking about other famous baseball images: Willie Mays's famous catch at the Polo Grounds, Jackie Robinson stealing home at Ebbets and so on.

Those ancient photos that I loved to study . . . what occupied those places now?

And what about all of the great ballparks that all of a sudden weren't around anymore? I remember being in Pennsylvania in the early 1970s when the abandoned Connie Mack Stadium caught fire. It stung to watch the local news reports. I remember when Forbes Field was torn down. And I felt then as I do now; that the ground of those ballparks was sacred, and should at least be identified. Put up a building if you must, create another parking lot if you have to, but please, let people know what happened there. Maybe even try to preserve a shred or two of what once stood. Make it known that there was once a field here, with bright green grass and fresh dirt. Where dreams came true and where hearts were broken. So if a father wanted to bring his child to a spot where he saw Roberto Clemente play, it will be easy.

Where the Giants (and the Yankees and the Mets) once roamed. Today the site of the Polo Grounds Towers.

So if two old-timers want to go re-create Enos Slaughter's frantic World Series run from first base, maybe they'll be able to. So if a kid wants to stand where one of his favorite pictures was taken, he'll be able to locate the spot.

Today, more and more it seems, inspired efforts have been undertaken all over the country to recognize baseball history. In both huge cities and small towns, museums, plaques, signs, markers and memorials are popping up more than ever. When I did make it to the site of Hilltop Park years later, I was thrilled to find a plaque in the shape of home plate had been placed near where the original one sat. So finally, I could map

Forbes Field, Pittsburgh, shortly before the wrecking ball.

the spot of that Charles Conlon photo. It gave me peace of mind, and an idea
. . . why not try and document all of these sites?

Hence, this book.

Some places have not been marked yet, but hopefully they will be
soon. (Maybe after someone reads about them in this book.) In addition to
the stadium sites, over the years I also became interested in other sites that
make up the fabric of the game's history. Birthplaces . . . museums . . . statues
. . . forgotten fields . . . final resting places. They all play a part in helping to
define why baseball remains our national pastime, and so they are all a part
of *Roadside Baseball.*

And while this book is about history, it is also about the emotions en-
countered on the quest for baseball's
past—the love, passion, dreams, courage, glory and pain found in places
like a school in Baltimore, where
Babe Ruth first picked up a mitt . . .
where he hit his first home run . . .
and his last.

From a hotel lobby where
Lou Gehrig told Yankee manager Joe
McCarthy that he was pulling himself
from the lineup later that day to the
spot where Jackie Robinson first took
the field, righting decades of terrible
wrong, to where Hans Lobert raced a
horse around the bases.

**Proof that you can go home again—home
plate at Hilltop Park, New York.**

From hometowns where locals lovingly erect signs for Walter Johnson, Tris Speaker, Grover Cleveland Alexander and others, and build shrines in their honor, to vacant lots where once there was the carnival smell of hot dogs, beer and cigars.

This is about small towns with big hearts that dedicate plaques and parks and monuments to their local heroes.

This is about playing catch on a diamond where Satchel Paige, Buck O'Neil and Josh Gibson once performed their magic.

This plaque marking the birthplace of "Cool Papa" Bell is in tiny Starkville, Mississippi.

Standing where Ruth, Williams, Speaker, Hornsby, Maris, Mantle and Musial waited for their pitch.

Where ghosts still might play, and where, in the dust and in the wind, you still might swear you can hear the distant crack of a bat and the faint echoes of a crowd.

This is about finding our own personal fields of dreams and reconnecting with the innocence of oiling our glove . . . keeping score with a #2 pencil . . . and lying awake at night, dreaming about some day playing in a Game 7.

This is about roadside baseball. So get ready to discover the heart and soul of baseball . . . ready? Let's hit the road.

—Chris Epting

The author (center) with his daughter, Claire (left), and son, Charlie (right), at the 2008 Red Sox-Dodgers contest that saw baseball return for one game to the Los Angeles Memorial Coliseum.

Introduction
to the Second Edition

"The field was even greener than my boy's mind had pictured it. In later years, friends of ours visited Ireland and said the grass there was plenty green all right, but that not even the Emerald Isle itself was as green as the grass that grew in Ebbets Field."   —Duke Snider

Five years ago, when this book was first published, who would have thought that the marquee names of the day—Mark McGwire, Barry Bonds, Sammy Sosa, Roger Clemens and Alex Rodriguez (among others)—would become so tarnished? That steroids would become such a prevailing issue in the game that congressional hearings would be held and that still so much ugly mystery would remain around this insidious issue? When I started seeing the mid-90s era through today being referred to as the "Steroids era," I thought of all the kids (including my own) who, all of a sudden, had their era snatched away by a thoughtless bunch of cheaters. Thank goodness they still had the Tony Gwynns and Cal Ripkens of the world, along with other players of character, to help ease the sting. Still, what a mess some of the game's best have left.

The stark reality of the "Steroids era" made me appreciate baseball's history even more. All of a sudden, the stories and places in *Roadside Baseball* seemed a lot more comforting, like an old blanket or a lazy dog at your feet. It's not to say that there weren't scandals before, or players of questionable character. But not since the 1919 "Black Sox" scandal had anything so nefarious tainted the game—threatening to ruin its reputation for many years. Who knows how it will shake out? But regardless of what happens, if the now suspicious home run races involving McGwire, Bonds and Sosa don't make you appreciate the accomplishment of Roger Maris, nothing will. For me, his single-season, modern-day record is still the only one that counts.

After this book came out, I had the pleasure of hearing from many baseball travelers—hundreds of emails from all over the US (and beyond) with tips, suggestions, stories and more. This book seemed to tap into the passion many of us feel about baseball road trips, and I've appreciated and enjoyed every message. In particular, though, are a few people I'd like to acknowledge who have helped bring what I consider to be the soul of roadside baseball to life.

The writer Joan M. Thomas told me, "Barbara Sheinbein, who is a board member of the Bob Broeg Chapter of SABR, conceived the idea of marking the locations of old ballparks when she went on a tour at a SABR convention in Cincinnati. None of the locations were marked, and she realized that the same was true of St. Louis. At the time she brought it up at a chapter meeting, I was there, and my book *St. Louis' Big League Ballparks* had just been released. As the parks are a pet subject of mine, I was more than happy to help." Together, along with other SABR members, the group has placed markers at several ballpark sites (the others of which are documented in this book).

Then there's Mike Reischl. Head of the Way Out in Left Field Society in Chicago, he first wrote and pointed out to me that the former site of old West Side Grounds in Chicago was not included in the book (it didn't make the final edit). So what has Mike done since? Spent years raising funds and getting permission (no small feat in Chicago) to have a marker placed at the site—a marker that's proudly included in this book.

Finally, there's David Stalker from Wisconsin. Since 2003, David has worked tirelessly to place no less than seven historical markers to players of the Deadball Era (they're all included in this book). He gets the permissions, raises the money, has the markers created and then placed. And what's more, as of this writing he has four more markers planned.

Folks like Joan, Barbara, Mike and David may not be pro ball players, but in their own ways they help restore my faith in the game by preserving and protecting the game's history. To fans like this we should be all be grateful—and so a tip of the hat to you four.

I hope you enjoy this new edition, which has many new sites added. Since the first book, a bunch of ballparks have come down, new markers have been placed and lots more. Whether you have a chance to travel to these places or just read about them, I hope that the spirit of the book comes through—this idea that baseball, history and the open road all have a beautiful relationship with each other. They are inextricably linked for many of us wanderers; we who still believe in the power of the game.

—Chris Epting

AUTHOR'S NOTE: I have tried my best to include all the sites that are out there, but I know there are still some stones left uncovered. If you know of a site that you feel should be included in the next edition of *Roadside Baseball*, please write me at chris@chrisepting.com. Thanks! (Any and all additional comments are always welcome too.)

ROADSIDE BASEBALL
THE EAST

HARWOOD BASEBALL SHOP
-1858-
Citizen and leading businessman Harrison Harwood built this factory to manufacture the original "League Ball", designed for professional baseball use. It was the first facility of its type.

Overlooking Natick Center from the base of Walnut Hill, the three-story, wooden building enhances the 19th century townscape by providing a punctuation mark at the northern end of Main Street.

Natick Center Historic District
National Register of Historic Places - 1977

Connecticut

The First Hit House

City: Bridgeport
Location: 274 Pembroke Street

To understand what makes this house special in terms of baseball history, consider the mission statement of a group called The First Hit, Inc.:

> Vision: To relocate, preserve and maintain the historic home of James Henry O'Rourke, presently located at 274 Pembroke Street, as an integral component of Bridgeport's re-energized waterfront. The house, a valuable example of Victorian architecture, will be transformed into a museum and education center for and about baseball in Bridgeport and Connecticut. Exhibits and activities will celebrate James O'Rourke and the city's one hundred-plus year legacy of professional and amateur baseball. The museum will foster an appreciation for the place of baseball in America and international culture as well as examine the game's impact on the diverse cultures that have found common ground on Bridgeport diamonds.

Now, what exactly did James O'Rourke do? And why should this house be saved? The statement makes it clear:

> James Henry O'Rourke, Bridgeport's only Baseball Hall of Fame member (elected in 1945), was born on the East Side of Bridgeport, Connecticut to Irish immigrants in 1850. Young James grew up playing baseball on his family's farm as well as on fields around the city. Recognized as an outstanding ballplayer he was signed in 1872 to play for the professional Middletown Mansfields. O'Rourke later be-

The "First Hit" house in Bridgeport.

came a star for the National Association's Boston entry. As a member of the Boston Red Caps O'Rourke is credited with the first hit in the first game during the National League's inaugural season on April 22, 1876. O'Rourke went on to establish a number of feats, some of which remained unbroken until recent decades. He was the batting champion of 1884. While a member of the New York Giants he attained a law degree from Yale University (Class of 1887).

Jim O'Rourke was a career .313 hitter and caught a game at age 54.

After completing a successful major league career that lasted 22 years Orator O'Rourke, nicknamed for his astounding verbal skills, returned to Bridgeport, the city he cherished. Always forward-thinking Attorney O'Rourke immediately established a popular Connecticut minor league that flourished for nearly half a century. During the Connecticut League's first fifteen years he served as team owner, manager and player for the Bridgeport Orators. In 1895 O'Rourke became the first professional Bridgeport manager to sign an African-American player. He also served in various executive offices as league president, secretary and treasurer. O'Rourke was involved in city politics, acted as umpire during Ivy League baseball contests, and was recognized as a national baseball legal expert.

O'Rourke built his Queen Ann Victorian home in 1891, not far from the place of his birth. James and his wife Annie raised seven children in the house. Until the time of his death, in 1919, the home was a center of local and national baseball activity.

Saving the sole remnant of this Victorian neighborhood helps preserve a vibrant aspect of signature New England architecture. The O'Rourke Home and Museum will anchor a re-energized waterfront while serving as an education center celebrating O'Rourke's legacy, baseball history, and Bridgeport's rich ethnicity.

Today, the house sits forlornly in a field by the highway. Its windows are boarded up and fencing surrounds the decrepit structure. But it's still there, and this group is fighting vainly to help save it. Hopefully, as you read this, the house still stands and perhaps, has even become a museum.

Roberto Clemente Baseball Field Park
City: Bridgeport
Location: Iranistan Avenue
Seaside Park

A monument to Clemente stands at this youth baseball field, which bears his name.

Roberto Clemente Memorial
City: Hartford
Location: Wawarme Avenue
Colt Park

This monument dedicated to the Pirates great is located behind field No. 3.

Wiffle Ball
City: Shelton
Location: 275 Bridgeport Avenue
203-924-4643

Wiffle ball was invented back in 1953 by David N. Mullany of Fairfield, Connecticut. Looking for a way to help his 12-year-old son throw a curve, he designed a ball that curved easily, without requiring any sort of special grip. As for the name, that came about when the son and some friends referred to each strikeout they'd toss with the unique ball as a "whiff." Today, a standard Wiffle ball is approximately the same size as a regulation baseball; however, it's made of hollow plastic no more than 1/8" thick. As many of us have learned from experience, this construction allows pitchers to throw a tremendous variety and size of curveballs, sinkers, risers and tailers. Wiffle balls are usually packaged with a hollow, hard plastic yellow bat that measures 31 inches in length and about 1.25 inches in diameter. The game of Wiffle ball became incredibly popular as a backyard/sandlot game in the 1960s and 1970s, and remains popular today. In fact, since 1980, the game has become an organized sport, with many successful sports leagues and tournaments now played across the United States and as far away as Europe. It's from here in Shelton that all Wiffle balls (and bats) are made today.

Jackie Robinson Park of Fame
City: Stamford
Location: Jackie Robinson Way
West Main Street

For more than 20 years, Jackie Robinson lived with his family in Stamford.

To honor him, the city erected a life-size bronze statue of the Brooklyn Dodgers star with an engraved base bearing the words "Courage, Confidence and Perseverance." The statue is in a park also named for the man who in 1947 broke the color barrier in modern Major League Baseball.

Jackie Robinson Park of Fame features a life-size bronze statue of the man who broke baseball's color barrier.

Yale Field
City: West Haven
Location: 252 Derby Avenue

Yale Field is home to the Yale University baseball team and the New Haven Ravens of the Class AA Eastern League. Renovated in 1927 after being an open field with just a few bleachers, the park has its own version of the "Green Monster"—a 35-foot-high metal scoreboard in center field. Yale's Bulldogs have played at this site since 1902. Babe Ruth once remarked that the playing surface at Yale Field was the best he had ever seen. The noted 1948 photograph of Ruth and Yale first baseman George Bush was taken here. Ruth was presenting a manuscript of *The Babe Ruth Story*, written by Bob Considine, to the Yale captain and future US president for delivery to the Yale Library.

Hall of Famers Buried in Connecticut

Morgan Bulkeley
Cedar Hill Cemetery
Hartford

Roger Connor
Old St. Joseph's Cemetery
Waterbury

Jim O'Rourke
St. Michael's Cemetery
Bridgeport

George Weiss
Evergreen Cemetery
New Haven

As general manager of the New York Yankees, George Weiss won seven World Series titles.

Delaware

Judy Johnson House

City: Marshallton

Location: Intersection of Newport Road and Kiamensi Street

This is the house where William Julius "Judy" Johnson and his wife, Anita, lived for 55 years. During a career that ran from 1921 through 1937, Johnson was considered the best third baseman in the Negro Leagues. He captained a legendary Pittsburgh Crawfords team that also featured future Hall of Famers Satchel Paige, Oscar Charleston, Josh Gibson and Cool Papa Bell. Johnson went on to serve as a major-league scout and helped sign such future stars as Dick Allen (for the Philadelphia Phillies) and Bill Bruton (for the Milwaukee Braves). This residence is listed in the National Register of Historic Places.

Judy Johnson Statue

City: Wilmington

Location: Judy Johnson Field at Daniel S. Frawley Stadium

801 South Madison Street

No Delaware-born player has ever made the Hall of Fame, but Negro Leagues star Judy Johnson made the state proud in 1975 when he was elected to Cooperstown. Johnson was born in Maryland, but he moved with his family to Delaware at an early age and developed his many skills on the sandlots of Wilmington. He died in 1989—four years before a statue of the third

Hall of Famer Judy Johnson, who is buried at Silverbrook Cemetery in Wilmington, batted over .300 most of his career and was considered the best third baseman in the Negro Leagues.

baseman was dedicated at Daniel S. Frawley Stadium, home of the Carolina League's Wilmington Blue Rocks. The field bears Johnson's name as a tribute to this soft-spoken, keen student of the game. Judy Johnson is buried at Silverbrook Cemetery.

Hall of Famers Buried in Delaware

Bill McGowan
Cathedral Cemetery
Wilmington

Vic Willis
St. John's Cemetery
Newark

Vic Willis recorded eight 20-win seasons in his career and pitched 45 complete games in 1902, a 20th-century NL record.

Bill McGowan, whose colorful antics made him a fan favorite, was known as baseball's best balls-and-strikes umpire and didn't miss an inning over a 16-year stretch.

Maine

Gravesite of Louis Sockalexis
City: Old Town
Location: Old Town Cemetery

Louis Sockalexis was the first major-leaguer known to be a Native American. He was born at Indian Island (Penobscot Indian Reservation) in Maine in 1871 and showed phenomenal athletic skill at an early age. He played baseball at Notre Dame and later was an outfielder for the Cleveland Spiders of the National League. Injuries, alcoholism and racial taunting contributed to a quick demise for Sockalexis, who batted .338 for Cleveland in 66 games in 1897 but wound up with only 367 at bats over three major-league seasons. Sockalexis spent his final years on the reservation, teaching boys how to play baseball until his death in 1913. Though for years it was suggested that the American League's Cleveland Indians chose their name in partial tribute to Sockalexis, that contention has never been substantiated.

Coombs Field
City: Waterville
Location: Colby College
4000 Mayflower Hill Drive

Jack Coombs, who went from Colby College to the Philadelphia A's, set an AL record in 1910 with 13 shutouts en route to a 31–9 record.

The baseball field at Colby College is named for right-hander "Colby Jack" Coombs, who went from the Waterville campus to the Philadelphia Athletics in 1906. Coombs and Boston's Joe Harris, matched up late in the '06 season, established an American League innings-pitched record for one game when both hurled all 24 innings of a game the A's won, 4–1. Rookie Coombs, who struck out 18 Boston batters, finished with a 10–10 record that year. (Harris struggled to a 2–21 mark and was 3–30 in his career.) Four years later, Coombs set an AL record with 13 shutouts en route to a 31–9 record. In the 1910 World Series, the Colby product defeated the Chicago Cubs three times. In 1911, Coombs compiled a 28–12 mark. After his retirement as a player, Coombs became a noted coach at Duke University, where the baseball field is also named in his honor.

Maryland
(and the Washington DC Area)

Cal Ripken Museum
City: Aberdeen
Location: Aberdeen City Hall, US 40 and Bel Air Avenue

The city of Aberdeen, just 30 miles from Baltimore and about 65 miles from Washington DC, is where the Ripken family has its roots, and this museum is the official repository for Cal's memorabilia. It's loaded with items from his record consecutive-games streak, including a huge display from game No. 2,131 and even a ball from Ripken's first game in the streak (May 30, 1982). The gift shop features items signed by the longtime Orioles star. Ripken Stadium, at 873 Long Drive, is home to the Cal Ripken-owned Aberdeen IronBirds of the New York-Penn League.

The Cal Ripken Museum features a huge display from Ripken's record-breaking 2,131st game, and the gift shop has items signed by the longtime Orioles star.

The Babe Ruth Birthplace and Museum in Baltimore.

Babe Ruth Birthplace and Museum
City: Baltimore
Location: 216 Emory Street

This brick row house is where "The Sultan of Swat" was born on February 6, 1895. Designated a National Historic Site, it features rare photos, films, radio broadcasts and other Babe Ruth-related artifacts (including items excavated from the site of the bar that Ruth's father ran—a bar that stood in the area of what is now center field at Oriole Park at Camden Yards). Located just three blocks from Camden Yards, this is also the official Baltimore Orioles Museum. Plus, there are exhibits honoring long-ago greats Lou Gehrig, Wee Willie Keeler and Jimmie Foxx and modern stars like Cal Ripken, Ken Griffey Jr. and Mark McGwire.

Oriole Park at Camden Yards
City: Baltimore
Location: 333 West Camden Street

When it opened in 1992, Camden Yards revolutionized the way ballparks looked and felt. Designed to resemble parks from the "good old days," it inspired the current trend toward "retro" parks that bring fans close to the field after years of being pushed away in multipurpose stadiums. Camden Yards features tributes to legendary local baseballers. On the Eutaw Street promenade, there is a large bronze statue of Babe Ruth. Strikingly, the left-handed Ruth is sporting a right-handed fielder's glove. Those who created the statue contend this is not a mistake—that back when the Babe played for St. Mary's Industrial School in Baltimore, the school didn't have left-handed gloves (thus the monument's "authenticity"). If you access the ballpark through the Eutaw entrance and walk alongside the old B & O Warehouse, you will notice brass, baseball-shaped plaques embedded in the walkway with names and dates on them. The plaques mark where tape-measure home runs landed on Eutaw. The one on the wall past the Orioles Store notes the spot where Ken Griffey Jr. hit the warehouse during the 1993 Home Run Derby competition at the All-Star Game. (No one has hit the warehouse during a game.) If you enter from the left-field side of the stadium, you'll see a plaza with monuments of the numbers retired by the Orioles. Cal Ripken Sr., the longtime Orioles coach and proponent of "The Oriole Way," is honored

The park that started the wave of retro ballparks, Camden Yards features a 60-foot promenade between it and the B & O Warehouse (left) that includes, among other amenities, culinary delights from Boog's Bar-B-Q.

with a commemorative plaque in the Baltimore dugout. Two Camden Yards seats are specially marked. One in left field (Section 86, Row FF, Seat 10) is red and indicates where Cal Ripken Jr. hit career home run No. 278 in 1993, breaking Ernie Banks's record for a shortstop. In the right-field bleachers, an orange seat (Section 96, Row D, Seat 23) marks where Eddie Murray hit his 500th career homer on September 6, 1996, one year to the day after Cal Jr. played in his 2,131st consecutive game. The foul poles here are from Memorial Stadium, where the Orioles played from 1954 through 1991.

Cardinal Gibbons School
City: Baltimore
Location: 3225 Wilkens Avenue

This formerly was St. Mary's Industrial School for Boys, where Babe Ruth first picked up a baseball. Ruth, deemed out of control by his parents, was placed at St. Mary's (a reformatory/orphanage) at age 7. St. Mary's was run by Jesuit missionaries, and it was Brother Matthias who made the greatest impact on Ruth. A man of discipline, guidance and support, he helped teach Ruth how to play baseball—and how to find more structure in his life. Ruth became an excellent pitcher, and he demonstrated the ability to hit a baseball to distant places. By his late teens, he had developed

The fields where Babe Ruth first picked up a baseball remain intact behind Cardinal Gibbons School, formerly a reformatory and orphanage.

into a major-league prospect. In February 1914, at age 19, Ruth entered the pro ranks when he signed a contract with Jack Dunn's Baltimore Orioles of the International League. Although some of the school's original buildings have been destroyed by fire, the fields where Ruth first played remain intact. A marker was recently placed there in tribute to Ruth.

Babe Ruth's First Professional Game
City: Baltimore
Location: American League Park
Grandstand was located at 29th Street and Greenmount Avenue

This was where Babe Ruth first played pro ball, on April 22, 1914. Pitching for Baltimore, he tossed a six-hitter as the Orioles defeated Buffalo, 6-0, in an International League game. Buffalo's second baseman was Joe McCarthy, who 17 years later became Ruth's manager with the New York Yankees. An industrial park now occupies the site.

Leon Day Park
City: Baltimore
Location: Franklintown Road

A marker here reads:

> "This park is named for Leon Day, an outstanding player in the Negro Leagues who was elected to the National Baseball Hall of Fame. A resident of southwest Baltimore, Day joined the Baltimore Black Sox in 1934 when African Americans could not play in the Major or Minor Leagues. He went on to excel as a second baseman and pitcher for several teams and returned to Baltimore in the 1940s as a member of the Elite Giants. He was inducted into the Hall of Fame in 1995 just a few days before he died."

Some more history about Leon Day: Day retired from baseball in 1955 and passed away from a heart attack in Baltimore, Maryland, at age 78 (in 1995). This was just six days after being told he had been elected to the Baseball Hall of Fame. Leon Day was the twelfth Hall of Famer chosen in the Negro League category to date, and the seventh to be chosen while he was still alive (Paige, age 71; Buck Leonard, 72; Irvin, 73; C.P. Bell, 74; Judy Johnson, 75; and Dandridge, 87). Leon Day is the only Hall of Famer to enter the Hall represented by a cap of a team outside the mainland United States; his plaque depicts him as an "Aguadilla Shark" (Los Tiburones de Aguadilla), the Puerto Rican team for which he had once played.

Memorial Stadium
City: Baltimore
Location: Bounded by center field (N), East 36th Street; third base (W), Ellerslie Avenue; home plate (S), 1000 East 33rd Street; first base (E), Ednor Road.

Memorial Stadium opened in 1950 to serve as home of the minor-league Orioles, who had played at Municipal Stadium (also called Venable Stadium and Babe Ruth Stadium) after Oriole Park was destroyed by fire in 1944. When the American League's Browns moved here from St. Louis in 1954 to become the major-league Orioles, a second deck was added to the stadium, increasing the park's capacity to nearly 48,000. In the park's

Memorial Stadium was named in honor of the Baltimore veterans who died in both world wars and the Korean War.

38-year history as a big-league venue, only Frank Robinson hit a home run that left the confines of Memorial Stadium. He did it on May 8, 1966, connecting against Cleveland's Luis Tiant. When the Washington Senators left the nation's capital after the 1971 season, Memorial Stadium inherited the spring ritual of US

Some Memorable Moments at Memorial Stadium

★ JULY 8, 1958: The American League won the All-Star Game, 4–3. There were no extra-base hits in the Midsummer Classic, attended by Vice President Richard M. Nixon and a crowd of 48,829.

★ SEPTEMBER 20, 1958: Knuckleballer Hoyt Wilhelm, in one of only 52 starts in a 21-season major-league career, tossed a no-hitter against the Yankees.

★ JUNE 10, 1959: Cleveland's Rocky Colavito slammed four home runs against the Orioles. Previously, no team—much less an individual—had hit more than three home runs in one game at the spacious ballpark.

★ OCTOBER 9, 1966: Dave McNally's four-hit shutout completed a sweep of the Dodgers, giving Baltimore its first World Series title.

★ SEPTEMBER 13, 1971: The Orioles' Frank Robinson hit his 500th career home run, connecting off Detroit's Fred Scherman.

★ SEPTEMBER 24, 1974: Detroit's Al Kaline collected his 3,000th career hit. His victim: Baltimore's McNally.

★ MAY 30, 1982: Cal Ripken, penciled into the lineup against Toronto, began a playing streak that would reach 2,632 consecutive games.

presidents throwing out the first ball on opening day (although the practice has become somewhat of a rarity). The Orioles played their last game here in 1991, and the stadium was torn down in 2001. Though there is nothing at the site now, a senior housing center and a YMCA are planned for the location.

Sports Legends Museum at Camden Yards

City: Baltimore
Location: 301 West Camden Street
410-727-1539

A senior housing center and a YMCA are planned for the grounds where Brooks Robinson once made so many spectacular plays at third base.

Sports Legends Museum at Camden Yards opened to the public on May 14, 2005. The museum occupies the basement and first floor of Camden Station with 22,000 square feet of artifacts and interactive exhibits, transforming the station into one of the most spectacular sports museums in America. The exhibits represent the two incarnations of the Baltimore Orioles (minor league and major league); local legends, including Babe Ruth and Cal Ripken Jr.; and the two Negro Leagues teams that once played in Baltimore. At one time, many of the items here were located at the nearby Babe Ruth Birthplace and Museum, which focuses more specifically on the Babe.

Walter Johnson High School

City: Bethesda
Location: 6400 Rock Spring Drive

Walter Johnson, "The Big Train" pitching star of the Washington Senators, became a prominent member of the Bethesda community. His standing in the area—he once served on the Montgomery County Council—is reflected by the naming of this high school in his honor. A monument to Johnson,

The author and his son, Charlie, at Walter Johnson High School in 1995. The marker on display once stood at Griffith Stadium in Washington DC.

who won 417 major-league games, stands at the front of the school, which opened in 1956. The memorial dates to 1947, the year after Johnson died. (President Harry Truman had unveiled the granite monument and bronze tablet in the presence of Johnson's mother in a ceremony at Griffith Stadium, and the memorial remained at the ballpark through the stadium's final season, 1961, before being moved to the high school.) A school newsletter is called *The Big Train*.

Walter Johnson House
City: Bethesda
Location: 9100 Old Georgetown Road

This private residence, recently designated a state landmark, was the home of Walter Johnson from 1926 to 1936. From 1936 until his death 10 years later, Johnson lived and worked on a farm in Germantown, about 20 miles from here. The property where the farm sat has been developed into a shopping center and is also the site of Seneca Valley High School.

William Beck Nicholson Marker
City: Chestertown

A marker here reads:

> "Swish"
> Philadelphia A.L., 1936
> Chicago N.L., 1939-1948
> Philadelphia N.L., 1948-1953
>
> Born Chestertown, Kent County, Eastern Shore of Maryland, 1914. Graduate of Washington College 1936. Feared and respected outfielder with fine arm who played the national game of baseball with great determination. Led National League in home runs, RBI 1943, 1944, runner-up for MVP 1944. 235 career home runs, had 8 career grand slams, tied a major league record for four home runs in a doubleheader and four home runs in four consecutive times at bat. The accolade "Swish" began at storied Ebbets Field, Brooklyn and spread to every ballpark. Legend has it that only Bill Nicholson and Babe Ruth have ever been walked intentionally with the bases loaded. Country boy who worked hard to become a major leaguer and star, ever helpful to rookies. Retired here in 1953.

He was nicknamed "Swish" due to his mighty swing, which often

whiffed as he tried to club the ball.
Still, Nicholson twice led the National League in home runs and
RBI. Playing briefly in the American
League for the Philadelphia Athletics in 1936, Nicholson went down
to the minors before being called
up to play for the Chicago Cubs in
1939. Updating some trivia from the
plaque: In 1944, Nicholson received
an intentional walk with the bases
loaded. He is listed as one of only six
players in major-league history to do

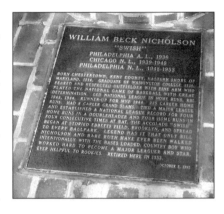

it. The others are Abner Dalrymple (1881), Nap Lajoie (1901), Del Bissonette
(1928), Barry Bonds (1998) and Josh Hamilton (2008).

Babe Ruth Gets Married

City: Ellicott City
Location: St. Paul the Apostle Catholic Church
3755 St. Paul Street

On October 17, 1914, Babe Ruth married Helen Woodford at this church in
suburban Baltimore. Ruth was just months removed from St. Mary's Industrial School for Boys when he met Helen at a Boston coffee shop in July 1914.
He was 19 years old; she was 17 (there were reports she might have been

Babe Ruth's first marriage
certificate in Maryland.

Babe Ruth was a 19-year-old rookie pitcher for the
Boston Red Sox when he married Helen Woodford in
this church in 1914.

even younger). The couple adopted a daughter, Dorothy, in 1921. Babe and Helen were living apart in 1929 when Helen died in a fire.

Charlie Keller's Horse Farm
City: Frederick
Location: Yankeeland Farms
8423 Yellow Springs Road

Yankeeland Farms was founded by former Yankees star Charlie Keller in 1955. Along with members of his immediate family, Keller built the 100-acre farm into a major East Coast Standardbred facility. Today, Yankeeland remains a family-run business and a leading breeding establishment. Its many success stories include trotter Fresh Yankee, who in the early 1970s exceeded $1 million in winnings.

Lefty Grove's 1931 MVP Trophy
City: Lonaconing
Location: George's Creek Public Library
76 Main Street

Hall of Fame pitcher Robert Moses "Lefty" Grove, who was born in Lonaconing in 1900, won exactly 300 games in the majors. In 1931, he compiled an astonishing 31–4 record for the Philadelphia Athletics and won the AL Most Valuable Player award. Grove donated the trophy to the local high school, and the award has since made its way to a showcase in the public library.

Lefty Grove had seven straight 20-win seasons, and his .680 career winning percentage (300–141) ranks number one of all time among 300-game winners.

Charlie Keller Plaque
City: Middletown
Location: Middletown Memorial Park
Between Church (Route 17) and Franklin Streets

Middletown native Charlie "King Kong" Keller hit .334 for the Yankees in his rookie season of 1939 and had five 100-RBI seasons for the Yankees in the 1940s. He also hit 30 or more homers five times. Keller appeared in four World Series with New York, but back problems eventually forced him into a reserve role and duty as a pinch hitter. On September 26, 1998, Middletown honored its hometown hero with a granite monument and plaque placed at the field where he played baseball as a youth.

The Eastern Shore Baseball Hall of Fame Museum

City: Salisbury
Location: US 50 and Hobbs Road
410-546-4444

This museum, located within Perdue Stadium (home of the Delmarva Shorebirds of the South Atlantic League), is a celebration of old-time Minor League Baseball. Exhibits feature uniforms, equipment, photos and other memorabilia from local low-classification minor leagues and semipro leagues of years gone by. Admission to the museum is included when you buy a Shorebirds game ticket.

Jimmie Foxx Statue

City: Sudlersville
Location: Church and Main Streets

Slugger Jimmie Foxx was born in Sudlersville in 1907. He began his professional baseball career in 1924 with manager Frank "Home Run" Baker's Easton, Maryland, club of the Eastern Shore League. "Double X" was the second player in major-league history to hit 500 home runs, reaching the landmark total in 1940 (11 years after Babe Ruth accomplished the feat). Foxx won American League MVP awards in 1932 and 1933 with the Philadelphia Athletics and in 1938 with the Boston Red Sox. In '33, he won the Triple Crown. He had 58- and 50-homer seasons, won three AL homer titles outright and shared the league lead in home runs once. Elected to the Base-

A three-time MVP, Jimmie Foxx's 534 career home runs ranked second of all time to Babe Ruth for many years.

ball Hall of Fame in 1951, he died in 1967. The statue was dedicated on October 25, 1997. In addition to this monument, there is Foxx memorabilia on display at the Sudlersville Train Station Museum.

Home Run Baker Park

City: Trappe
Location: 4200 Main Street

The famed John Franklin "Home Run" Baker played third base from 1908 to 1922 and helped the Philadelphia Athletics win three World Series (1910, 1911 and 1913). Baker's legacy has grown over the years and he is thought by many to be the best third baseman of the prewar era. He led the American League in home runs in 1911, and earned the nickname "Home Run" during the 1911 World Series. It happened after he hit a go-ahead home run off Rube Marquard in Game 2 and a ninth-inning game-tying blast off Christy Mathewson in Game 3. Baker's home run crown would be the first of four consecutive seasons leading the American League in home runs.

The park that's dedicated to Frank "Home Run" Baker celebrates the Deadball Era hero.

But the totals are not that impressive by today's standards. He hit 11 home runs in 1911, 10 in 1912, 12 in 1913, and 9 in 1914.

The plaque here reads:

> This Park is Dedicated to Hall of Fame Inductee John Franklin "Home Run" Baker (1886–1963) Baseball's First Home Run Hero and 'As fine a citizen as any town could have.' Of all the players in the history of baseball, it may sound unusual that the one who ended up named for the game's most identifiable feat, the home run, hit only twelve in his best season. During baseball's Deadball Era (1900–1919), before Babe Ruth and Jimmie Foxx—when the ball was less lively and ballparks generally had very large outfields—most home runs were of the inside-the-park variety. A ball hit over the fence was truly an extraordinary clout, and very few players were identified with the long ball.

Famous Baseball Catch

City: Washington DC
Location: Washington Monument

Charles Evard "Gabby" Street was a catcher, manager, coach and radio broadcaster during the first half of the 20th century. As a catcher, he participated in one of the most publicized baseball stunts of the century's first decade. On August 21, 1908, Street achieved a measure of immortality by catching a baseball dropped from the top of the Washington Monument, a distance of 555 feet—after muffing the first 12 balls, thrown by journalist Preston Gibson, he made a clean reception of number 13. An article written shortly after the

The Washington Monument was the scene of one of baseball's most famous catches.

feat quoted Street: "The ball I caught hit my mitt with terrific force, much greater than any pitched ball I have ever caught, and I have caught some pitchers who are given credit for having wonderful speed. Though my mitt is three or four inches thick, the force of the ball benumbed my hand." In the fall of 2008, a ball purported to be the actual one dropped that day went up on the auction block, but then the auction house issued this statement: "Subsequent to the publishing of the auction catalog, it was brought to our attention that a baseball purported to be the one caught by Street is within the collection of the Baseball Hall of Fame. While Heritage would contend that an American League baseball with Street family provenance makes a more compelling argument than the Hall of Fame's National League baseball with provenance from the family of the man who tossed the ball from the Monument, this issue must be disclosed nonetheless." The ball did not sell.

Griffith Stadium
City: Washington DC
Location: Seventh Street and Florida Avenue NW

While the Washington Senators were at spring training in 1911, the club's National Park burned down. (Just the year before, William Howard Taft had begun the presidential tradition of throwing out the first ball at the season-opening game in Washington.) On the same site of the old National Park, a new park bearing the same name was hastily constructed, with steel and concrete among the components. In 1920, National was renamed Griffith Stadium in honor of Senators owner Clark Griffith. That same year, a second deck was added to the stadium, which was known for its unusually long distance to left field (adjusted from time to time, the distance often was more than 400 feet). Although the Senators won the World Series in 1924 and repeated as AL champions in 1925, the club became a perennial second-division team beginning in the mid-1930s and fan support faltered. After the 1960 season, the Senators were relocated to Minnesota and Washington was awarded an expansion team. The new Senators played at Griffith Stadium in 1961, then moved into new District of Columbia Stadium (later renamed Robert F. Kennedy Stadium). Griffith was demolished in 1965. Today, Howard University Hospital occupies the site of the old ballpark. After the 1971 season, the new Senators skipped town, too, fleeing to Arlington, Texas, to become the Texas Rangers.

Though many remember Griffith as the stadium where William Howard Taft began the presidential tradition of throwing out the first ball, many also recall the indent in center field where the fence detoured around five duplexes (the owner wouldn't sell).

Memorable Moments at Griffith Stadium

★ JULY 5, 1924: The Yankees got a big scare when Babe Ruth, furiously pursuing a fly ball, crashed into the right-field wall. After several anxious moments, Ruth got up and stayed in the game. Shaken but hardly unnerved, Ruth went 3-for-3 in the game, which was the opener of a doubleheader.

★ OCTOBER 10, 1924: The Senators won their only World Series title, defeating the Giants in Game 7 when Earl McNeely's 12th-inning bad-hop grounder drove in the winning run.

★ APRIL 13, 1926: Walter Johnson, making his 14th and last opening-day start, out-dueled Philadelphia's Ed Rommel in a 15-inning, 1–0 game in which both pitchers went the distance.

★ JULY 7, 1937: Cardinals ace pitcher Dizzy Dean suffered a toe fracture when struck by a line drive in the All-Star Game. The Yankees' Lou Gehrig doubled, homered and drove in four runs in the AL's 8–3 victory.

★ APRIL 17, 1953: Batting right-handed, New York's Mickey Mantle crushed a Chuck Stobbs pitch and sent it caroming off the side of the football scoreboard in left field. The ball, which landed in a backyard across the street, traveled an estimated 565 feet.

Hall of Famers Buried in Maryland

Leon Day
Arbutus Memorial Park
1101 Sulphur Spring Road
Baltimore

Richard "Rube" Marquard
Baltimore Hebrew Cemetery
2100 Belair Road
Baltimore

Pitcher Rube Marquard had a record 19-game winning streak in 1912.

Wilbert Robinson, Ned Hanlon, Joe Kelley, John McGraw
New Cathedral Cemetery
4300 Old Frederick Road
Baltimore

Frank "Home Run" Baker
Spring Hill Cemetery of
Talbot County
Hanson and Aurora Streets
Easton

Frank "Home Run" Baker

Robert "Lefty" Grove
Frostburg Memorial Park
70 Green Street
Frostburg

Clark Griffith
Fort Lincoln Cemetery
3401 Bladensburg Road
Brentwood

Sam Rice
Woodside Cemetery
Haviland Mill Road
Brinklow

Clark Griffith

Walter Johnson
Rockville Union Cemetery,
1 mile east of Highway 28
on Baltimore Road
Rockville

Smokey Joe Williams
Lincoln Memorial
Cemetery
4001 Suitland Road
Suitland

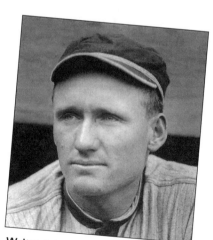
Walter Johnson

Massachusetts

The "Black Sox" Hatch Their Scheme

City: Boston
Location: Hotel Buckminster
645 Beacon Street

It was in this hotel near Fenway Park that Chicago White Sox players, in town to play the Red Sox, conspired to fix the 1919 World Series against the Cincinnati Reds. Bitter about the perceived greed of White Sox owner Charles Comiskey, Sox first baseman Chick Gandil invited bookie Joseph "Sport" Sullivan to his hotel room on September 18, 1919, and told him: "I think we can put it in the bag." (The Sox, comfortably in first place, were obviously Series-bound.) Gandil demanded $80,000—a figure later raised to $100,000—and then approached Chicago pitcher Eddie Cicotte to take part in the plan. Cicotte agreed, provided he got $10,000 up front. Gandil also sold the idea to teammates Lefty Williams, Swede Risberg and Fred Mc-Mullin. Sox star "Shoeless Joe" Jackson insisted that when Gandil offered him $10,000, then $20,000, he refused to join the scheme. Gandil allegedly told Jackson to take it or leave it because the fix was arranged anyway. In all, eight players and several gamblers were indicted for conspiracy to de-

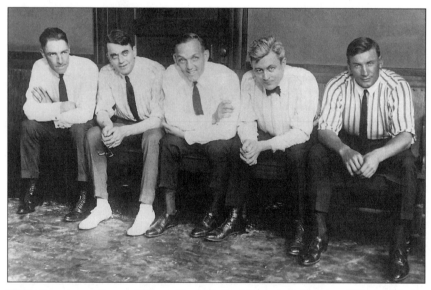

White Sox players Swede Risberg (far left), Buck Weaver (middle) and Happy Felsch (far right) wait outside the courtroom with their attorneys during a break in the 1921 Black Sox trial.

fraud the public. (The other players involved were Happy Felsch and Buck Weaver.) All were acquitted at the trial after transcripts of confessions by Cicotte and Jackson disappeared from the court files, but the eight players ultimately were banned from baseball for life by commissioner Kenesaw Mountain Landis. Landis said the players' "crookedness" was evident throughout the trial.

Ted Williams Tunnel
City: Boston

Ted Williams, the last major-leaguer to hit .400, had a life-time batting average of .344.

The city of Boston's third harbor tunnel is named after Ted Williams. Williams officially became part of the Boston family in December of 1937, when the Red Sox acquired him from the San Diego Padres. From the outset, Beantown knew they had a winner. Williams hit his first home run in an exhibition game at Holy Cross College in Worcester, on April 14, 1939. His last one came in his last career at bat on September 28, 1960, at Fenway Park. In between, the fiery superstar, fisherman and patriot carved out one of the all-time great careers. "The Splendid Splinter" was the last major-league player to hit for a .400 average or better for a full season. He was voted the league's most valuable player in 1946 and 1949 and won the Triple Crown in 1942 and 1947.

During his major-league career he had a lifetime batting average of .344, batted in 1,839 runs, hit 521 home runs, and was batting champion of the American League six times (1941, 1942, 1947, 1948, 1957, 1958). In 1966, Williams was elected to the Baseball Hall of Fame. The Ted Williams Tunnel opened on December 15, 1995, and connects South Boston to East Boston and Logan Airport.

Braves Field
City: Boston
Location: Nickerson Field
Boston University
Harry Agganis Way

Home to the Boston Braves from 1915 until their move to Milwaukee after the 1952 season, Braves Field also was home to Red Sox home games in the 1915 and 1916 World Series because the NL park had a larger seat-

While only a portion of Braves Field exists today—as Nickerson Field, where Boston University plays its football and soccer games—the Gaffney Street ticket office that was located down the right-field line remains intact, as a child-care center and security office for Boston University.

ing capacity than the American Leaguers' new Fenway Park. Today, a portion of the ballpark remains, albeit as part of Boston University's Nickerson Field, where lacrosse and soccer are played today. The virtually unchanged Gaffney Street ticket office that was located down the right-field line is now a child-care center and security office for Boston University. Directly behind the ticket office building is a grandstand that made up the right-field bleachers at Braves Field. A plaque near the ticket office building com-

Some Memorable Moments at Braves Field

★ JUNE 16, 1916: Boston's Tom Hughes hurled the first no-hitter in Braves Field history, baffling the Pirates, 2–0.

★ MAY 1, 1920: Major League Baseball's longest game, a 26-inning, 1–1 tie between the Dodgers and Braves, was played here. Joe Oeschger went the distance for the Braves and Leon Cadore pitched all the way for the Dodgers.

★ OCTOBER 6, 1923: The third unassisted triple play in regular-season major-league play was pulled off by Braves shortstop Ernie Padgett in a game against the Phillies.

★ JULY 7, 1936: The National League won the All-Star Game here, 4–3, as Dizzy Dean beat Lefty Grove.

★ JUNE 19, 1942: The Braves' Paul Waner got his 3,000th career hit, achieving the milestone blow against Pittsburgh's Rip Sewell.

★ OCTOBER 11, 1948: In the third and last World Series game played at Braves Field, Boston lost to Cleveland, 4–3, in decisive Game 6 of the Fall Classic.

★ Only 281,278 fans attended Braves home games in 1952, spurring relocation of the franchise to Milwaukee.

memorates the historical significance of this site. In addition, a crumbling, peeling portion of the original right field wall still stands.

Huntington Avenue Grounds

City: Boston
Location: Left field (NW), Huntington Avenue; third base (SW), Bryant (Rogers) Street, now Forsyth Street; first base (SE), New Gravelly Pt. Road and New York, New Haven and Hartford Railroad tracks; right field (NE), New Gravelly Pt. Road.

Before the 1912 opening of Fenway Park, Huntington Avenue Grounds was home to the Boston Red Sox. In fact, it was their very first ballpark. Built for $35,000 in 1901, Huntington Avenue Grounds originally seated only about 9,000 fans. However, there was room for thousands more (albeit via standing room) beyond ropes in the outfield and in the huge foul territory. With just a single entrance (and one turnstile), the simple structure was home field to the team known as the Boston Americans, who won their first game played here on May 8, 1901, defeating Connie Mack's A's, 12-4, behind the pitching of Cy Young. Nearly three years later, on May 5, 1904, Young tossed the first perfect game in American League history when he stopped the A's, 3-0, here. In use for only 11 years, Huntington Avenue Grounds is notable because of what is conveyed on a plaque that sits near the original spot of home plate: Dedicated in 1993, the inscription reads: "On October 1, 1903 the first modern World Series between the American League champion Boston Pilgrims (later known as the Red Sox) and the National League champion Pittsburgh Pirates was played on this site. General admission tickets were fifty cents. The Pilgrims, led by twenty-eight game winner Cy Young, trailed the series three games to one but then swept four consecutive victories to win the championship five games to three." Now located on the campus of Northeastern University, there is also a life-size statue of Cy Young located near where the pitcher's mound used to be (in the Churchill Hall Mall). Additionally, there is a World Series Exhibit Room in the nearby Cabot

A plaque in the shape of home plate marks the spot where modern baseball's first World Series took place. About 60 feet away stands a statue of a hunched over Cy Young (background).

Physical Education Center with memorabilia from the 1901–1911 Red Sox teams and a plaque attached to the side of the building marking where the left-field foul pole stood.

South End Grounds

City: Boston
Location: Columbus Avenue and Walpole Street. Walpole ran behind home plate, Columbus along the first-base side of the field. The New York, New Haven and Hartford Railroad tracks ran along the third-base side. Behind the outfield was a railroad roundhouse, and behind that was Gainsborough Street.

In early Boston baseball, this was the home to the Doves, Red Caps and finally the Braves. And from 1871–1914, three baseball parks were located on the site known as the "South End Grounds." Located across the street from Huntington Avenue Grounds, the most famous of the parks that stood here was the Grand Pavilion, which was used from 1883–1894. A majestic, double-decked, six-spired masterpiece, it was destroyed by fire in 1894 and replaced with a less distinctive structure. This park served as home of the Boston Braves for 20 years, until Braves Field was built. (The Miracle Braves of 1914 played their World Series games at the larger Fenway Park before moving into their Braves Field the following season.) At the Ruggles T Station today, a plaque reads:

"South End Grounds: Professional baseball games were regularly played here from 1871–1914. Boston's only double-decked ballpark was topped with distinctive twin towers, and was regarded as the latest in sports

A parking lot now covers what was once the right field (left) and infield (right) of South End Grounds in Boston.

stadiums when it opened in 1888. Also known as the Walpole Street Grounds, the park burned in 1894 during a ball game. It was rebuilt and served as the home of the National League's Boston Braves."

Fenway Park
City: Boston
Location: 4 Yawkey Way

After two rain delays, Fenway Park finally hosted its first American League game on April 20, 1912. Coincidentally, Tiger Stadium (Navin Field) in Detroit opened the same day. On opening day, the Red Sox defeated the New York Highlanders (later known as the Yankees) in an 11-inning thriller, 7–6. (The park's grand opening was overshadowed on the news pages because of the continuing coverage of the sinking of the *Titanic* in the Atlantic.) Today, Fenway Park is the oldest major-league park in use and its basic configuration remains much like it was on opening day. The mythical left field wall,

Young fans in Fenway Park's center-field bleachers eagerly await a home run ball during batting practice at the 1999 All-Star Game.

Some Memorable Moments at Fenway Park

★ Site of the 1946, '61 and '99 All-Star Games.

★ OCTOBER 1, 1967: Jim Lonborg defeated the Twins, clinching Boston's "Impossible Dream" pennant.

★ OCTOBER 21, 1975: Carlton Fisk's 12-inning home run decided Game 6 of the World Series.

★ SEPTEMBER 12, 1979: Carl Yastrzemski collected his 3,000th hit in a game against the Yankees.

★ APRIL 29, 1986: Roger Clemens struck out a major league-record 20 Seattle Mariners.

known as the "Green Monster," is synonymous with Boston baseball, and so is the so-called "Curse of the Bambino," which has seemingly doomed the team from winning a World Series since the Red Sox sold Babe Ruth to the Yankees in January 1920. Also, its manually operated scoreboard and peculiar shape (including the only ladder in play in the majors) make Fenway Park one of the most classic and revered landmarks in baseball history—a gem that helps connect the past with the present. Excellent tours are offered here at what some purists call "Boston's Sistine Chapel."

Sports Museum of New England
City: Boston
Location: TD Banknorth Garden
100 Legends Way
617-624-1234

Opened in 1987, the Sports Museum of New England is located on the fifth and sixth levels of the TD Banknorth Garden. Although it includes historic memorabilia from all major Boston sports teams, there is a good deal of emphasis on Boston baseball. (The museum also displays artifacts loaned from private collectors and other museums, such as the Baseball Hall of Fame.) The Sports Museum was also the first museum ever to bring an outside exhibition to the Baseball Hall of Fame when it presented "Boston Braves 1876–1952" at Cooperstown in 1990.

Mickey Cochrane Monument

City: Bridgewater
Location: Legion Field at the
Mickey Cochrane Sports Complex
Bridgewater State College
508-531-1200

Born here in Bridgewater on April 6, 1903, Mickey Cochrane attended local public schools and played on one of the towns semipro baseball teams known as the Old Bridgewater Club. In 1925, he made his professional baseball debut as a catcher for the Philadelphia Athletics. He started for the A's for nine consecutive seasons, which included three World Series appearances. In 1933, Cochrane was traded to the Detroit Tigers and helped lead the team to the American League pennant in 1934. The season after that, the Tigers won the World Series. Un-

Mickey Cochrane was known as one of the smartest and toughest players in baseball history.

fortunately, Cochrane's career ended after he was knocked unconscious by a Bump Hadley fastball at Yankee Stadium on May 25, 1937. Cochrane was elected to the Baseball Hall of Fame in 1947 and died in Lake Forest, Illinois, on June 28, 1962, at age 59. Interestingly, Mickey Mantle was named after Cochrane—Cochrane was the favorite player of Mantle's father.

The house in the background at the end of Connie Mack Drive is where the legendary manager grew up. East Brookfield holds an annual parade in his honor.

Birthplace of Connie Mack

City: East Brookfield
Location: East Main Street

Cornelius Alexander McGillicuddy, better known as Connie Mack, was born on December 22, 1862, here in East Brookfield. A major-league manager for over 50 years with the Philadelphia Athletics, the "Tall Tactician" left a huge mark in the town he still visited occasionally after becoming a legend. The house in which he lived on East Main Street is marked with a plaque. Each year the town holds a Memorial Day parade along Connie Mack Drive and July 4th celebrations end with fireworks at Connie Mack Field. Also, signs welcoming visitors into town make note of their hometown hero.

First Game Played under the Lights
City: Nantasket Bay
Location: On the lawn behind Nantasket's Sea Foam House

On September 2, 1880, two amateur teams played a nine-inning, 16–16 tie game at Nantasket Beach in Hull, Massachusetts. What made the game special is that it was played at night, under temporary lights, as staged by the newly formed Northern Electric Light Company. (Edison had invented the incandescent lightbulb just the year before.) The teams were actually representing two popular Boston department stores, Jordan Marsh and R. H. White. The *Boston Post* reported the next day that "a clear, pure, bright light was produced, very strong and yet very pleasant to the sight," by the 12 carbon-arc electric lamps. More specifically, 36 lamps were placed on three 100-foot wooden towers. They were powered by two engines and three generators, emitting just 30,000 candlepower of light. For the next 50 years, the night game experiments continued. While several promoters used the gimmick of portable lighting to illuminate the field as their exhibition teams traveled around the country, the first "official" major-league game played under the lights happened in Cincinnati on May 24, 1935 (with President Franklin Roosevelt throwing the light switch from the White House 600 miles from old Crosley Field).

The Harwood Baseball Factory
City: Natick
Location: Walnut Street

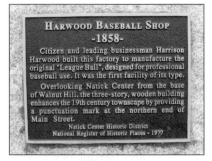

The spot in Natick where baseballs were once manufactured.

Ellis Drake first developed the figure-eight stitched baseball cover in the 1840s. It was then mass-manufactured in 1858 by H. Harwood & Sons of Natick, the first baseball factory in the United States, which was even used at times by the Cincinnati Red Stockings during their 1868 and 1869 tour. Harwood had earlier purchased the pattern for the current figure-eight stitch baseball from a Natick shoemaker named John Walcott and for more than 100 years the factory turned out hundreds of thousands of Official League Baseballs. The center-wound balls were made with horsehide covers and, later, softballs were made using cowhide. Some facts from the Natick Historical Society:

Another image of the former baseball factory in Natick.

> Harwood could never perfect a machine that could stitch the balls as well as hand sewing. Local women at their homes sewed much of the balls. Carts brought the cores from the factory and picked up the finished balls. Also, it took approximately ten minutes from start to finish to sew the cover on a ball. Harrison Harwood was posthumously elected to the Major League Baseball Hall of Fame in 1959. An 1871 *New York Times* article reports that the factory produced 30,000 dozen balls in that year. In 1891 the price of a Harwood baseball ranged from a nickel to $1.25. There is enough yarn in a Harwood baseball to go around the bases three times!

America's first baseball factory was converted to 20 condominiums and one commercial unit in 1989. Over the years, downtown Natick has grown up around this historic building, and today the baseball factory is in the heart of downtown Natick.

Jack Chesbro Plaque

City: North Adams
Location: Joe Wolfe Baseball Field at the Noel Field Complex
State Street

Born here on June 5, 1874, Hall of Famer "Happy Jack" Chesbro was one of baseball's early spitball aces. Among his career highlights was his 1904 performance with the New York Highlanders. The numbers almost defy logic. He started 51 games, completed 48 of them. In all, he was the victor in 41 of those games and tossed a total of 454 2/3 innings. And from

Family members at the Jack Chesbro marker unveiling.

1901 to 1906, Chesbro won 153 games—an average of more than 25 per season. He played for pennant winners in Pittsburgh and New York, and led the league in winning percentage three times. After retiring in 1909, Chesbro returned to North Adams to start a career as a merchant, running both a saw mill and lumberyard in town. North Adams honored him with a plaque at Joe Wolfe Field, named for a former local minor-league ballplayer who revived the North Adams Babe Ruth League in addition to working in other local youth-related baseball groups.

Wahconah Park
City: Pittsfield
. Location: Wahconah Street

Another classic little ballpark that harkens back to another era. Nestled in a working-class neighborhood, Wahconah Park is one of the last remaining ballparks in the United States with an original wooden grandstand. It was built way back in 1919, and today seats 4,500. At the close of the 2003 season, the Berkshire Black Bears allowed their lease to expire. That's when former major-league pitcher Jim Bouton proposed that the park be renovated without any public dollars as a means of bringing professional baseball back. In fact, the park was the subject of the book *Foul Ball* by Bouton, his first diary since the famous, controversial *Ball Four* back in 1970. In the book, Bouton recounted his adventure trying to save old Wahconah Park. As I said, Bouton and his partners offered the community a terrific deal—a locally owned professional baseball team and a privately restored

Wahconah Park in Pittsfield harkens back to another era.

city-owned ballpark at no cost to the taxpayers. However, the generous plan was opposed by a group of power brokers who wanted to build a new $18.5 million stadium—a ballpark that the people had voted down three different times! Nevertheless, on July 3, 2004, a record crowd of 5,000 watched a vintage baseball game that Bouton organized here at Wahconah Park between Pittsfield and Hartford. The game was broadcast live on ESPN Classic as *America's Pastime: Vintage Baseball, Live*. On air for the game were Bouton, former professional ballplayer Bill Lee, actor Tim Robbins, and baseball historians John Thorn and David Pietrusza. The stadium has been home to the Pittsfield Dukes of the New England Collegiate Baseball League since 2005 and with its newfound support, hopefully this ballpark will be around for a long time to come. Some interesting trivia surrounding Wahconah is that because it was built before the concept of night baseball, home plate was designed to face the setting sun, which still results in "sun delays" several times a season. Also, the name *Wahconah* is derived from a Mahican legend of an Indian maiden.

Babe Ruth's Farmhouse
City: Sudbury
Location: 558 Dutton Road

Babe Ruth bought this then-80-acre farm in 1916 for $12,000, using his $4,000 World Series check as the down payment. It was Ruth's primary residence while he was a member of the Boston Red Sox. Today, most of the acreage has been developed into other homes, but the former Ruth house remains as a private residence.

Where Babe Ruth lived while a member of the Boston Red Sox.

Babe Ruth's Piano
City: Sudbury
Location: Willis Pond

The legend of Babe Ruth's piano finding its way into this pond lives on. While Ruth definitely spent off-season time at a cabin here, the facts about the piano are difficult to nail down. One story is that Ruth, "under the influence" during one of his many parties, pushed the piano onto the frozen pond to show off his strength. Another version is that Ruth shoved the piano

onto the pond to entertain youngsters at a singalong he was hosting. After the kids left, he supposedly forgot about the piano,
which eventually sank once the
ice gave way. Whatever the case,
there has been enough interest
in the goings-on to compel div-
ers to survey the murky bottom
of the pond with high-tech sonar
equipment. So far, the missions
have proved fruitless.

Christy Mathewson Gets His Start

City: Taunton
Location: Whittenton Athletic
Grounds
Pleadwell Street and
4th Avenue

Babe Ruth, shown here with his first wife,
Helen, rented a cottage near Willis Pond in
1917 and 1918.

In 1899, Christy Mathewson was
a budding college superstar at
Bucknell University in Pennsylvania. After his freshman year, he joined his
first professional baseball team, the minor-league Taunton Herrings (of the
New England League). Taunton's home field was called the Whittenton Athletic Grounds, today known simply as the Whittenton ball field. Mathewson
first pitched here on July 24, 1899, and was shelled by the Brockton Shoe-
makers, losing 13-4. By the next season, Mathewson had moved over to play
for Norfolk in the Virginia League where he had a 20-2 record. In 1901, he
was pitching for the New York Giants, going 20-17 in his first full major-
league season. In 1994, a plaque was placed at the Whittenton field, used today by Little Leaguers and softball players. It states that this is where Christy
Mathewson spent his first season in professional baseball.

Site of Baseball's First Perfect Game

City: Worcester
Location: Current site of Becker College
61 Sever Street

In 1880, the Worcester Agricultural Fairgrounds was located here, and the
fairgrounds field was home to the National League's Worcester team. On

This marker sits where fans entered the park at Worcester Agricultural Fairgrounds, home of the NL's Worcester team.

June 12, 1880, it was here that Worcester's Lee Richmond tossed the first perfect game in major-league history. In the last season in which the pitching distance was 45 feet, Richmond mowed down Cleveland, 1–0. Just five days later, Providence's John Montgomery Ward pitched a perfect game against Buffalo. Incredibly, the third perfect game in National League history did not occur until 1964, when the Phillies' Jim Bunning accomplished the feat against the Mets. The spot where the Worcester marker sits today—in front of Becker's Main Academic Building—is where fans entered the park.

Hall of Famers Buried in Massachusetts

John Clarkson

BOSTON METROPOLITAN AREA

George Wright
Holyhood Cemetery
Heath Street
Brookline

Tim Keefe and John Clarkson
Cambridge Cemetery
76 Coolidge Avenue
Cambridge
617-349-4890

Mike "King" Kelly
Mount Hope Cemetery
355 Walk Hill Street
Mattapan
617-635-7361

Hugh Duffy

Tommy Connolly

Jack Chesbro won 41 games in 1904— the most single-season wins in the 20th century.

Hugh Duffy and Tommy McCarthy
Mount Calvary Cemetery
Harvard Street and
Cummins Highway
Mattapan
617-296-2339

Frank Selee
Wyoming Cemetery
205 Sylvan Street
Melrose
Pine Banks Section, Lot 200
781-665-0405

Tommy Connolly
St. Patrick's Cemetery
Pond Street
Natick

Eddie Collins
Linwood Cemetery
US Highway 20 and
Linwood Avenue
Weston
781-893-8695

OTHER AREAS

Joe Cronin
St. Francis Xavier Cemetery
Pine Street (one half mile off
Strawberry Hill Road)
Centerville

Jack Chesbro
Howland Cemetery
Shelburne Falls Road
Conway

Billy Hamilton
Eastwood Cemetery
Old Common Road
Lancaster

Walter "Rabbit" Maranville
St. Michael's Cemetery
1601 State Street
Springfield
413-733-0659

Candy Cummings
Aspen Grove Cemetery
95 Pleasant Street
Ware
413-967-9626

Jesse Burkett
St. John's Cemetery
260 Cambridge Street
Worcester
508-757-7415

Rabbit Maranville played more games at shortstop than any other NL player.

Jesse Burkett had a .338 career batting average.

New Hampshire

Sunset Baseball
City: Concord
Location: Red Eastman Field
White Park
Washington Street

New Hampshire sandlots and youth programs have produced such well-known major-leaguers as Carlton Fisk, Mike Flanagan and Bob Tewksbury. But there's more distant baseball history to be found in this park. It's the site of the Sunset League, known as the "oldest after-supper amateur baseball league in the United States." Organized in 1909 at this very park, the league was the training ground for the likes of Red Rolfe, a New York Yankees standout in the late 1930s. Today, the league consists of five teams—four from Concord and one from Manchester. Players are at least 17 years old, teams are locally sponsored and a 16-game schedule is played. A marker was placed in the park in 1984, and the field was recently re-dedicated in honor of Red Eastman, the man who ran the league for three decades.

Red Rolfe Field

City: Hanover
Location: Dartmouth College

Red Rolfe batted .300 or better four times and scored 100 or more runs in seven of his 10 seasons with the New York Yankees.

This playing site, formally named Red Rolfe Field in 1971, has been home to Dartmouth baseball for almost 100 years. It honors Robert A. "Red" Rolfe, a former Dartmouth star who was a key player on the Yankees team that won four consecutive World Series titles beginning in 1936 and captured five Series crowns and six American League pennants in a seven-year span. Third baseman Rolfe led the AL in hits, doubles and runs scored in 1939. He later managed Detroit for 3½ seasons, guiding the club to a 95–59 record and a second-place finish in 1950. He then served as Dartmouth athletic director from 1954 to 1967.

Holman Stadium

City: Nashua
Location: Amherst Street
(From Route 3, take exit 7E onto Amherst Street. Holman Stadium is approximately one mile on the left.)

Opened in 1937, Holman Stadium is now home to the Nashua Pride of the independent Atlantic League. Unquestionably, though, the park's claim to fame dates to 1946, when it was home field for Roy Campanella and Don Newcombe, who played for the Nashua club of the New England League. The '46 season marked the integration of modern Minor League Baseball, and the Brooklyn Dodgers led the way with Jackie Robinson starring for their Class AAA affiliate in Montreal and Campanella and Newcombe standing out for Brooklyn's Class B Nashua team (which, under manager Walter Alston, won the New England League playoffs). Campanella drove in 96

Roy Campanella (left) and Don Newcombe (right) integrated modern Minor League Baseball in 1946 by starting for the Brooklyn Dodgers' Class B team in Nashua, New Hampshire. Jackie Robinson started that season for their AAA club in Montreal.

runs in 113 games for Nashua; Newcombe compiled a 14–4 record and finished with a 2.21 ERA.

After his playing days were over, Babe Ruth was a frequent visitor to the inn owned by his daughter and son-in-law.

Babe Ruth Slept Here

City: North Conway
Location: Cranmore Mountain Lodge
859 Kearsarge Road
603-356-2044

In the 1940s, this bed-and-breakfast inn was owned by Babe Ruth's daughter and son-in-law. The Bambino spent many vacation days here after his baseball career ended. His favorite room, No. 2, has been maintained with the original furnishings from Ruth's days at the ski-country lodge.

New Jersey

Bacharach Park

City: Atlantic City
Location: 500 North South Carolina Avenue

In the mid-1920s, this was home to the Bacharach Giants of the Eastern Colored League. The mayor of Atlantic City, Henry Bacharach, had been to Jacksonville, Florida, and was so enamored with the black baseball team he saw play there that he brought it home and built a park to showcase its talents. The park was home to Game 2 of the 1926 Negro League World Series. Today, it's the site of the Carver Hall housing development.

John Henry Lloyd Park

City: Atlantic City
Location: Martin Luther King Jr.
Boulevard at US Route 30

John Henry Lloyd was one of the best black players of the dead-ball era. A soft-spoken gentleman off the field, Lloyd was a ferocious competitor on it, drawing glowing comparisons to legendary Pittsburgh shortstop Honus Wagner. Lloyd's career spanned many teams from 1905 to 1931, includ-ing the New

John Henry Lloyd Park is a tribute to the Hall of Fame player considered by many to be the finest shortstop in Negro Leagues history. After retiring as a player, Lloyd organized and managed many youth leagues in the Atlantic City area.

York Lincoln Giants, Brooklyn Royal Giants, New York Bacharach Giants, Atlantic City Bacharach Giants, Columbus Buckeyes, Hilldale Daisies and the Harlem Stars. Over the course of a 27-year career, Lloyd was one of the Negro Leagues' most prolific hitters. After retiring as a player, Lloyd helped organize and manage youth leagues here in the Atlantic City area, often serving as commissioner of the city's youth baseball leagues. For his rich contribution to the area, John Henry Lloyd Park was dedicated in his honor in 1949. Lloyd was elected to the Hall of Fame by the Special Committee on Negro Leagues

A plaque honoring "Pop" Lloyd stands outside the stadium that bears his name.

in 1977, and died in Atlantic City in 1965. There is an inscribed plaque at the stadium honoring Pop Lloyd.

Lloyd is buried at Atlantic City Cemetery (south side of Washington Avenue between Doughty Road and New Road), Pleasantville, 609-646-2260, in Section S, Lot 910.

Sports Hall of Fame of New Jersey
City: East Rutherford
Location: Izod Center
50 Route 120
201-935-8500

More than 30 inductees have been enshrined here in the New Jersey Sports Hall of Fame since May 1993, when the first class was inducted. The list includes baseball players Yogi Berra and Phil Rizzuto, plus such other Jersey legends as Franco Harris, Bill Bradley, Althea Gibson, Paul Robeson, Vince Lombardi and Bill Parcells. Plaques honoring the inductees are on permanent display in the box office lobby of the Izod Center at the Meadowlands Sports Complex.

Some consider an 1846 game at Elysian Fields the start of organized baseball. Soon after, the sport took off.

The Birth of Baseball?
City: Hoboken
Location: Elysian Fields
Corner of 11th and
Washington Streets

It's a fact that Frank Sinatra was born in Hoboken . . . but was baseball? Perhaps. We know several games similar to baseball had been played in Europe and America as far back as the 1600s, but it wasn't until the 1800s that baseball's closer cousin, "Town Ball," began to take shape. But certain facts do appear clear. In 1842, several men, including Alexander Cartwright and Daniel "Doc" Adams, began drafting rules for a game called "baseball." In 1845, they formed the first actual baseball "club," the Knickerbocker Baseball Club, and adopted 20 rules not previously included in earlier editions of

the game, including three strikes per batter, three outs per inning, tags and force-outs in lieu of trying to hit the batter with the ball and the inclusion of an umpire. On June 19, 1846, the Knickerbocker Baseball Club, under these new rules, played the first ever organized game versus the New York Nine. With Cartwright umpiring, the Knickerbockers lost the four-inning game, 23-1. Soon after, with these rules, the sport caught on. In 1869, the first professional team, Cincinnati's Red Stockings, was formed and in 1871, the first nationwide professional league was founded. Was this the first game ever; the so-called birth of baseball? It's hard to say for sure. But until something displaces the seminal games that took place here, it is hard to dispute.

The Lineup from the 1846 Game

New York Knickerbocker Club vs. New York Nine
June 19, 1846
Elysian Fields
Hoboken, New Jersey

Knickerbockers	New York Nine
Turney	Davis
Adams	Winslow
Tucker	Ransom
Birney	Murphy
Avery	Case
H. Anthony	Johnson
D. Anthony	Thompson
Tryon	Trenchard
Paulding	Lalor

FINAL SCORE: New York Nine, 23, Knickerbockers, 1 (4 innings)
UMPIRE: Alexander Cartwright

Jackie Robinson Statue

City: Jersey City
Location: Journal Square
Transportation Center
2815 Kennedy Boulevard
201-659-8823

This monument to Jackie Robinson commemorates his professional debut game at nearby Roosevelt Stadium (no longer standing) on April 18, 1946. In arguably the most important minor-league game in baseball history, Jackie Robinson's Montreal Royals defeated the Jersey City Giants to mark the beginning of the

Jackie Robinson made his minor-league debut at the now defunct Roosevelt Stadium in Jersey City.

racial integration of baseball. Robinson's first pro game was impressive: He hit a three-run homer, singled three times, stole two bases and drove in four runs. One year later, Robinson shattered Major League Baseball's color line as a member of the Brooklyn Dodgers, earning distinction as the National League's Rookie of the Year.

Roosevelt Stadium

City: Jersey City
Location: Society Hill
Apartments
Area bounded by Danforth
Avenue (first base side), Route
440 (right field), Hackensack
River (third base).

This was where Jackie Robinson made his professional debut in April of 1946 as a member of the minor-league Montreal Royals. Built in 1936, it was once home of the minor-league Jersey City Giants and Jerseys. The Brooklyn Dodgers played 15 games here in 1956 and 1957, and Willie Mays hit the only ball ever to sail completely out of the park in 1956 to beat the Dodgers 1-0. Roosevelt Stadium was torn down in 1984 and today is the site of an apartment complex. A marker here commemorates the stadium's history.

Yogi Berra Museum & Learning Center

City: Little Falls
Location: On the campus of Montclair State University
8 Quarry Road
973-655-2378

Yogi Berra remains one of baseball's great characters, gentlemen and ambassadors for the game. A resident of Montclair for more than 40 years, he has received an honorary doctorate from Montclair State University and a baseball stadium has been named in his honor on campus. His museum is located next to the stadium. The Yogi Berra Museum & Learning Center's mission is "to educate and inspire all people, especially children, with culturally diverse, inclusive sports-based educational programming. The Museum's programs foster literacy, as well as a better understanding of social justice, mathematical and scientific principles and the history

The Yogi Berra Museum features permanent and rotating exhibits about baseball, Yankees history and the storied career of Yogi Berra.

and contemporary role of sports in our society." There are permanent exhibits as well as special rotating exhibits featuring memorabilia from Yogi's storied career, lots of Yankee history and a celebration of baseball the way it used to be played. Admission to the Yogi Berra Museum & Learning Center is $6 for adults; $4 for children and students. Programs are free with admission (unless otherwise noted). Hours are Wednesday through Sunday, noon to 5 PM. As Yogi might say, one visit to the museum is like déjà vu all over again.

Michelin Field

City: Milltown
Location: Sheridan Avenue and Lafayette

In 1907, the Michelin Tire Company of France set up shop in this small New Jersey borough, changing it forever. By 1919, the company had not only erected more than 200 houses for its employees, it had also built a small stadium called Michelin Field, where it fielded its own local team. Made up of both employees and local athletes, the team took on all comers, including teams featuring Casey Stengel and Babe Ruth and even the legendary House of David squad. In 1930, Michelin closed down and returned to France, leaving such street names as Lafayette, Joffre, Foch and Our Lady of Lourdes Church, which all recall when Milltown was predominantly French in population. It also left Michelin Field, which sits today where it always did and is used more than ever by the community.

Ruppert Stadium
City: Newark
Location: 262 Wilson Avenue

Ruppert Stadium once stood in Newark, New Jersey, in the area that is now known as the Ironbound. It was originally called Davids' Stadium, and was home to the minor-league Newark Bears of the International League from 1926 to 1949. It was also where the Newark Eagles of the Negro Leagues played from 1936 to 1948. Additionally, Ruppert Stadium was the home field of the short-lived Newark Bears of the first American Football League in 1926. The stadium was razed in 1967, but a plaque can be found at Wilson Avenue and Avenue K commemorating the former home of the Newark Eagles.

Hinchliffe Stadium
City: Paterson
Location: Walnut, Spruce and Liberty Streets

Grand old Hinchliffe Stadium is a historic 10,000-seat municipal stadium situated in Paterson, New Jersey. Erected during 1931–32, it remains one of only a handful of ballparks still standing that once played host to significant Negro League baseball during America's Jim Crow era. It's a large concrete oval with seating laid out like a classical amphitheater, and it was inspired by the "stadium movement" in the 1920s, which saw the arrival of several interesting ballparks. It was named for Mayor John Hinchliffe, who was instrumental in the ballpark being realized, and the first game was played here on September 17, 1932.

The venerable Hinchliffe Stadium in Paterson still stands today.

The stadium initially played host to Negro League and "barnstorming" exhibition games. The first full baseball season ended in 1933 with the Colored Championship of the Nation, the

Negro League equivalent of the World Series. That same season, the New York Black Yankees called the stadium their home, which was the case until 1945. This situation was interrupted only once, when the team played at Triborough Stadium on Randall's Island in New York for the 1938 season. After World War II, the Black Yankees left Hinchliffe and headed north, taking up residency at Red Wing Stadium in Rochester, New York.

Over the years, the baseball played at Hinchliffe Stadium was some of the best and most competitive in the game, including famed players such as Satchel Paige, Josh Gibson, Oscar Charleston, and "Cool Papa" Bell, among many others. Hall of Famer Larry Doby, the legendary player who broke the American League color barrier in 1947, grew up in Paterson playing football and baseball in Hinchliffe Stadium for Paterson's Eastside High School, and was scouted from Hinchliffe for the Newark Eagles in 1942.

And there was more than baseball at Hinchliffe. It was also an important venue for boxing (Diamond Gloves, precursor to the Golden Gloves), auto racing (precursor to NASCAR featuring pre-Indianapolis racing events), and professional and semipro football. Victory Bond rallies held at the stadium during World War II drew sports stars and New York and Hollywood celebrities by the dozens. Among the many notable events headlined at Hinchliffe were shows performed by the famed comic duo Abbott and Costello. (Lou Costello was born and raised in Paterson's Eastside section.)

So what's next for Hinchliffe Stadium? Well, it continues to exist on the public radar even as it continues to deteriorate. Currently, there is a movement to preserve it, even though it has become dilapidated. As it is for many landmarks such as this, there are some big challenges ahead and perhaps in the next edition of *Roadside Baseball*, there will be some resolution to include involving this wonderful stadium.

Lou Costello Park
City: Paterson
Location: At Cianci and
Ellison Streets

Famous comedian Lou Costello hailed from Patterson, New Jersey, growing up near the current location of a life-size statue dedicated to him. It's called *Lou's on First*, a play upon the brilliant "Who's on First" comedy routine Costello performed for years with partner Bud Abbott.

Paterson native Lou Costello (right), shown with his "Who's on First" comedy partner Bud Abbott, was honored with a park and a life-size statue in his hometown.

Clarke Field

City: Princeton
Location: Princeton University
609-258-3000

The diamond used by the Princeton Tigers baseball team is named in honor of Bill "Boileryard" Clarke, who went to school and later coached here. Clarke shared catching duties with Wilbert Robinson on three consecutive first-place Baltimore (National League) teams (1894–96). In 1901, the American League's first season, he was the Senators' first baseman. Clarke Field is one of the finest fields in Northeast collegiate circles, and has been the site of NCAA regional tournament games as well as the host of New Jersey state high school playoff and all-star games.

Lena Blackburne Baseball Rubbing Mud

City: Near Willingboro

Since 1938, a special variety of Jersey muck, Lena Blackburne Baseball Rubbing Mud, has been removing the sheen from baseballs for just about every professional baseball team in the country. It all began when an umpire complained to Lena Blackburne, a third base coach for the old Philadelphia Athletics, about the sad condition of the baseballs used by the American League. Back then, a ball was prepped simply with mud made of water and dirt from the playing field. The result was that the ball's cover was too soft, leaving it open for tampering. Something was needed to take off the shine but not soften the cover. So Blackburne headed to New Jersey looking for a certain kind of mud.

Blackburne had visited many streams to dig up mud, which he then rubbed on new baseballs to make them easier to grip. Finally, Blackburne found a stream in the Delaware River near Willingboro, New Jersey, that had a certain kind of mud on the bottom that, when rubbed on a new baseball, would not change the baseball's color, but would improve its grip. Bingo. He kept the location of this stream a secret, and began to dredge the mud up from the bottom, package it in cans, and sell it to Major League Baseball. Soon the entire American League was using the amazing gunk. Later, the National League took to using it. Before Blackburne's death in the late '50s, every major and most minor leagues in the United States were using his baseball rubbing mud.

When Blackburne died, his friend, John Haas, continued packaging and selling the special mud. Haas eventually turned over the enterprise to his son-in-law, Burns Bintliff. Burns in turn passed it on to son Jim and his family. Lena Blackburne Baseball Rubbing Mud is still used today in Major League Baseball. There is even a can of the mud on display at the Baseball

Hall of Famers Buried in New Jersey

Leon "Goose" Goslin
Baptist Cemetery
Yorke Street
Salem

Goose Goslin batted .300 or better 11 times.

Hall of Fame in Cooperstown, New York, and the place where it is found in New Jersey is still a well-kept secret. But know that each July, the Bintliff team heads a boat out to the "ole mud hole" and scoops up hundreds of pounds of the stuff that's been a part of the game since 1938. They bring back just enough for one season. Then the mud rests in barrels until the next spring when it's packed and shipped to each of the major-league and minor-league teams, most independent leagues and many colleges in time for opening day. Think of it as one of baseball's last "dirty little secrets."

New York

War Memorial Stadium
City: Buffalo
Location: Johnnie B. Wiley Amateur Athletic Sports Pavilion
1100 Jefferson Avenue

Though primarily a football stadium, War Memorial (referred to locally as "The Rockpile") was also used by Buffalo's Class AAA Bisons team. It was built in the 1930s and torn down in the 1980s, but what secures War Memorial Stadium's place in baseball history was its transformation into a vintage 1939 park for the 1984 filming of Bernard Malamud's novel *The Natural*,

Two of the archways from War Memorial Stadium in Buffalo still stand today.

starring Robert Redford. Though the stadium is gone, the pillars at the entranceway were preserved at what is now a public park facility. The flagpole from War Memorial Stadium also was moved and now sits alongside a plaque outside the right-field bleachers at the new home of the Bisons, Dunn Tire Park, at 275 Washington Street.

Greater Buffalo Sports Hall of Fame
City: Buffalo
Location: HSBC Arena
1 Seymour H. Knox III Plaza

The Greater Buffalo Sports Hall of Fame honors many local athletes, including baseball legends Luke Easter, Sal Maglie and Warren Spahn. The museum is free and located on the lower level of the HSBC Arena atrium in downtown Buffalo. Memorabilia, information, interactive computer kiosks and video presentations are displayed in honor of these athletes.

Cooperstown Bat Company
City: Cooperstown
Location: 118 Main Street
888-547-2415

If you visit the Hall of Fame in Cooperstown, I recommend a trip to the Cooperstown Bat Company. They've been making interesting, authentic bats here for more than 25 years. Their line of vintage baseball bats and balls have been used and enjoyed for years by baseball history enthusiasts. Plus, they handcraft historic bats representing periods from the Civil War era through the turn of the 20th century and into the very first days of the modern game.

How do they maintain accuracy? Well, each bat is reproduced from profiles researched just down the road from their factory at the National Baseball Hall of Fame & Museum's Library and Archives. From custom engraving to high quality bats for players and collectors, the Cooperstown Bat Company has been crafting bats since 1981. As they say, "The store is less a tourist attraction than an American way of life, celebrating America's favorite pastime in an elegant presentation and thoughtful customer service. It is a must-stop for any baseball aficionado when visiting Cooperstown." Agreed (and I have the bat I bought to prove it).

Doubleday Field

City: Cooperstown
Location: The Baseball Hall of Fame
25 Main Street

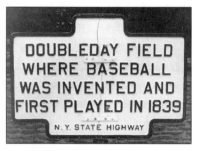

Located just a block from baseball's Hall of Fame, Doubleday Field sits on a former cow pasture called Phinney's Farm.

Abner Doubleday probably was nowhere near Cooperstown during the summer of 1839 when he allegedly laid out the first baseball diamond and limited the number of players per side to nine. But enough baseball has been played on this field to give it a special history, Doubleday or no Doubleday. Here, at the "mythical" birthplace of baseball, a former cow pasture called Phinney's Farm, two professional baseball games are played during each Hall of Fame induction weekend. The annual Hall of Fame game is the feature presentation; the other is hosted by the Oneonta Tigers, who play their New York-Pennsylvania League home games at nearby Damaschke Field.

Two pro games, one by major-league teams and another by minor leaguers, are played during each Hall of Fame induction weekend at Doubleday Field.

The field is just a block from the Baseball Hall of Fame, the granddaddy of all sports museums and the ultimate baseball shrine. The Baseball Writers' Association of America elected its charter class in 1936: Ty Cobb, Babe Ruth, Honus Wagner, Christy Mathewson and Walter Johnson. Three years later, on June 12, 1939, the Hall of Fame officially was dedicated. Of the 26 players who had been elected to that point, 11 were still alive and all but Cobb visited Cooperstown for the spectacular celebration. Today, annual attendance at the Hall of Fame and Museum approaches 350,000 and twice has topped 400,000. The shrine is open year round. The busiest months are July and August, when the annual induction weekends take place.

Dunn Field
City: Elmira
Location: 546 Luce Street
607-207-0159

Dunn Field is a quaint historic stadium located down on the banks of the Chemung River. Since first opening in 1939, it's been home to various incarnations of the Elmira Pioneers. The site itself has a lot of history. The first stadium at the site was known as the Maple Avenue Driving Park. Interestingly, on November 21, 1902, the stadium was the site of the first National Football League night game (the Philadelphia Athletics football team defeated the Kanaweola Athletic Club, 39-0). In the late 19th century, the stadium also served as an alternate home for baseball's National League Buffalo Bisons. The Maple Avenue Driving Park was replaced by Recreation Park, which burned down in 1938. A new stadium was built to replace it and the name came from a local businessman, Edward Joseph Dunn, who agreed to donate some land to the city on which to build the ballpark.

Along with being the home field of the Elmira Pioneers, many other events have taken place here over the years. There's been wrestling, boxing matches, high school sports, and even concerts (case in point: a well-attended Beach Boys show held here in 1984). Dunn Field was also home field for both the Elmira Free Academy and Southside High School football teams for many years until each team built their own stadiums. Many great baseball players played their home games on this field during part of their minor-league careers, including Wade Boggs, Curt Schilling, and Jim Palmer. Former player and major-league manager Don Zimmer was even married on Dunn Field in 1951 (pictured in *Sports Illustrated* magazine, and his autobiography). Dunn Field has a capacity of 4,020 people, including 312 box seats.

Headin' Home Filming Site
City: Haverstraw
Location: Babe Ruth Field
Broadway

During part of the summer of 1920, Babe Ruth came to the village of Haverstraw in Rockland County (about an hour north of New York City) to film scenes for a silent film called *Headin' Home.* The *New York Times* gave this synopsis of the plot, which was adapted from a short magazine story by Wid Gunning:

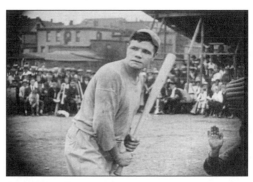

A still from the silent film *Headin' Home,* shot in Haverstraw, New York.

> Babe Ruth plays Babe Dugan, home run whiz of the Los Angeles Angels. Babe's habit of chewing tobacco makes him the bane of the Snow White Laundry, which has to clean his juice-stained uniforms after every game. Laundress Vernie (Anna Q. Nilsson) attends an Angels game to see for herself just how one man can be so messy. Babe hits a fly ball, which hits Vernie in the eye. From this bad start, a romance develops, culminating in an engagement. On the eve of the wedding, Babe and Vernie have a rhubarb over his tobacco habit. She walks out, and Babe goes into a slump. But during a crucial game (bases loaded in the ninth, natch!) Vernie shows up in the stands and tosses Babe a flesh [sic] plug of tobacco. He stuffs the wad in his mouth and hits the deciding homer. Conceding that it was Vernie's love and not the "chew" that inspired him to win, Babe swears off tobacco forever.

Haverstraw had a small ballpark back then where a local farm team played and it was used extensively in *Headin' Home.* Today, the spot where these action scenes were shot is preserved as Babe Ruth Field.

Russell E. Diethrick, Jr. Park Baseball Marker

City: Jamestown
Location: 285 Falconer Street

According to the city of Jamestown, New York:

> Jamestown enjoys a long heritage of baseball. Organized baseball has been played here since the Civil War. It continues today with professional, semi-pro and amateur teams calling the Jamestown area "home base." Players from the area have gone on to the Major Leagues and World Series

games. Empty fields and city parks accommodated the early teams. Celoron Park and Allen Park had ball fields that served the area before Municipal Stadium (now Russell E. Diethrick, Jr. Park) was opened in 1941. Early Major League teams and barnstorming teams played exhibition games at available ball fields. Amateurs and semi-pros continue to play here and in recent years Diethrick Park has hosted college tournament teams and Babe Ruth World Series teams from around the country. Jamestown has been a part of the Major League farm club system for close to fifty years. Baseball could not have flourished here without the interest of the community–the fans. For almost 150 years, the Jamestown area has been involved and interested in baseball.

Because of this dedication to the game of baseball, a plaque was placed in town that reads:

Baseball

An enduring part of Jamestown's heritage this marker recognizes the baseball players and spectators of yesteryear and salutes the present and future players and fans.

Eddie Collins Park
City: Millerton
Location: Route 22

There's a ball field named for him here because Hall of Fame second baseman Eddie Collins was born in this small Dutchess County town on May 2, 1887. He signed his first major-league contract in 1906 and then went on to play 25 seasons after that. Part of the renowned $100,000 infield for the Philadelphia Athletics, he also played for the Chicago White Sox. Collins, a member of the 3,000-hit club, was elected to the Hall of Fame in 1939.

Lou Gehrig Wedding
City: New Rochelle
Location: 5 Circuit Road

In 1933, Lou Gehrig married Eleanor Twitchell at this private home. As any baseball fan knows (or anyone who saw the classic film, *Pride of the Yankees*), the marriage ended sadly on June 2, 1941. That's when Lou Gehrig passed away from amyotrophic lateral sclerosis–the disease that today bears his name. After Gehrig died, Eleanor never remarried. Rather, she lived quietly in her apartment on Manhattan's East Side for more than 40 years. From time to time, she visited her upstairs neighbor, the famed boxer Jack Dempsey. She'd also visit Yankee Stadium with Mrs. Babe Ruth to attend old-timers' games or the World Series. Eleanor Gehrig was once quoted as saying: "I had the best of it with Lou. I would not have traded two minutes of my life with that man for 40 years with another." The great love story of Eleanor and Lou Gehrig inspired the movie *Pride of the Yankees*, which stars Teresa Wright and Gary Cooper as the well-respected couple.

Monument Park at Yankee Stadium (now found at the new Yankee Stadium)
City: New York
Location: 161st Street and River Avenue
The Bronx

When Yankee owner Jacob Ruppert was asked by the Giants to vacate the Polo Grounds, he didn't blink. The Yankees were outdrawing their tenants and he expected fans to relocate with them. At a site just across the Harlem River from the Polo Grounds, Ruppert built a massive, state-of-the-art stadium that would become one of the most legendary sports venues in the world. Yankee Stadium, opened in 1923, closed recently. Monument Park, which had been located behind the left-center field fence, was a reflec-

Plaques honoring Babe Ruth and Joe DiMaggio are among the many memorials and retired-number tributes at Monument Park, located beyond the left-center field fence at Yankee Stadium.

tion of that success, and can be found today in the new ballpark. It is filled with monuments and plaques honoring former Yankee greats and a special area is dedicated to uniform numbers retired by the Yankees.

Parish of the Yankees
City: New York
Location: St. Angela Merici Church
917 Morris Avenue
The Bronx

Babe Ruth and Joe DiMaggio were parishioners at this church during their playing days with the Yankees. Ruth, his wife and daughter, in fact, donated the church's marble altar, explaining why their names appear on a plaque in the church.

Edward L. Grant Memorial Highway

City: New York
Location: From Jerome Avenue to Martin Luther King Boulevard (about six blocks north of Yankee Stadium)
The Bronx

This stretch of road was named in 1945 for former New York Giants player Eddie Grant, who holds the sad distinction of being the first major-league player killed in wartime action. The former third baseman led a mission in the Argonne Forest offensive to rescue the "Lost Battalion" trapped behind German lines during World War I. He was killed by machine gun fire and was subsequently honored at the Polo Grounds with a plaque and monument in center field. Every Memorial Day, the Giants held a wreath-laying ceremony at the plaque, which mysteriously disappeared after the Giants left the Polo Grounds. Grant, a Harvard graduate, had retired from baseball in 1915 to practice law in New York City before the war.

Yankee Stadium

City: New York
Location: East 161st Street and River Avenue
The Bronx

Is it really not being used anymore? It's sad, but true. As almost every fan knows, Yankee Stadium was the home of the New York Yankees from 1923 through 2008. The park had a capacity of 57,545 and over the years hosted 6,581 Yankees regular-season home games during its illustrious 85-year history. It was also the former home of the New York Giants football team, and host of 20 of boxing's most renowned fights and three Papal masses. Yankee Stadium's nickname, "The House That Ruth Built" harkens back to the iconic Babe Ruth, arguably the most famous player in history, whose prime years paralleled the dawn

Opening day at the old Yankee Stadium, 1923.

of the Yankees' winning history. In 2006, after years of speculation surrounding a new park, the Yankees actually began construction on a new $1.8 billion stadium in public parkland adjacent to the original Yankee Stadium. The team is expecting to open their new home in 2009, just as this edition of this book is published. Once the new baseball palace opens, most of the old stadium, including the above-ground structure, is slated to be demolished to become parkland.

A recent image of the old Yankee Stadium, former home of the Yankees.

The first game at Yankee Stadium was held on April 18, 1923, and the Yankees defeated the Boston Red Sox, 4-1. The final game at the stadium was held on September 21, 2008, with the Yankees beating the Baltimore Orioles, 7-3. To create a proper send-off, on November 8, 2008, former Yankees Scott Brosius, Paul O'Neill, David Cone and Jeff Nelson, all members of the 1998 world championship team, joined 60 children from two Bronx-based youth groups, Youth Force 2020 and the ACE Mentor Program, in ceremoniously digging up home plate, the pitcher's rubber and the surrounding dirt of both areas and transporting them to the same areas of the new Yankee Stadium. This gesture symbolically and physically linked the two stadiums, passing a bit of the torch from one to the other.

A portrait of Charles Ebbets.

Charles Ebbets Home
City: New York
Location: 1466 Glenwood Road
Brooklyn

Charles Ebbets, the man for whom Ebbets Field was named, was born in New York City and was originally not a baseball man, but rather a draftsman and architect who designed numerous New York City buildings. Ebbets also served on the Brooklyn City Council for four years and in the New York State Assembly for one year. He started his baseball career as a bookkeeper with the Dodgers in 1883, the team's first year, and he became a shareholder in 1890. Ebbets took an active role in marketing baseball (and the Dodgers) to families and took over team operations in 1898. He also managed the Dodgers that year, but it was a bit of a bust—the team finished tenth in the league. After the 1898 season, Ned Hanlon, owner and manager of the Baltimore Orioles, bought some of the remaining stock in the Dodgers and brought in some of the strongest players from his Baltimore operation to the Brooklyn team. Thanks in part to that, the Dodgers won pennants in both 1899 and 1900. In 1905, Hanlon wanted to move the team to Baltimore but Ebbets bought out his shares. He'd then go on to become one of the most famous owners in history; an innovative executive who helped change the game for the better. Today, we remember Charles Ebbets as the man who invented the concept of the rain check and of proposing a player draft favoring teams that finished low in the standings. He also financed the building of the beloved Ebbets Field in 1912 by selling half his shares in the team. Charles Ebbets died of heart failure at the age of 65 in New York City and is buried in Green-Wood Cemetery in Brooklyn. This house was his primary residence when he was the owner of the Brooklyn Dodgers. There is no marker and it is a private residence today.

Jackie Robinson School/PS 375
City: New York
Location: 46 McKeever Place
Brooklyn

Though a number of schools around the country are named for Jackie Robinson, this one is located closest to where he actually made history. It is in Brooklyn, at the point where the third base foul line at Ebbets Field used to be. The school, built in the late 1960s, features a large mural of Robinson on its outside facade.

Ebbets Field
City: New York
Location: Bedford Avenue and
Montgomery Street
Ebbets Field Apartments
Crown Heights
Brooklyn

One of the most storied, romanticized venues in baseball history was opened by Dodgers owner Charles Ebbets in 1913. It was a raucous, sometimes-zany ballpark that became known for its colorful

The Ebbets Field apartments now dominate the Bedford Avenue and Montgomery Street location once occupied by Ebbets Field.

fans, interesting charac-
ters and unusual, always
offbeat atmosphere. It
was a place of the heart
for legions of neighbor-
hood fans, who loved
their Dodgers with unre-
lenting passion. Among
its trademark fans and
memories were Hilda
Chester, the cowbell-
ringing bleacher regu-
lar; the right and left
field walls, plastered
with such advertise-
ments as the memora-

Ebbets Field, pictured just after its opening, circa 1915.

ble Schaefer Beer sign atop the right field scoreboard that gave fans the
official scorer's ruling on hits and errors, and the bottom-of-scoreboard Abe
Stark ad that challenged batters to "Hit sign, win suit."; and the Dodgers
Sym-Phony band, a collection of "Brooklyn Bum" musicians who wandered
the stadium, entertaining fans while pounding out off-key music. But all of
the characters, the local color and the teams that won nine National League
pennants and one World Series couldn't keep owner Walter O'Malley from
seeking greener pastures. After the 1957 season, O'Malley relocated the
beloved Bums to sunny Los Angeles. Just 6,673 fans attended the final game
at Ebbets Field and the park was torn down in 1960. Today, the Ebbets Field
apartments occupy the site, with only a cornerstone left to salute the former
location of a once-proud ballpark.

Only a cornerstone marker (left) remains at the former site of Ebbets Field, but other
reminders are visible throughout the borough.

Some Memorable Moments at Ebbets Field

★ JUNE 15, 1938: Cincinnati's Johnny Vander Meer pitched his second consecutive no-hitter, defeating the Dodgers, 6-0, in the first night game at Ebbets Field.

★ OCTOBER 5, 1941: Catcher Mickey Owen's passed ball on what would have been the final pitch of a Dodgers' Game 4 World Series victory over the Yankees allowed the Bronx Bombers to pull out a shocking 7-4 win over Brooklyn.

★ APRIL 15, 1947: Jackie Robinson made this an opening day for the ages as he became the 20th century's first black player while contributing to a 5-3 victory over Boston.

★ AUGUST 31, 1950: Dodgers first baseman Gil Hodges hit four home runs and a single in a 19-3 rout of the Boston Braves.

The Location of the Ebbets Field Flagpole
City: New York
Location: Corner of Utica Avenue and Farragut Road
Brooklyn

The original Ebbets Field center field flagpole still stands at this former VFW Hall (now a casket company). Though there was some talk of moving it to the new Brooklyn minor-league stadium, Keyspan Park (home of the Cyclones), that plan has been put on hold. A plaque at the base of the flagpole identifies it as being from Ebbets Field.

Home of the Brooklyn Excelsiors
City: New York
Location: 133 Clinton Street
Brooklyn Heights
Brooklyn

A plaque on the building at this address commemorates it as the former home of the Brooklyn Excelsiors, Brooklyn's first professional baseball team. The Excelsi-

During the Civil War era, the Excelsiors taught the game of baseball to soldiers from various states, thus spreading the popularity of the game.

ors, according to the plaque, helped spread the game throughout the country in the post-Civil War years.

Jackie Robinson Parkway
City: New York

On April 14, 1997, the Interborough Parkway was renamed after Jackie Robinson to commemorate the 50th anniversary of him breaking the major-league color barrier with the Brooklyn Dodgers. Over his 11 seasons, Robinson helped the Dodgers win six National League pennants and one World Series—a seven-game 1955 thriller against the hated Yankees. Robinson was inducted into the Hall of Fame in 1962. The Parkway serves as a link between the Kew Gardens (Grand Central Parkway-Van Wyck Expressway) interchange in central Queens and Pennsylvania Avenue in East New York, Brooklyn. It also passes the cemetery in Cypress Hills where Robinson was buried in 1972.

Washington Park
City: New York
Location: Left field (NW), 3rd Avenue; third base (SW), 3rd Street; first base (SE), 4th Avenue; right field (NW), 1st Street.
Brooklyn

This was the location for the original home of the Brooklyn Dodgers, the first ballpark erected by Charles Ebbets. Opened in 1898 when the team was called the Superbas, they played here until 1912, at which point they moved into their new home, Ebbets Field. (Casey Stengel made his professional debut at Washington Park as a member of the 1912 Dodgers.) After the Dodgers vacated Washington Park, it was used by the Brooklyn entry in the Federal League in 1914 and

Old Washington Park in Brooklyn. Today, only a piece of the outfield wall remains.

1915. Soon after the Federal League folded, the stadium was torn down. Amazingly, part of Washington Park's clubhouse wall still stands. It is now the 3rd Avenue wall to the Con Edison yard at 222 1st Street in Brooklyn. This is thought to be the oldest remaining piece of any major-league stadium still standing and preservationists are battling to keep the ballpark relic from being demolished.

Parade Grounds

City: New York
Location: Prospect Park (southern end)
Bounded by Parkside Avenue on the north, Parade Place on the east, Caton Avenue on the south and Coney Island Avenue on the west.
Brooklyn

When Caton Avenue was constructed in 1926, Brooklyn added a small triangular section of its unused land to the project. By the late 1930s, the Parade Grounds' baseball diamonds attracted an average crowd of 20,000 daily to watch such soon-to-be-discovered players as Sandy Koufax. In the 1950s, a new recreation building was added to the Parade Grounds. In addition to housing Parks Department offices, a comfort station, a concession area and several indoor tennis courts, the Grounds also provided space for Brooklyn's 74th Police Precinct. As the loosely formed baseball "leagues" continued to develop (becoming a breeding ground for professional and semipro ballplayers), the *Brooklyn Daily Eagle* covered Parade Grounds games, ran box scores and even provided highlights of the more important games. A peak of 140 teams were once registered to play at the Parade Grounds. Although some baseball is still played today on the site, tennis courts, soccer fields and football fields now take up a good portion of the real estate.

Jackie Robinson Signs— Brooklyn Dodgers Headquarters

City: New York
Location: 215 Montague Street
Brooklyn

It was in August of 1945 (three weeks after the atomic bomb was dropped on Hiroshima) that Jackie Robinson

The historic meeting between Jackie Robinson and Branch Rickey, where Robinson signed his contract to play pro ball, occurred at the former headquarters of the Brooklyn Dodgers. A plaque marks the site of meeting.

secretly sat down in an office once located at this address and signed a contract to play baseball for the 1946 Class AAA Montreal Royals. For integration to work, Dodgers boss Branch Rickey knew Robinson would have to turn the other cheek—ignore the ugly comments he'd surely hear and not be confrontational in the face of certain cruelty. Rickey insisted that, no matter how foul the treatment Robinson got from fans or opposing players, he could not retaliate for two years. "What I'm looking for is more than a great player," Rickey told Robinson. "I'm looking for a man that will take insults, take abuse—and have the guts not to fight back." With grace, honor and courage, Robinson honored the agreement and thus changed baseball. A plaque identifies this as the former headquarters of the Brooklyn Dodgers—and salutes the historic meeting that occurred here.

Gil Hodges Way
City: **New York**
Location: **On Bedford Avenue between Avenues L, M and N (three blocks)**
Brooklyn

In April 2001, just a couple of miles from where Ebbets Field used to sit, then-New York mayor Rudy Giuliani was on hand to rename Bedford Avenue, between Avenues L and M (the street on which Gil Hodges and his family lived), "Gil Hodges Way." Hodges's widow, Joan, was there for the ceremony. Hodges came to New York in 1943 as a 19-year-old rookie catcher for the Brooklyn Dodgers and, like many players of his generation, saw his career interrupted by service in World War II. He returned to the Dodgers in 1947 and became a staple at first base, hitting 370 career home runs and driving in 1,274 runs. His lifetime batting average of .273 was forged around 1,921 career hits. Hodges also was an outstanding fielder, earning three Gold Gloves, and he represented the National League at first base in eight All-Star

Former Dodgers first baseman Gil Hodges was always a fan favorite in Brooklyn.

Games. Nearing the end of his playing career, Hodges played for the New York Mets and gained distinction as the first Mets player to hit a home run in their expansion season of 1962. In 1968, he became Mets manager and led the team to its first World Series—the "miracle" championship of 1969.

Other Gil Hodges-Related Landmarks in Brooklyn

★ PS 193 is called the Gil Hodges School, located at 2515 Avenue L.

★ There is a Gil Hodges Little League Field on Knapp Street between Avenues V and W.

★ The Marine Parkway-Gil Hodges Memorial Bridge connects Floyd Bennett Field in Brooklyn with Fort Tilden in the Rockaways. A sign and bust of Hodges are at the entrance to the bridge.

The Birth of the National League
City: New York
Location: Grand Central Hotel
673 Broadway, just south of West 3rd Street
Lower Manhattan

It was at this site in 1876 that a small group of men led by Chicago businessman William Hulbert and pitching star Albert Spalding met to form the National League. As a result, eight teams were created to start the 1876 season. In 1952, a plaque was placed on the hotel stating that it was the "Birthplace of major league baseball. On this site the National League of Professional Baseball Clubs was organized on February 2, 1876." In 1973, the hotel collapsed after years of weakening and the plaque was lost. Today, a New York University law school dorm is located on the site.

Polo Grounds
City: New York
Location: Polo Grounds Towers
West 157th Street and Eighth Avenue
Washington Heights
Manhattan

The New York Giants originally played baseball at a city polo field on 110th Street and Sixth Avenue. When owner John Brush moved the team to Coogan's

This view from Coogan's Bluff shows Polo Grounds Towers covering the area where the legendary stadium once stood.

Bluff in 1891, he kept the name "Polo Grounds." In April 1911, the wooden Polo Grounds burned to the ground. The stadium was quickly rebuilt with steel and concrete in time to host the Philadelphia Athletics in the 1911 World Series. An odd "bathtub-shaped" ballpark, the Polo Grounds was home to some of the greatest legends in baseball history. Mel Ott, Willie Mays, Christy Mathewson and Carl Hubbell are just a few of the famous Giants who carved out history here. (The Polo Grounds was even home to the Yankees for 10 seasons until Yankee Stadium opened in 1923.)

In 1957, Giants owner Horace Stoneham devastated the city when he announced that he was moving the Giants to San Francisco. The Polo Grounds remained for seven more years, serving as home to the New York Mets for the 1962 and 1963 seasons. In 1964, the stadium was demolished and now the Polo Grounds Towers, a housing project, occupies the site. All that is left of the original Polo Grounds is an old staircase on the side of the cliff that once led to the ticket booth. On one of the landings of the stairway is a

The horseshoe-shaped Polo Grounds was the site of many of baseball's most memorable moments.

All that remains of the Polo Grounds is the staircase fans would walk down as they approached the stadium

A vintage image, circa 1909, of the Polo Grounds.

Some Memorable Moments at the Polo Grounds

★ SEPTEMBER 23, 1908: Fred Merkle neglected to touch second base on an apparent game-ending hit against Chicago, triggering a controversy that eventually cost the Giants a 1908 pennant.

★ AUGUST 16, 1920: Cleveland Indians shortstop Ray Chapman was killed by a pitch thrown by Yankee Carl Mays. Chapman remains the only major-leaguer ever to die after being struck by a pitched ball.

★ JULY 10, 1934: Pitching in the All-Star Game, Giants screwballer Carl Hubbell struck out Babe Ruth, Lou Gehrig, Jimmie Foxx, Al Simmons and Joe Cronin consecutively.

★ AUGUST 1, 1945: Giants slugger Mel Ott became the third member of baseball's 500-homer club with a shot off Boston's Johnny Hutchings.

★ OCTOBER 3, 1951: Bobby Thomson fired the "Shot Heard 'Round the World"— the legendary homer that beat the Dodgers, 5–4, to give the Giants a dramatic National League pennant.

★ SEPTEMBER 29, 1954: Giants center fielder Willie Mays hauled in a 460-foot blast by Cleveland's Vic Wertz, one of the most memorable catches in World Series history.

A plaque marks the former location of the Polo Grounds' home plate.

marker that states: "The John T. Brush Stairway Presented by the New York Giants." The stairway was used by fans to get to the ticket booth behind home plate. A plaque marks the approximate site where home plate once sat.

Hank Greenberg Ball Field
City: New York
Location: 663 Crotona Park North
Manhattan

This ball field was named in honor of the great Major League Baseball player Henry Benjamin "Hank" Greenberg. "Hammerin' Hank," as he was also called, Greenberg was renowned for his strong right-handed hitting, and he constantly challenged some of the great hitters of his era. Greenberg lived at 663 Crotona Park North, next door to Crotona Park, where he continually worked on his game, which makes this park so much more meaningful for Greenberg fans who visit.

Born into a Jewish-Romanian family in Greenwich Village on January 1, 1911, Hank came here to the Bronx as a young boy. He played first base on the James Monroe High School baseball team and once remarked, "My baseball greatly improved, due to the fact that we moved to the Bronx across the street from Crotona Park. I did have a whole army of kids in the outfield shagging balls." Known for his strenuous work ethic, Greenberg spent many hours at this very site improving his batting and fielding.

Like other gifted young players of his era, Greenberg was desired by a number of teams. In fact, in 1929, Greenberg was offered contracts by three teams, including the local New York Yankees. Greenberg, an up-and-coming first baseman, deferred to Lou Gehrig (the Yankees' iconic first baseman) and passed on the Yankees' offer. In 1930, Greenberg began his pro career when he signed a minor-league contract with the Detroit Tigers for $9,000 ($1,000 less than the Yankees were offering). He was 19 then, a strapping young athlete who stood six feet four inches tall and weighed 210 pounds. The powerful Greenberg quickly proved his value to the team soon after joining.

In 1933, he was called up to the major leagues, and as a rookie he hit .301 with 12 home runs, and 87 RBI. In his second major-league season, he won his first of three major-league MVP awards, and is one of only three players to win MVP honors at two different positions, first base and left field. In 1935, Greenberg helped the Tigers win their first World Series in club history and in 1938, he hit 58 home runs, nearly breaking Babe Ruth's single-season record of 60 home runs. This is a fact that has been forgotten by many over the years.

In 1941, Greenberg was drafted into military service, along with many other young players. Assuming he would be back in time for the '42 season, Greenberg instead volunteered to stay in the war for its duration when Pearl Harbor was attacked in December of 1941. He returned home in the summer of 1945 and, several weeks later, crushed a grand slam in the ninth inning, to clinch the American League pennant for the Detroit Tigers. Greenberg played with the Tigers until 1946, when a contract dispute forced him to join the National League Pittsburgh Pirates in 1947. Greenberg was notable as one of the few players to openly welcome Jackie Robinson into the league. Robinson had kind words for Greenberg, saying, "He [Greenberg] suddenly turned to me and said, 'A lot of people are pulling for you to make good. Don't ever forget it.' I never did."

In total, Greenberg played nine seasons and yet, despite this short career, he still managed to hit 331 career home runs. He played his final game on September 18, 1947, and was the first Jewish player to be inducted into the Hall of Fame in 1956. He died September 4, 1986, in California, but he is remembered here at the spot where he first learned about baseball.

Joe DiMaggio's Apartment
City: New York
Location: 400 West End Avenue
Manhattan

The great Yankee ballplayer, Joe DiMaggio, is almost as famous for his marriage to actress Marilyn Monroe as he is for his playing career, but many are not aware that the Yankee Clipper was married before he ever even knew the blonde bombshell. In November 1939, DiMaggio was married to another attractive blonde actress, a woman by the name of Dorothy Arnold. They were married in St. Peter and Paul Church in North Beach, California (the place where, 60 years later, DiMaggio's funeral would be held). The couple would go on to have one son, Joe Jr., who was born in 1941. They lived here at 400 West End Avenue but the marriage did not last long. Arnold divorced DiMaggio in 1944 and moved to Reno, taking their 13-month-old son along with her. Joe DiMaggio Jr., the star's only child, served as a pallbearer at his father's funeral service (he had not talked with his father in more than two years). Five months after his father died, Joe DiMaggio Jr. died as the result of a heart attack. The apartment still stands today.

Christy Mathewson and John McGraw's Apartment
City: New York
Location: 76 West 85th Street
Manhattan

How good was Christy Mathewson? In his first full season for the Giants, the great Hall of Fame pitcher won 20 games and lost 17. On Opening Day in

1902, he blanked Philadelphia but ended up that season with a losing record of 14 wins and 17 defeats. The next season, he started a 12-year stretch of domination in which, amazingly, he averaged 26 wins a season and compiled four 30-win years. Mathewson won 317 games and lost only 133 games in that span. He was the dominant pitcher in the National League, leading his league in wins four times, in earned run average five times, and in strikeouts five times.

The renowned manager/strategist John McGraw immediately took Christy Mathewson under his wing after becoming Giants manager in 1903. In fact, his tutelage of the gifted pitcher extended off the field. That spring, Mathewson and his new wife, Jane, a Sunday school teacher, celebrated their honeymoon at the Giants' training camp. Soon after, McGraw's wife, Blanche, formed a bond with Jane Mathewson. When the team returned to New York City, the McGraws and Mathewsons actually shared a home together, living under one roof in this ground-floor apartment near Central Park, a strange arrangement even by today's standards. It remains the same today as it was back then, and it's interesting to imagine these two legends leaving for work and returning each day together after the game was done.

Roy Campanella's Liquor Store
City: New York
Location: 198 West 134th Street
Manhattan

The legendary Brooklyn Dodger catcher Roy Campanella lived in Glen Cove, New York, on the North Shore of Long Island. However, the liquor

The site of Roy Campanella's liquor store, today.

store he owned was located at this site in Harlem. "Campy," as he was called, ran the store himself during the baseball off-season, and on January 28, 1958, after shutting the store for the night, he headed home to Glen Cove. En route, traveling at about 30 MPH, his car (a rented 1957 Chevrolet sedan) skidded across a patch of ice, careened into a telephone pole and overturned, breaking Campanella's neck. He fractured the fifth and sixth cervical vertebrae and compressed the spinal cord. Tragically, the accident left Campanella paralyzed from the shoulders down. After a lot of physical therapy, Campy was eventually able to gain some use of his arms and hands, along with being able to feed himself, shake hands, and gesture while speaking. However, he needed a wheelchair to get around for the rest of his life.

After his playing career ended, Campanella remained active with the Dodgers. In January 1959, the team made him assistant supervisor of scouting for the eastern part of the United States and a special coach of the team's annual spring training camp in Vero Beach, Florida, serving each season as a mentor and coach to up-and-coming young catchers in the organization. In 1978, Campanella moved to California and became an assistant to the Dodgers' director of community relations, Campanella's former teammate in Brooklyn and longtime buddy, Don Newcombe.

Campanella died of a heart attack on June 26, 1993, in his Woodland Hills, California, home. He was cremated by the Forest Lawn, Hollywood Hills Cemetery in Los Angeles.

Hilltop Park

City: **New York**
Location: **New York-Presbyterian Hospital/Columbia University Medical Center**
622 West 168th Street
Washington Heights
Manhattan

Opened in 1903, Hilltop Park was the New York Yankees' first home. Originally called American League Park, the stadium was renamed because it sat on high ground and the New Yorkers were called, appropriately, the Highlanders. From this perch, when seated behind home plate, spectators could enjoy scenic views of the Hudson River. Hilltop was shared by the Giants for a short period in 1911 when their Polo Grounds home was destroyed by fire. After the 1912 season, the Giants reciprocated, allowing the Yankees to become tenants of their rebuilt Polo Grounds. Hilltop Park, now empty, was razed in 1914 and the Columbia University Medical Center opened on the site in 1928. Today, a plaque marks the spot where home plate once sat.

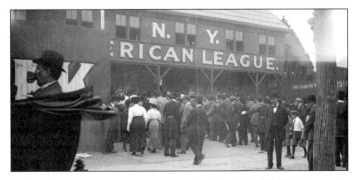

A vintage shot of Hilltop Park, where the New York Highlanders (soon to be Yankees) played.

Some Memorable Moments at Hilltop Park

★ JUNE 28, 1907: The Washington Senators stole 13 bases off Yankees catcher Branch Rickey and posted a 16–5 victory over the New Yorkers.

★ JUNE 30, 1908: Cy Young, at age 41, hurled his third career no-hitter, defeating Boston, 8–0.

★ SEPTEMBER 7, 1908: Washington's Walter Johnson pitched his third shutout against the New York Giants in a four-day span.

★ MAY 15, 1912: Detroit's Ty Cobb jumped into the Hilltop stands and began punching a handicapped fan who had been insulting him. Cobb was suspended for the ugly incident.

Babe Ruth Gets Married

City: New York
Location: St. Gregory the Great
144 West 90th Street
Manhattan

Babe and Claire Ruth

In the mid-1920s, Babe Ruth met and became seriously interested in a young widow, Claire Hodgson. Claire had come to New York from Georgia with her young daughter, Julia, in 1920 to work as a model and actress. On April 17, 1929, Ruth and Hodgson were married at St. Gregory the Great Catholic church in New York, scheduling the ceremony at 6:00 AM to keep it private. Word leaked out, however, and hundreds of well-wishers waited on the street for a glimpse of the couple.

Babe Ruth's Apartment

City: New York
Location: 110 Riverside Drive and West 83rd Street
Manhattan

This is the Upper West Side building where Babe Ruth lived with wife Claire in an 11-room apartment from 1942 until his death in 1948. Claire remained at the apartment for another 28 years after the Babe died. When the couple got married in 1929 (Ruth had been separated from his first wife, who later died in a fire), Babe and Claire resided at 345 West 88th Street, occupying the entire seventh floor. A plaque on the side of that building honors Ruth. After several years there, they moved to 173 Riverside Drive, at the corner of 89th Street, and eventually to the 110 Riverside Drive address.

The Babe Dies

City: **New York**
Location: Memorial Sloan-Kettering Hospital
424 East 68th Street
Manhattan

This was where Ruth died on August 16, 1948, at 8:01 PM. Diagnosed with throat cancer about two years earlier, doctors attributed the disease to Ruth's heavy smoking and tobacco chewing. Ruth's body laid in state for two days at Yankee Stadium while thousands of mourners gathered to pay their respects.

An impressive monument at Gate of Heaven Cemetery marks the gravesite of former Yankees slugger Babe Ruth and wife Claire Hodgson in New York.

Babe Ruth is buried (with wife Claire) at Gate of Heaven Cemetery, 10 West Stevens Avenue, Hawthorne. (Billy Martin was buried just behind Ruth's grave.)

Hubert's Flea Circus and Museum

City: **New York**
Location: 228 West 42nd Street (in Times Square)
Manhattan

This was where Hall of Fame pitcher Grover Cleveland Alexander ended up after his career ended in 1930. Home to various sideshow acts like Lydia the Contortionist and Waldo the Sword Swallower, Alexander joined the circus and regaled customers with tales of his life and baseball feats. All it cost was 25 cents to hear the legend speak for a while and Alexander was good for 10 or more "shows" per day. The circus closed in 1965.

Willie Mays Home

City: New York
Location: 80 Saint Nicholas
Avenue
Manhattan

Where Willie Mays would play stickball with neighborhood kids.

In the 1950s, during his years with the New York Giants, this is where the great center fielder Willie Mays lived. In fact, the famous photos and movies of Mays playing stick-ball on the streets near the Polo Grounds were taken just outside this building. Nicknamed "The Say Hey Kid," Willie Mays was elected to the Baseball Hall of Fame in 1979, in just his first year of eligibility. Today, many consider Mays to be the greatest all-around player in history. When he was inducted into the Hall of Fame, Mays was asked to name the best player that he had seen during his career. Mays replied, "I don't mean to be bashful, but I was." Ted Williams once said "They invented the All-Star Game for Willie Mays."

Joe DiMaggio Highway

City: New York
Location: From Battery Park Place to West 72nd Street
Manhattan

In 1999, Mayor Rudolph Giuliani was present to rename the West Side High-way in honor of Yankees legend Joe DiMaggio. Adorned with crossed bats and baseballs, new green-and-white signs were posted on the southbound side of the West Side Highway at 70th Street and on the northbound side at West Street between Morris and Thames near the Brooklyn Battery Park Tunnel in tribute to the "Yankee Clipper."

First Baseball Game Ever Televised

City: New York
Location: Columbia University
Andy Coakley Field
Broadway and West 218th Street
Manhattan

The first televised game was broadcast from Columbia University's Baker Field by New York experimental NBC station W2XBS on May 17, 1939. The second game of a college doubleheader between the Princeton Tigers and Columbia Lions was shot with one camera standing on a platform behind home plate. (Approximately 400 people watched the game at home.) Three months later, on August 26, W2XBS broadcast its first major-league game, the first game of a doubleheader between the Brooklyn Dodgers and Cincin nati Reds from Ebbets Field. Broadcasting legend Red Barber handled the first play-by-play and interviewed rival managers Leo Durocher (Dodgers) and Bill McKechnie (Reds) in the first post-game show.

Ray Chapman Death Site
City: New York
Location: St. Lawrence Hospital
457 West 163rd Street
Manhattan

Raymond Johnson Chapman played his entire career as a shortstop for the Cleveland Indians. An excellent ballplayer, in 1918, Ray Chapman led the American League in runs scored and walks. A skilled bunter, Chapman ranks sixth on the all-time list for sacrifice hits (only Stuffy McInnis boasts more sacrifices for right-handed batters). Chapman was also a gifted short-stop who led the league in putouts three times and assists once. He also batted .300 three seasons, and led the Indians in stolen bases four times. He set a team record of 52 stolen bases in 1917, a mark that stood until 1980. But as good as he was, the main reason many of us remember Chapman is that he is the second of only two Major League Baseball players to have died as a result of an injury received in a game (the first was Mike "Doc" Powers in 1909). Chapman was hit in the head by a ball thrown by Yankees pitcher Carl Mays on August 16, 1920. His death led Major League Baseball to establish a rule requiring umpires to replace the ball whenever it became dirty. His death was also one of the examples used to point out the crucial need for wearing batting helmets (although the rule was not officially ad-opted until over 30 years later). Chapman's death was also partially the rea-son MLB banned the spitball after the season. St. Lawrence Hospital, where Chapman died, no longer stands. Bonus location: After he died, Chapman was taken to the James McGowan Funeral Home in New York City, which was located at 1879 Amsterdam Avenue.

Mickey Mantle's Restaurant
City: New York
Location: 42 Central Park South
Manhattan
212-688-7777

When he was still living in New York, this is where you might have found "The Mick," hanging out with old pals and teammates, relaxing in his favorite booth. Today, the restaurant continues to dazzle patrons with memorabilia, a well-supplied gift shop and classic American fare. Mickey Mantle's is to today's diner what it once was to a great sports hero: a place to relive baseball's past, to hang out and to have fun.

Ansonia Hotel

City: New York
Location: 2109 Broadway, between 73rd and 74th Streets (now a co-op apartment)
Manhattan

Babe Ruth spent most of the 1920s at this onetime grand hotel—an ornate, Beaux Arts-style masterpiece that catered to stars from all walks of life. Famed tenor Enrico Caruso lived here, as did boxer Jack Dempsey, composer Igor Stravinsky and many other notables. But it also was here in 1919 that eight members of the Chicago White Sox (the so-called "Black Sox") plotted among themselves to throw the 1919 World Series to the Cincinnati Reds. The Ansonia was the first air-conditioned building in New York. Today, the grand apartments have mostly been divided into studios and one-bedroom units, almost all of which retain their original architectural detail.

The restaurant opened by former Yankees star Mickey Mantle remains a popular New York hangout.

Lou Gehrig, who went on to fame as the New York Yankees' Iron Horse, was born in the Yorkville section of Manhattan.

Lou Gehrig's Birthplace

City: New York
Location: 1994 Second Avenue and East 103rd Street
Upper East Side
Manhattan

Yankee Hall of Famer "Ironman" Lou Gehrig was born in upper Manhattan on June 19, 1903. In 1953, Gehrig's birthplace, a four-story apartment building (which later became a laundry), had a memorial plaque, which read: "This plaque marks the site of the birthplace of Henry Louis Gehrig." Christina Gehrig, Lou's mother, was at the unveiling ceremony. Today, both the apartment and the plaque are gone, but a new marker was placed in the last several years at the site (where a garden center can be found). After growing up in the neighborhood, Lou Gehrig attended PS 132 in the Washington Heights section of Manhattan and then went to Commerce High School, where he graduated in 1921. Gehrig went to Columbia University for

The home where Lou Gehrig was born used to stand here.

two years, but did not graduate. While at Columbia, he was a member of the Phi Delta Theta fraternity. Initially, Gehrig was not eligible to play intercollegiate baseball for the Columbia Lions because he had played baseball for a summer pro league during his freshman year. At that time, he was unaware that this would harm his eligibility to play any collegiate sport. Gehrig was ruled eligible to play on the Lions' football team and was a star fullback. Later, he gained baseball eligibility and joined the Lions' baseball team, too.

Gehrig first attracted national attention for his baseball talents while playing in a game at Cubs Park (now Wrigley Field) on June 26, 1920. His New York School of Commerce team was battling a team from Chicago's Lane Tech High School, and with his team winning 8–6 in the top of the ninth inning, Gehrig crushed a grand slam completely out of the park. Of course, this was an unheard-of feat for a 17-year-old high school boy.

More Gehrig trivia: On April 18, 1923, the same day that Yankee Stadium opened for the first time and Babe Ruth inaugurated the new stadium with a home run, Columbia pitcher Gehrig struck out 17 for a team record. However, Columbia lost the game.

Lou Gehrig is buried about 45 minutes from New York City at the Kensico Cemetery in Valhalla, New York (in Section 93, Lot 12686, ashes placed in the center of the headstone).

The Sports Museum of America
City: New York
Location: 26 Broadway
Manhattan
212-747-0900

The Sports Museum of America opened on May 7, 2008, as the United States' first national sports museum dedicated to the history and cultural significance of sports in America. It's the first museum ever to represent all sports, and it partnered with over 50 of the individual sport Halls of Fame to create an amazing array of artifacts. There are over 600 individual pieces, 1,100 photos, 20 original films and 19 galleries for people to explore, as well as two dozen interactive exhibits. The museum will also be the full-time home of the Heisman Trophy and the Women's Sports Foundation International Women's Sports Hall of Fame (within the Billie Jean King International Women's Sports Center). Like dozens of other sports halls of fame and museums, the National Baseball Hall of Fame has loaned numerous artifacts for display, and so this is a place that baseball fans will not want to miss.

Dexter Park

City: New York
Location: North side of Jamaica Avenue between Dexter Court and 76th Street
Woodhaven
Queens

In the first half of the 20th century, Dexter Park played host to many of the top baseball stars of the majors and Negro Leagues. (Babe Ruth even played here in

A marker at the former site of Dexter Park.

1928, after promoting a rodeo with Lou Gehrig.) But it primarily served as home for a team called the Bushwicks, which hired players on their way up or down from the major leagues. The Bushwicks were among the best semipro teams in America for 40 years, and their legendary Sunday afternoon games against the top Negro League teams often outdrew the Brooklyn Dodgers at Ebbets Field. Dexter Park was torn down in the mid-1950s and the site is now occupied by two-family homes. There is no marker to commemorate what happened here.

Jackie Robinson Home

City: New York
Location: 112–40 177th Street
Queens

In April 2008, the *New York Daily News* reported:

> Two years after breaking the Major League Baseball color barrier, Jackie Robinson settled into the tony Addisleigh Park, Queens, home where he would live from his 1949 MVP season through one of his final years with the Brooklyn Dodgers. But the pioneering athlete's house was never

designated by the city Landmarks Preservation Commission, meaning a developer can legally buy and destroy the structure linked to one of the nation's most indelible sports stars. "We used it to move on to the next stage of our lives," said Rachel Robinson, Jackie's widow. "We had moved around and hadn't been sure of anything—whether Jack would make it with the Dodgers, or if we could ever afford a home." Asked about the Robinson home, commission spokeswoman Lisi de Bourbon said it's "under review," adding that the commission is "looking" at the area as a potential historic district that would bar demolitions.

As of this writing, the house still stands. After living here, Jackie Robinson and his family moved to North Stamford, Connecticut, where Robinson died at age 53 in 1972.

Shea Stadium

City: New York
Location: 12601 Roosevelt Avenue
Queens

William A. Shea Municipal Stadium, usually shortened to Shea Stadium, was, until recently, located in the borough of Queens, in Flushing Meadows–Corona Park. Home to the New York Mets from 1964 to 2008, Shea was originally erected as a multipurpose stadium. It was also the home of the National Football League's New York Jets until 1983. Shea Stadium was demolished at the end of 2008 to create additional parking spaces for the adjacent Citi Field, which was under construction to replace Shea in 2009. The Mets' inaugural season was played at the Polo Grounds, located closer to Yankee Stadium, and the original plan was for the team to move to a new ballpark in 1963. However, construction was delayed, and the Mets played at the Polo Grounds a second season. The original name for Shea was Flushing Meadow Park Municipal Stadium—the name of the public park on which it was built—but a fervent movement was undertaken to name it in honor of William A. Shea, the man who fought to bring National League baseball back to New York. Earlier, New York City official Robert

Shea Stadium, former home of the New York Mets.

Moses tried to interest Brooklyn
Dodgers owner Walter O'Malley
in this property as the location
for a new Dodger stadium, but
he and O'Malley were unable to
come to terms.

Shea Stadium being razed, January 2009.

In addition to the Mets,
the New York Yankees played
their home games in Shea Stadium during the 1974 and 1975
seasons while Yankee Stadium
was being enhanced. Also, on April 15, 1998, the Yankees played one home
game at Shea after a beam collapsed at Yankee Stadium two days before,
destroying several rows of seats.

More Shea history: One of the most significant concerts in music
history occurred at Shea Stadium on Sunday, August 15, 1965, when The
Beatles opened their 1965 North American tour at Shea Stadium to a record
audience of 55,600. The Beatles' set list included only 12 songs that night.
After that, Shea hosted numerous concerts over the years, the most recent
being a two-night engagement by Billy Joel on July 16th and July 18th of
2008. The shows were called the "Last Play at Shea," and featured many
special guest appearances, including former Beatle Paul McCartney, who
closed the second show with an emotional rendition of the Beatles classic
"Let It Be." Other artists that joined Joel on stage for the show were former
Shea performer Roger Daltrey of The Who, Tony Bennett, Don Henley, John
Mayer, John Mellencamp, Garth Brooks, and Steven Tyler of Aerosmith.

The Lights from Ebbets Field

City: New York
Location: Downing
Stadium
Randall's Island

Recently torn down,
this one-time track
stadium (also used for
Negro League base-
ball) attained some
degree of notoriety
when it was learned
that some of the Ebbets
Field lights were put to

The lights from Ebbets Field (left) were later put to good
use at Downing Stadium, the one-time home of professional soccer's New York Cosmos.

use here after the fabled Brooklyn park was torn down in 1960. Originally opened as the Triborough Stadium (to coincide with the 1936 completion of the Triborough Bridge), the stadium was renamed Downing Stadium in 1955. Over the years, the stadium hosted baseball and concerts and served as home to the New York Cosmos, a professional soccer team, during the 1970s. In 1991, the United States National Track and Field Championships returned to the stadium after a 25-year absence. It is not known today what has become of the Ebbets Field lights.

Scouts Wall of Fame
City: New York
Location: Richmond County Bank Ballpark
Staten Island

This is the home of the Staten Island Yankees Minor League Baseball team (a New York-Pennsylvania League affiliate of the New York Yankees). It was opened in 2001 on the former site of the B & O Railroad yards, which were adjacent to the Staten Island Ferry Terminal in St. George.

The ballpark is also home to the only Professional Baseball Scouts Wall of Fame, an interesting section in what is now called "Pinstripe Alley." This wall was created as a tip of the hat to one of the most underrated group of people in baseball: the scouting community. For instance, this is the text from three markers placed here for the Class of 2005:

> Gil Bassetti has worked in baseball for over 44 years, first as a player then as a scout. He has worked with the Cardinals, Twins, and Dodgers. He has signed players such as John Franco and Eric Young and has had seven players reach the big leagues during his career. He was a professional scout covering the Northeast for the Baltimore Orioles as of 2005.

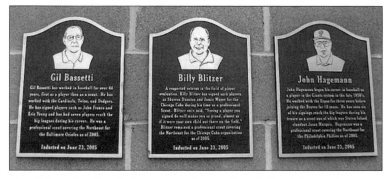

The oft-forgotten baseball scouts are honored at a ballpark in New York.

Billy Blitzer, a respected veteran in the field of player evaluation has signed players [such] as Shawon Dunston and Jamie Moyer for the Chicago Cubs during his time as a professional Scout. Blitzer once said, "Seeing a player you signed do well makes you so proud, almost as if it were your own child out there on the field." Blitzer remained a professional scout covering the Northeast for the Chicago Cubs organization as of 2005.

John Hagemann began his career in baseball as a player in the Giants system in the late 1950's. He worked with the Expos for three years before joining the Braves for 18 years. He has seen six of his signings reach the big leagues during his tenure as a scout, one of which was Staten Island standout Jason Marquis. Hageman was a professional scout covering the Northeast for the Philadelphia Phillies as of 2005.

This is a novel tribute to a part of the sport that, while visible during contract time, ignores the bulk of the folks who are in the field all year, combing high school fields and sandlots looking for that next big-league phenom.

John McGraw Field

City: Olean
Location: St. Bonaventure University
3261 West State Road

St. Bonaventure University has a long and storied baseball history. The famed player/manager John McGraw and star player Hugh Jennings went there and actually perfected the "Baltimore chop" hitting style in the basement of one of the buildings on campus. Babe Ruth and the 1923 Yankees came to speak at the school and barnstorm. When the campus baseball field opened in 1925, McGraw came with his Giants and played the school team. In honor of the days he spent coaching at St. Bonaventure, St. Bonaventure University named its athletic fields after McGraw and his teammate, fellow coach, and fellow Hall of Famer Hugh Jennings.

After the 1899 season, Jennings entered Cornell Law School. While attending there, he managed the Cornell baseball team while at the same time studying law. While there, he came to the decision that he was destined to become a manager. Jennings continued as a scholar-athlete until the spring of 1904, when he left campus early to go manage the Orioles. Although Jennings never completed his law degree at Cornell, he did go on to pass the Maryland bar exam in 1905 and from there he started a law practice. Jennings continued to practice law during the off-season through the remainder of his baseball career.

Damaschke Field

City: Oneonta
Location: Main Street and Neahwa Place (Exit 15 off I-88)
607-432-6041

Damaschke Field, a legendary minor-league park, is the current home of the Oneonta Tigers in the New York-Pennsylvania League. Since opening in 1940, this cozy, unpretentious stadium, formerly home of the Oneonta Yankees, has played host to such greats as Babe Ruth, Lou Gehrig, Joe DiMaggio, Mickey Mantle, Don Mattingly, Bernie Williams and many more. Called Neahwa Park Field when it opened in 1940, it was renovated and renamed Damaschke Field in 1968, after Ernest Damaschke, the longtime chairman of the Oneonta Parks & Recreation Commission.

Troy Baseball Monument—Birth of the Giants

City: Troy
Location: Knickerbacker Park
Lansingburgh

Many people don't realize that the origin of the San Francisco Giants baseball club lies here in upstate New York, where the legendary Troy Haymakers played in the late 19th century. In 1871, the National Association of Professional Base Ball Players (the first organized professional baseball league) was founded in New York City, and the Troy Haymakers were one of its original nine teams. Playing its first game here on May 9, Troy lost to the Boston Red Stockings, 9–5. That year, the Haymakers ended up a mediocre sixth place, going 13–15. The Haymakers disbanded, primarily for financial reasons, before the next season was over, but from 1879 to 1882, the National League's Troy Trojans were part of the major-league scenery. Voted out of the league after the 1882 season, Troy left quite a professional baseball legacy. Five future Hall of

The five Hall of Famers who played for Troy in its brief major-league history have been memorialized by a town monument.

Famers played there: Dan Brouthers, Roger Connor, William "Buck" Ewing, Tim Keefe and Mickey Welch. After the Troy Trojans were kicked out of the league, the franchise was moved to New York City and was renamed the New York Gothams. The nickname was eventually changed to Giants and the franchise prospered in New York through 1957, at which point Horace Stoneham relocated to San Francisco. The Troy Baseball Monument, erected in 1992, honors Troy baseball history as well as such local major-league products as George Davis and Leo Durocher. The monument is located in the northern section of Troy, an area called Lansingburgh. To get there, enter Knickerbacker Park at 103rd Street and drive straight into the parking lot. The monument is about 200 yards straight ahead. The park, once the playing field for the Troy Haymakers, is now a recreation area.

John McGraw Statue

City: Truxton
Location: Center of town at the four corners on Route 13

John J. McGraw, the longtime czar of New York baseball, hailed from this small upstate town about 20 miles from Syracuse. Born April 7, 1873, the fiery baseball legend always kept a spot in his heart for his hometown, even paying in the 1920s to build a grandstand at what became known as John J. McGraw Field. That park, which still stands, was the site of a 1938 game between the New York Giants and the local Truxton team. Four years after McGraw's death, his former team came to town to play an exhibition game that would raise money for a statue that was erected in 1942. Inter-

Managerial giant John McGraw never lost connections with his hometown in Truxton, New York.

estingly, the location of the marker in the center of town is where McGraw learned to play baseball as a child.

Dan Brouthers Monument

City: Wappingers Falls
Location: North Mesier Avenue, about two blocks off East Main Street

Dan Brouthers's career touched four decades, 1879–1904. Over that period, he won more major-league batting crowns (five) than any other 19th-century player. Playing for teams in Boston, Brooklyn, Baltimore, Detroit, Philadelphia and New York, Brouthers led his leagues in slugging seven times and was one of a handful of players to hit 100 or more homers before the 20th century. His lifetime batting average of .342 ranks among the all-time leaders and he was elected to the Hall of Fame by the Committee on Old-Timers in 1945. A monument was erected to Brouthers, a native son, in 1971.

Dan Brouthers is buried at St. Mary's Cemetery, on Convent Avenue, in Wappingers Falls.

The Dan Brouthers monument was dedicated in 1951.

Hall of Famers Buried in New York

Joe McCarthy
Mount Olivet Cemetery
4000 Elmwood Avenue
Tonawanda

John Evers
St. Mary's Cemetery
54 Brunswick Road
Troy

Jimmy Collins
Holy Cross Cemetery
2900 South Park Avenue
Lackawanna

**NEW YORK CITY
METROPOLITAN AREA**

Frank Frisch
Woodlawn Cemetery
Webster Avenue and
East 233rd Street
The Bronx

Joe McCarthy is considered by many as the greatest manager of all time.

Frank Frisch had a lifetime batting average of .316.

Ford Frick was a sports-writer, NL president and baseball commissioner.

Henry Chadwick invented the box score and wrote the first rule book.

Ford Frick
Christ Church Columbarium
17 Sagamore Road
Bronxville

Jackie Robinson
Cypress Hills Cemetery
833 Jamaica Avenue
Brooklyn

Henry Chadwick
Green-Wood Cemetery
500 25th Avenue
Brooklyn

**Mickey Welch and
Willie Keeler**
Calvary Cemetery
49-02 Laurel Hill Boulevard
Queens

John Montgomery Ward
Greenfield Cemetery
650 Nassau Road
Uniondale

Lou Gehrig and Ed Barrow
Kensico Cemetery
Commerce and
Lakeview Avenue
Valhalla

Pennsylvania

Home of John Montgomery Ward
City: Bellefonte
Location: 236 East Lamb Street

John Montgomery Ward was a trailblazer. In addition to being a star pitcher/ infielder (150-plus victories, more than 2,000 hits), he also was an attorney and union activist who fought the game's reserve clause and helped form the Brotherhood of Professional Baseball Players. The brotherhood brought the short-lived Players League into existence. Ward was also a golf star and authored one of the first books on baseball. A marker reads: "Baseball pioneer, born in Bellefonte, grew up here. Played for Providence, N.Y. Giants, Brooklyn, 1878–94. Pitched professional baseball's 2nd perfect game, 1880. Formed first players' union, 1885, & Players League, 1890. In Baseball Hall of Fame."

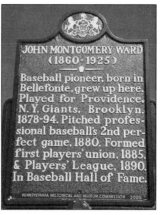

A plaque in Bellefonte, Pennsylvania, honors the considerable accomplishments of Hall of Fame native John Montgomery Ward.

Chief Bender Marker

City: Carlisle

Location: Indian Field

Carlisle Barracks

Off US 11

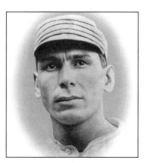

Chief Bender won 212 games during his 16-year Major League Baseball career.

"Chief" Bender was born in Crow Wing County, Minnesota, a member of the Ojibwa tribe. Throughout his career, Bender faced discrimination, not least of which was the stereotyped nickname ("Chief"), which is how history remembers him today. In 1981, writers Lawrence Ritter and Donald Honig included him in their book, *The 100 Greatest Baseball Players of All Time.* A plaque here reads: "One of baseball's great pitchers. Bender played for the Philadelphia Athletics from 1903–14, helping them to win 5 pennants and 3 world championships. After winning 212 games over 16 seasons and becoming one of the first World Series stars, he was inducted into the Baseball Hall of Fame in 1954. His mother was one-half Chippewa, and he attended Carlisle Indian Industrial School on this site from 1898–1901."

The Birthplace of Honus Wagner

City: Carnegie

Location: Mansfield Boulevard and Chartiers Avenue

Like Christy Mathewson, Honus Wagner was a member of the first class of Hall of Fame inductees. Over a 21-year career, the gritty, fearless, barrel-shaped shortstop batted .329, stole 720 bases and amassed 3,430 hits (sixth on the all-time list). In 1905, Wagner became the first player to have his signature burned into a Louisville Slugger bat. In the first decade of the 20th century, he was a superstar on Pirates teams that won four pennants and one World Series title. A marker reads: "The 'Flying Dutchman' was hailed as baseball's greatest shortstop and one of its finest all-around players. A lifelong Carnegie resident, born to German immigrants. Played for Louisville Colonels, 1897–99, and Pittsburgh Pirates, 1900–17; a Pirates coach, 1933–51. He set many National League records, including one for eight seasonal batting titles. Known for his modesty and sportsmanship. Charter member, Baseball Hall of Fame, 1936."

Former Pirates shortstop Honus Wagner was one of baseball's premier talents in the early 1900s.

Wagner is buried at Jefferson Memorial Park in Pittsburgh.

Home of John K. Tener

City: Charleroi
Location: 6th and Fallowfield Streets

A marker here honors John K. Tener, who pitched in 61 major-league games and had a 15-15 record for Cap Anson's 1889 Chicago NL club. It reads: "Governor of Pennsylvania, 1911–1915. Highlights of his administration included creation of statewide primary elections and a state highway system; establishment of the Department of Labor and Industry and Pennsylvania Historical Commission. Member of Congress, 1909–11. Professional baseball player, 1885–90; president, National League, 1913–18. Born in Ireland, he came to the US at age 9. Resident of Charleroi after 1891."

Hometown of Christy Mathewson

City: Factoryville
Location: Marker at US 6 and US 11 in front of Keystone College (in the adjoining town of La Plume)

Christy Mathewson won 373 major-league games. Only Cy Young and Walter Johnson posted more victories. A popular and highly respected player, Mathewson used his fadeaway pitch to win 22 or more games for 12 consecutive years. He reached 30 or more wins in three straight seasons. In one of the greatest pitching performances of all time, he tossed three shutouts over six days in the 1905 World Series. He later managed the Reds and was president of the Braves. Mathewson died of tuberculosis at 45, having possibly contracted the disease as the result of being gassed during a World War I training exercise. The marker reads: "The famed baseball pitcher was born in Factoryville. Attended Keystone Academy, 1895-98; Bucknell University, 1898-1901. He was with the New York Giants, 1900-16, and Cincinnati Reds, 1916-18; pitched 373 winning games, achieving a National League record. Served overseas in World War I. One of the first five players in the Hall of Fame (1936), he was seen as a gentleman in a rough-and-tumble baseball era."

Christy Mathewson, befitting the "Factoryville" city in which he was born, was a workhorse for John McGraw's New York Giants.

Other Christy Mathewson-Related Sites

★ At Bucknell University in Lewisburg, Pennsylvania, a monument called the Christy Mathewson Gateway sits across a field from Christy Mathewson-Memorial Stadium, which houses a plaque that honors the Hall of Famer.

★ Mathewson is buried at Lewisburg Cemetery.

The Birthplace of Eddie Plank
City: Gettysburg
Location: Carlisle Street and West Lincoln Avenue

Eddie Plank pitched more shutouts (64) and completed more games (387) than any other left-hander in history. Plank, who played little baseball as a youth, joined the Athletics after graduating from Gettysburg College. He spent 14 seasons with the A's, one with the St. Louis club of the Federal League and two with the St. Louis Browns. A marker here reads: "Baseball great. One of the most dominant pitchers of the 20th Century. 'Gettysburg Eddie' compiled a record of 326-194 throughout his career (1901-17), mostly with the Philadelphia Athletics. He won 20 games or more eight times and helped the A's win six pennants and three world championships. Plank was born here, attended Gettysburg Academy. He retired and died in Gettysburg. Elected to Baseball Hall of Fame, 1946."

Eddie Plank is buried at Evergreen Cemetery.

A marker dedicated to local hero Eddie Plank in Gettysburg.

Harrisburg Giants Marker

City: Harrisburg
Location: Roadway between
Walnut Street Bridge and
Commerce Bank Park
City Island

The Harrisburg Giants joined the Eastern Colored League (ECL) for the 1924 season with renowned Hall of Fame center fielder Oscar Charleston as their playing manager. The Giants became known primarily for their hitting; along with Charleston, outfielder/ first baseman Heavy Johnson, winner of the batting Triple Crown for the 1923 Kansas City Monarchs, was signed away from the rival Negro National League. Speedy outfielder Fats Jenkins, a well-known professional basketball player and member of the New York Rens, also played for Harrisburg throughout its tenure in the ECL. Harrisburg finished in the middle of the league in its debut season, winning 26 and losing 28 for a fifth-place finish (out of eight teams). In 1925, the Giants improved, challenging the defending champion team, Hilldale, before just missing the mark with a 37–19 record. In 1926, the Giants added shortstop/third baseman John Beckwith from the Baltimore Black Sox, and they finished second again, this time behind the Bacharach Giants. In 1927, the Harrisburg Giants sank to fourth place, with a 41–32 record. The club dropped out of the ECL the following year to play an independent schedule, which is when most of its star players signed on with other teams. The Giants returned to participate in the American Negro League in 1929.

A marker here, placed in honor of the notable team reads: "Harrisburg-based Negro League baseball team founded around 1900 and operated by Colonel William Strothers until his death in 1933. One of 27 major Negro League teams across the nation, the Giants finished in second place in the Eastern Colored League in 1925. Among well-known players were Hall-of-Famer Oscar Charleston, Spottswood Poles, Ben Taylor, John Beckwith, Fats Jenkins & Rap Dixon. They played here at Island Park through 1957."

Philadelphia Athletics Historical Society
City: Hatboro
Location: 6 North York Road
1-800-318-0483

This organization is dedicated to preserving the legacy of the Philadelphia Athletics (and keeping alive other baseball history throughout the area). There is a terrific museum here and a gift shop loaded with books, jerseys, hats and more.

Plaque Honoring the Homestead Grays
City: Homestead
Location: West Street and East Eighth Avenue

A marker sits on the former site of the Andrew Carnegie Homestead Steel Works, where more than a century ago a group of black mill workers formed a sandlot baseball team called the Blue Ribbon. A little more than a decade later, the Blue Ribbon club became the Homestead Grays. The Grays and the Pittsburgh Crawfords, their metropolitan-area rivals, became forces among the great black teams that were formed in the days before

A team portrait of the Homestead Grays.

the integration of modern Major League Baseball. The marker reads: "Legendary baseball team that dominated the Negro Baseball Leagues during the first half of the 20th Century. Founded by steelworkers in 1900, the Grays inspired African Americans locally and across the nation. Led by Cumberland Posey Jr., they won 12 national titles, including nine in a row, 1937-45. Players included Hall of Famers Josh Gibson, Buck Leonard and Smokey Joe Williams. Disbanded in 1950."

Bernice Gera Marker
City: Indiana
Location: Blue Spruce Park
1128 Blue Spruce Road
724-463-8636

A historical marker honoring Bernice (Shiner) Gera is located here near this beautiful park's ball field. A native of nearby Ernest, Gera made history as

baseball's first female umpire. Barred
by Minor League Baseball for five
years, Gera won a landmark lawsuit allowing her to work as an umpire. Her
one and only game as a professional
umpire took place on June 24, 1972, in
a New York-Pennsylvania League game
in Geneva, New York. At the Baseball
Hall of Fame in Cooperstown, New
York, Gera's photograph, pink whisk
broom and complete umpire uniform
are on display.

Bernice Gera, an Indiana, Pennsylvania,
product made history as baseball's
first female professional umpire.

Pete Gray Marker
City: Nanticoke
Location: Front Street, Hanover
section

The legendary Pete Gray was born as Peter Wyshner in the mining town of
Nanticoke. He was a right-hander until he lost his right arm at age 6. He
accidentally slipped while riding a farmer's wagon and his right arm was
trapped in the spokes. Sadly, the arm had to be amputated above the elbow.
However, Gray's love of the game led him to learn to bat and field one-
handed, catching the ball in his glove and then quickly removing his glove
and transferring the ball to his hand in one motion. The marker to him here
in his hometown reads: "The only one-armed man to play major league baseball. Born and resided in Nanticoke's Hanover section. As a child, he lost
his right arm in an accident. Named Most Valuable Player of the Southern
Assn. while playing for the Memphis Chicks in 1944. In 1945, he played 77
games as an outfielder for the St. Louis Browns and batted .218. His on-field
exploits set an inspirational example for disabled servicemen returning from
World War II."

African American Baseball in Philadelphia Marker
City: Philadelphia
Location: Belmont and Parkside Avenues

A marker here reads: "For 85 years, starting with the Pythians and Excelsiors in 1867, Black ball clubs were a significant part of the Philadelphia
scene. The Giants, formed 1902, were soon 'World's Colored Champions.'
The Hilldales, Eastern Colored League Champions, 1923-25, won the Colored World Series, 1925. The Philadelphia Stars from 1933-52; they were in

the Negro National League, 1933-48, and many of their games took place at this site."

Alfred James Reach Marker

City: Philadelphia
Location: 1820 Chestnut Street

In 2003, the state of Pennsylvania honored Alfred James Reach, the man who brought the Philadelphia Phillies to town and served as the team's owner and president for 20 years, with a historical marker. He is the first Phillies' official honored by the state with a marker, and it was installed at the site of Reach's sporting goods store. It reads:

The Alfred James Reach marker in Philadelphia.

Alfred J. Reach (1840-1928) Pioneer baseball professional; a great early 2nd baseman. Played for the Philadelphia Athletics, 1865-1875. Phillies' first owner & president, 1883-1902. Published "Official Base Ball Guide." His A.J. Reach & Co., maker of sporting goods, was here.

Reach (1840-1928), after becoming one of the early stars of baseball in the National Association, went on to become an influential executive, publisher, sporting goods manufacturer and spokesman for the sport.

Al Reach was born in London, moved to America as a young man, and soon became a regular player for the champion Eckford club of Brooklyn in the early 1860s (before moving to the Philadelphia Athletics in 1865). When the National Association was formed, Reach helped them win the first professional baseball pennant in 1871. In 1875, after retiring, he helped found the Philadelphia Phillies franchise. From 1883 to 1902, Reach served as the team's president. Later, in a move that mirrored what Al Spalding did, Reach formed a sporting goods company and earned a fortune. In fact, Reach sold his company to Spalding in 1889. Al Reach maintained his stake in the Phillies franchise, finally selling out in 1903 to the owner of the Pittsburgh Pirates. Al Reach passed away at age 87 in Atlantic City, New Jersey, and he is buried in West Laurel Hill Cemetery in Bala Cynwyd, Pennsylvania.

Roy Campanella's High School
City: Philadelphia
Location: Simon Gratz High
18th Street and Hunting Park Avenue

Roy Campanella was one of the most beloved players of the modern era. A three-
time MVP in the National League, he
helped Brooklyn to its only World Series
title in 1955 and was a mainstay on five
pennant-winning Dodgers teams. In 1953,
Campanella set a major-league record
(since broken) for home runs in a season
by a catcher (40) and he led the league
with 142 RBI. (He hit another homer that
season as a pinch hitter.) His career ended
in 1958 when he was paralyzed in a car
accident just months before the Dodgers
were to begin their first season in Los Angeles. Campanella remained a part of the

Philadelphia-born Roy Campanella
was an offensive and defensive
backbone for the Brooklyn teams
that won five pennants and the
1955 World Series.

Dodgers' organization until his death on June 26, 1993. A historic marker at
the school reads: "A record-breaking catcher with Brooklyn Dodgers, 1948–
57. He began his professional baseball career while in high school here. In
Negro League, 1937–42, '44–45. MVP, National League, 1951, '53, '55. All-
Star, '49–'56. Baseball Hall of Fame, 1969."

Baker Bowl
City: Philadelphia
Location: Broad Street and Lehigh Avenue

Opened for the Phillies in 1887, 18,000-seat Baker Bowl was a simple wooden

Baker Bowl, home of Phillies baseball from
1897 to 1938, was generally regarded as the
game's first "modern" ballpark.

grandstand with a 40-foot-high
right-field wall (later increased
to 60 feet). The park was heavily
damaged in an 1894 fire. Fans
were seated in temporary stands
for the rest of the '94 season
and only a small portion of the
exterior outfield wall remained
(the wall was incorporated into
a newly constructed stadium).
The next version of Baker Bowl
opened on May 2, 1895. It seat-

ed 18,800 and is generally regarded as the first "modern" park built for baseball. Misfortune struck again at Baker Bowl in August 1903 when a section of stands collapsed, killing 12 people. As years passed, the park became obsolete as steel and concrete facilities such as Shibe Park and Yankee Stadium went up. The Phillies played here until 1938, at which point the park had become dilapidated. They joined the Athletics at Shibe Park in July of that season. Recently, a marker was placed at the site (which is now home to an industrial park): "The Phillies' baseball park from its opening in 1887 until 1938. Rebuilt 1895; hailed as nation's finest stadium. Site of first World Series attended by U.S. President, 1915; Negro League World Series, 1924–26; Babe Ruth's last major league game, 1935. Razed 1950."

Some Memorable Moments at Baker Bowl

★ JUNE 9, 1914: Pittsburgh's Honus Wagner became the second member of the 3,000-hit club (Cap Anson was the first) when he doubled off the Phillies' Erskine Mayer. (Cleveland's Nap Lajoie joined the club later that season.)

★ MAY 14, 1927: During a game between the Phils and Cardinals, 10 rows of stands collapsed and hundreds of fans fell on those sitting below. There was one death—and it was caused by a stampeding crowd.

★ MAY 30, 1935: Babe Ruth, then with the Boston Braves, played only the first inning of the opening game of a doubleheader against the Phillies and went 0 for 1. It was his final major-league appearance.

★ JUNE 30, 1938: The Phillies played their final game at the old park and lost to the Giants, 14-1.

Shibe Park/Connie Mack Stadium
City: Philadelphia
Location: 21st Street and Lehigh Avenue

Shibe Park opened in 1909, replacing Columbia Park as the home of the Athletics. A's owner Ben Shibe built the structure entirely of steel and concrete—an architectural first for a ballpark. Shibe Park originally had a capacity of 23,000, which could be increased significantly by allowing fans to stand in

Shibe Park just several years before its destruction in the mid-1970s.

an area in deep center field. Shibe featured an ornate French Renaissance facade, complete with a Beaux Arts tower, at its main entrance, giving the park the appearance of a European church. A mezzanine level was added in 1930, bringing the capacity to 35,000. There was a 12-foot wall in right field, but buildings across the street enabled fans to watch games for free if they could gain access to a rooftop. Until 1935, fans on the roofs still had a bird's-eye view, but A's management—tired of fans beating the system—raised the wall to 50 feet. (The barrier was known locally as the "Spite Fence.") Lights were added, and the first night game was played on May 16, 1939. Shibe Park was renamed Connie Mack Stadium in 1953 in honor of the legendary manager of the A's. When the A's moved to Kansas City after the 1954 season, the Phillies bought the stadium and played there (as they had done since mid-1938) until Veterans Stadium opened in 1971. A fire destroyed much of the interior of Connie Mack Stadium in '71, and the park rotted for five years. A marker at the site (where a

A church, fittingly, now stands at the former site of Shibe Park, which enjoyed a long, religious-like relationship with Philadelphia fans.

Some Memorable Moments at Shibe Park

★ MAY 18, 1912: Detroit players went on strike to protest the suspension of Ty Cobb, who had recently gone into the stands in New York in pursuit of a heckler. To avoid a forfeit and a fine, the Tigers recruited Philadelphia-area sandlot players to take on the Athletics. The A's won, 24–2.

★ OCTOBER 12, 1929: With the Cubs breezing, 8–0, in Game 4 of the World Series and on the brink of tying the Fall Classic at two victories apiece, the Athletics stunned the National League champions with a 10-run seventh inning and seized a three games-to-one advantage. The Cubs wound up losing to the A's in five games.

★ JUNE 3, 1932: The Yankees' Lou Gehrig became the first American League player to hit four home runs in one game. The Yanks outslugged the A's, 20–13.

★ APRIL 8, 1934: The Phillies and Athletics squared off in a "City Series" exhibition game—the first legal Sunday baseball game played in Philadelphia.

★ MAY 24, 1936: Another Yankee, Tony Lazzeri, teed off against the Athletics. Lazzeri connected for three home runs—two of them grand slams—and drove in an American League-record 11 runs in New York's 25-2 rout of the A's.

★ SEPTEMBER 28, 1941: On the last day of the season, Boston's Ted Williams had a .39955 batting average—rounded off, it was .400—heading into a doubleheader against the A's. He could have sat out the two games and protected his .400 mark. Instead, he played both games and went 6 for 8. His final average: .406.

★ JULY 13, 1943: The American League defeated the NL, 5–3, in the first All-Star Game played at night.

church now stands) reads: "Early major league baseball park opened here, 1909. Renamed, 1953. Home to Athletics, 1909-1954; Phillies, 1938-1970. Site of three Negro League World Series; five A's World Series victories. Among first to host night games. Razed, 1976."

Home of Connie Mack

City: Philadelphia
Location: 604 Cliveden Street

Although he began his career as a catcher, Connie Mack made his mark as a manager. After
heading up the Pirates for a brief time, Mack
took over the Athletics of the fledgling American League in 1901 and managed the team for
an unfathomable half-century. "The Tall Tactician," who retired at age 88, guided the A's
to five World Series titles and helped craft two
dynasties. He led the A's to four pennants in
one five-year stretch (1910 through 1914) and to
three consecutive AL flags beginning in 1929.
A marker reads: "'Grand Old Man of Baseball.'
He started as a catcher in New England, 1883.

Scorecard-waving A's
manager Connie Mack was
a staple of Philadelphia
baseball for more than a
half-century.

As manager of the Philadelphia Athletics, 1901-1950—a record 50 years—he
led the team to nine American League pennants, 1902-31, and five World
Series championships, 1910-30. In baseball's first All-Star Game, he managed the victorious American League team, 1933. Elected to the Baseball
Hall of Fame, 1937. He lived on Cliveden Street here."

Connie Mack is buried at Holy Sepulchre Cemetery.

Home of Baseball Pioneer Jacob C. White Jr.

City: Philadelphia
Location: 1032 Lombard Street

In tribute to White, one of the city's most notable citizens of the 19th century,
a marker reads: "A black educator who lived here, White was the principal
of the Robert Vaux School for 40 years. He was a founder of the city's first
black baseball club, the Pythians, and the first president of the Frederick
Douglass Memorial Hospital."

Veterans Stadium

City: Philadelphia
Location: Broad Street and Pattison Avenue

Philadelphia Veterans Stadium (know by locals as "The Vet") was located at
the northeast corner of Broad Street and Pattison Avenue in Philadelphia as
part of the South Philadelphia Sports Complex. It was home to the Philadelphia Eagles of the National Football League from 1971 through 2002 and the
National League's Philadelphia Phillies from 1971 through 2003. The listed ca-

The former site of Veterans Stadium, Philadelphia.

pacity for baseball in 1971 was 56,371, and 62,000 for football. The 1976 and 1996 Major League Baseball All-Star Games were held at the venue. The Vet also hosted the annual Army-Navy football game 17 times, first in 1976 and last in 2001. In addition, numerous concerts were performed here by artists ranging from the Rolling Stones and Genesis to Bruce Springsteen and Pink Floyd (on their final US tour in 1994). The venue also played host to Live Aid in 1985 and religious events from annual Jehovah's Witnesses conventions to a Billy Graham crusade in 1992.

The Phillies played their very first game at the Vet on Saturday, April 10, 1971, defeating Montreal, 4–1. Hall of Famer Jim Bunning was the winning pitcher that day while Expo pitcher Bill Stoneman took the loss. Larry Bowa had the stadium's first hit and Don Money hit the first home run.

The last game ever played here was September 28, 2003. The Phillies lost to the Atlanta Braves that afternoon, but a heartfelt ceremony was held at the conclusion of the game. For the event, both former general managers, Paul "Pope" Owens and Tug McGraw, made their last public appearances at the park that day. Sadly, later that winter, both men passed away. The last publicly broadcast words ever uttered in the park were by legendary announcer Harry Kalas, who helped christen the ballpark back on April 10, 1971, paraphrasing his trademark home run call: "And now, Veterans Stadium is like a 3–1 pitch to Jim Thome or Mike Schmidt. *It's on a looooooong drive . . . It's OUTTA HERE!!!*" The team moved into Citizens Bank Park in 2004, with the first game being played there on April 12, 2004.

The physical end for the 33-year-old stadium came with a record-setting (62 seconds) implosion on March 21, 2004. Driscoll/Hunt Construction Company's project manager, Nick Peetros, pressed the "real" button to implode the stadium while former Phillies slugger Greg Luzinski

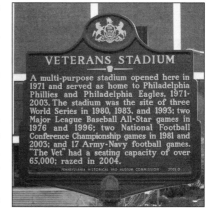

Another marker at the former site of Veterans Stadium.

pressed a placebo plunger for the fans. A parking lot for the current sporting facilities was constructed on the site in 2004 and 2005. On June 6, 2005, before playing Arizona, the Phillies dedicated the anniversary of D-Day with a plaque and monument to commemorate the spot where the stadium stood and a memorial for all veterans. On September 28th of that year, the second anniversary of the final game, a historical marker commemorating where the ballpark once stood was dedicated. And they've made it easy to get a sense of where things used to be: granite spaces mark the former locations of home plate, the pitching mound, and the three bases for baseball, as well as the goalpost placements for football, were added onto the parking lot in April 2006 in western parking lot U. The Veterans Stadium marker joins more than 2,500 historical markers installed throughout the state of Pennsylvania.

Forbes Field

City: Pittsburgh
Location: 230 South Bouquet Street

From mid-1909 through June 1970, Forbes Field was the home of the Pittsburgh Pirates. (It was also the occasional home of the Homestead Grays and Pittsburgh Crawfords of the Negro Leagues.) The classic park featured a huge foul territory behind home plate, and a spacious outfield that featured ivy-covered brick walls.

Remnants of Forbes Field can still be found at its former Schenley Park location, now part of the University of Pittsburgh campus.

A left-field bullpen area was added in 1947 to reduce the daunting home run distance faced by Pirates acquisition Hank Greenberg. The slugging Greenberg benefited from "Greenberg Gardens" for just one season before he retired, but the shortened barrier was a big help to Ralph Kiner during the rest of his stay with the Pirates. After Kiner was traded to the Cubs

Forbes Field, one of baseball's first steel-and-concrete stadiums, enjoyed a long, gloried history as home of the Pittsburgh Pirates.

Memorable Moments at Forbes Field

★ OCTOBER 8, 1909: In the first World Series game played at the park, rookie Babe Adams pitched the Pirates past Ty Cobb and the Tigers, 4-1. Adams won three times in that Series as Pittsburgh won the Fall Classic for the first time.

★ OCTOBER 2, 1920: In the only triple-header in modern big-league history, the Pirates managed to win only the third game against Cincinnati.

★ MAY 25, 1935: Babe Ruth, playing for the Boston Braves, slugged the final three homers of his career. The last one, No. 714, was the first smash ever hit over the right-field roof.

★ JULY 10, 1936: The Phillies' Chuck Klein hit four homers against Pittsburgh.

★ MAY 28, 1956: Pirates first baseman Dale Long, connecting off Brooklyn's Carl Erskine, became the first major-leaguer to hit home runs in eight consecutive games.

★ OCTOBER 13, 1960: Bottom of the ninth inning, Game 7 of the World Series against the Yankees, Mazeroski delivered the knockout punch with his home run off Ralph Terry. The Pirates' 10-9 triumph gave the club its first Series crown in 35 years.

A Memorable Non-Moment

★ No one ever pitched a no-hitter at Forbes Field.

in 1953, "Kiner Korner," as it became known, came down and the bullpens were returned to foul territory.

Though the field is gone, remnants of Forbes Field are still around. A sizable part of the outfield wall still stands, as does the flagpole. A sidewalk plaque marks the spot where Bill Mazeroski's World Series-winning home run in 1960 cleared the wall. Also, the last home plate used at Forbes remains on display near its final location—only now it is under glass at the University of Pittsburgh's Posvar Hall (formerly the Forbes Quadrangle Building).

PNC Park

City: Pittsburgh
Location: 115 Federal Street
For tours, call: 412-325-4700

The Pirates' glittering new home (it opened in 2001), which features a remarkable view of the Pittsburgh skyline, pays tribute to past stars with a series of statues and monuments. The old Honus Wagner statue, originally placed at Forbes Field and then moved to Three Rivers Stadium,

PNC Park is a jewel on the Allegheny River, in the shadow of Pittsburgh's impressive downtown skyline.

stands out front. The Roberto Clemente statue from Three Rivers is positioned outside the right-field wall; in the statue's base, under glass, is dirt from Forbes Field. A statue honoring Willie Stargell was unveiled at PNC two days before the Pirates played their first official game at the park (Stargell died the very day the Pirates played their opener), and the Barney Dreyfuss monument from Forbes Field has been relocated here. (Dreyfuss, former owner of Louisville's National League team, bought controlling interest of the Pirates in 1900 and brought such Louisville stars as Honus Wagner and Fred Clarke to Pittsburgh. Dreyfuss owned the Pirates for more than three decades.) Around PNC, the "Roberto Clemente Bridge" (formerly known as the Sixth Street Bridge) can be used as an entrance to the park, and the street that runs down the right-field line has been renamed "Mazeroski Way."

Tribute to Josh Gibson

City: Pittsburgh
Location: Ammons Field
2217 Bedford Avenue

Considered the "Babe Ruth of the Negro Leagues," catcher Josh Gibson was one of the game's greatest power hitters. He was also a noted battery mate of Satchel Paige. Gibson, known for his distant home runs, died at age 35, just three months before Jackie Robinson integrated modern Major League Baseball. The marker here reads: "Hailed as Negro leagues' greatest slugger, he hit some 800 home runs in a baseball career that began here at Ammons Field in 1929.

A marker is all that's left of Ammons Field, where Hall of Famer and Negro League star Josh Gibson pounded out his first home runs.

Played for Homestead Grays and Pittsburgh Crawfords, 1930–46. Elected to the Baseball Hall of Fame, '72."

Josh Gibson is buried at Allegheny Cemetery in Pittsburgh.

Greenlee Field

City: Pittsburgh
Location: 2500 Bedford Avenue, between Chauncy and Duff

Greenlee Field was the first black-owned and black-built major baseball field in the United States. It was built thanks to Gus Greenlee, owner of the Pittsburgh Crawfords. Greenlee was irritated that his team and others in the league could not use the dressing rooms at white-owned parks like Forbes Field or Ammons Field, so he did something about it. By 1932, when the park opened, Satchel Paige, Josh Gibson and Oscar Charleston all played for the mighty Crawfords. In 1933, permanent lights were added. Given that the Cincinnati Reds didn't do this at Crosley until 1935, many consider this to be the first permanent lighting system in a ballpark. However, toward the end of the decade, interest in the Crawfords waned, and the park was demolished in December of 1938. There is nothing here to hint of its existence, though a group is currently involved in trying get a marker placed in honor of it.

First World Series Plaque

City: Pittsburgh
Location: Riverwalk near PNC Park

A marker in Pittsburgh where the first World Series was played.

PNC Park, where the Pittsburgh Pirates play today, is built right by where Three Rivers Stadium used to sit, which in turn was built next to where old Exposition Park was. A plaque here reads: "In October 1903, National League champion Pittsburgh played American League champion Boston in major league baseball's first modern World Series. Boston won the best-of-9 series, 5 games to 3; prominent players included Pittsburgh's Honus Wagner and Boston's Cy Young. Games 4 through 7 were played near this site at Exposition Park, Pittsburgh's home from 1891 to 1909." Exposition Park was one of two ballparks (along with Boston's Huntington Avenue Grounds) that hosted the first modern Major League Baseball World Series in 1903. Exposition Park was located on the north shore of the Allegheny River directly across from downtown Pittsburgh in Allegheny City. The design of the field was laid out like this: Left field was bounded to the south by the B & O Railroad tracks and the Allegheny River; third base was bounded to the east by School (later Scotland) Street; first base was bounded to the north by South (later Shore) Avenue; and right field was bounded to the west by Grant (later Galveston) Street. Today, this exact location is situated between the site of Heinz Field and the current Pittsburgh Pirates' home, PNC Park. Exposition held 16,000 fans, and after 18 1/2 seasons at the mostly wooden ballpark, the Pirates moved into the steel-and-concrete Forbes Field, which was located in the Oakland neighborhood of Pittsburgh. That park opened on June 30, 1909. Exposition Park enjoyed a brief second life from 1913 to 1915 as the home of the Pittsburgh Rebels of the short-lived Federal League. Some improvements were made to the park at that time, including roofing one of the open bleacher sections and also removing the obsolete turrets on the grandstand roof. After that, the park was razed and its property was taken over by the rail yards. Pittsburgh has done a good job recently of marking historic baseball sites, especially in this exact area that played such a big part in Pirate history over the years.

Western Pennsylvania Sports Museum
City: Pittsburgh
Location: Located in the Smithsonian wing of the Senator John Heinz History Center, the Western Pennsylvania Sports Museum includes a breathtaking 20,000 square feet of exhibit space over the span of two floors.
412-454-6000

It's a "museum within a museum" that captures the area's evolution and sports history, covering more than the past 100 years. The Sports Museum commemorates unforgettable moments and lore in Pittsburgh through the display of hundreds of artifacts, more than 70 hands-on interactive exhibits and 20 audiovisual programs. Just a few of the things you can see outside of baseball include Franco Harris's "Immaculate Reception" shoes and Mario Lemieux's hockey skates. As for baseball, you'll see Satchel Paige's baseball glove and the pitching rubber from the 1960 World Series, to name but a few artifacts. There is a strong focus on baseball at this museum, and the lasting legacy that baseball in Pittsburgh represents.

Ed Walsh Marker
City: Plains
Location: North Main Street at Carey Street

In his prime, Ed Walsh was the greatest practitioner of the legal spitball, throwing it when it was still a legal pitch. He won two games for the White

Sox in the 1906 World Series, as the "Hitless Wonders" upset the rival Cubs. In 1908, Walsh won an incredible 40 games, and his team finished third. Born near this site, Walsh had a brief but truly remarkable major-league career. Walsh made his major-league debut in 1904, pitching for the Chicago White Sox. His first full season was in 1906, and he compiled a 17–13 record with a 1.88 ERA and 171 strikeouts. Through 1912, Walsh averaged 24 victories, 220 strikeouts and posted an ERA below 2.00 five times. He also led the league in saves five times during this time period. His best individual season was in 1908, when Walsh went a phenomenal 40–15 with 269 strikeouts, 6 saves and a 1.42 ERA.

Here near his birthplace, there is a marker that reads: "Inducted into the Baseball Hall of Fame, 1946. As a pitcher for the Chicago White Sox, 'Big Ed' Walsh averaged 24 victories a year during a seven-year span, 1906–12. He twice pitched over 400 innings in a single season. In 1908, he won 40 games, pitched 11 shutouts, and won both games of a doubleheader as a starting pitcher. Walsh finished his playing career in 1920 with a 1.82 earned run average. He was born nearby in Plains on May 14, 1881."

Rube Waddell Marker

City: Prospect
Location: Route 488, next to Fire Hall

A marker dedicated to the great pitcher Rube Waddell that was placed here reads: "One of the greatest pitchers in baseball history. With the Philadelphia Athletics 'Rube' Waddell led the American League in strikeouts 6 straight years, topping 20 wins in each of his first 4 years. During his career he won 193 games. He was known for his colorful & eccentric personality and was one of baseball's first true matinee idols. Born in Bradford, PA, and raised here in Prospect, Waddell was named to the Baseball Hall of Fame in 1946." Connie Mack said of the pitcher, "He had more stuff than any pitcher I ever saw. He had everything but a sense of responsibility."

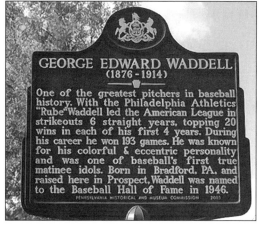

A marker dedicated to Philadelphia A's legend Rube Waddell.

Monument Honoring Stan Coveleski
City: Shamokin
Location: Market Street

Upon Stan Coveleski's election to the Baseball
Hall of Fame in 1969, the twin communities of
Shamokin and Coal Township honored their native son with a monument. The highlight of Coveleski's career came in the 1920 World Series
against the Brooklyn Dodgers, when he tossed
a shutout for Cleveland in the clinching game
and won three times overall. He pitched nine
shutouts in 1917 and had five 20-victory seasons
in the majors.

Stan Coveleski was a hero of
the 1920 World Series.

Boyhood Home of
Jacob Nelson "Nellie" Fox
City: St. Thomas
Location: 7417 Lincoln Highway (US 30) W

Nellie Fox was a spark plug on the "Go-Go" White Sox teams of the late
1950s and early 1960s. He was the American League's MVP in 1959, helping the Sox to their first World Series appearance in 40 years. He hit .306 in
'59, drove in 70 runs and led AL second basemen in fielding percentage. He
punched out 2,663 career hits and batted .368 in All-Star Game competition.
He was a master bunter and bat handler. A marker near the home reads:
"1997 Baseball Hall of Fame inductee. Second baseman for the Chicago
White Sox (1950-1963). Known for his passion and work ethic, Fox was an
AL MVP (1959), a three-time Gold Glove Award winner and a 12-time All-
Star. His boyhood home stands nearby."
　　　Nellie Fox is buried at St. Thomas Cemetery.

Birthplace of Little League Baseball
City: Williamsport
Location: Lycoming County Courthouse
48 West Third Street

A plaque conveys the county's history—and the impact that Little League
Baseball has had on the area. It reads: "Formed April 13, 1795 out of Nor-
thumberland County. The name (from a Delaware Indian word) honors Lycoming Creek. Williamsport, the county seat, became a borough, 1806, and
a city, 1866. Once a great lumbering center. Birthplace of Little League
baseball."

Peter J. McGovern Little League Museum
City: Williamsport
Location: Route 15
South Williamsport

Located just minutes from where the Little League World Series is played, the Peter J. McGovern Little League Museum celebrates Little League Baseball and Softball, past and present. It features pictures, displays and films about the players, equipment, history, rules and games. Plus, there are interactive exhibits.

A must-see attraction near the Williamsport home of Little League baseball is the Peter J. McGovern Little League Museum, which features pictures, displays, films and various interactive exhibits.

The Original Little League Field
City: Williamsport
Location: West Fourth Street

Founded in Williamsport in 1939 by Carl Stotz, Little League Baseball has become the largest youth sports program in the world. It is played by approximately three million children in 103 countries. In '39, a $30 donation was enough to purchase uniforms for each of the first three teams, named after their sponsors: Lycoming Dairy, Lundy Lumber and Jumbo Pretzel. A plaque honoring Stotz reads: "Founder of Little League baseball and commissioner through 1955. Stotz developed the Little League idea in 1938; in the next year three teams played 24 games. It was at this site that Stotz established field distances for the pre-teenage players. The first 12 Little League World Series were played on this field, 1947–1958, and during these years the number of teams grew from 60 to thousands in many nations."

Bowman Field
City: Williamsport
Location: 1700 West Fourth Street

This quaint 1920s-era park plays host to the Williamsport Crosscutters of the Class A New York-Penn League. A marker reads: "Bowman Field, one of the nation's oldest operating parks. Built 1926. Long noted as Pennsylvania's oldest operating minor-league baseball park and the nation's second oldest. The first professional game here was played April 27, 1926, between the Williamsport Grays and the Negro League Harrisburg Giants. Over the years this park became home to successive Williamsport teams and hosted many major-league teams for exhibition games. Originally Memorial Field; renamed 1929 for J. Walton Bowman."

The Hilldale Athletic Club (Darby Daisies) Marker
City: Yeadon
Location: Cedar Avenue and MacDade Boulevard

The Hilldale Athletic Club (also called the Hilldale Daisies and Darby Daisies) was a Negro League baseball club based in Darby, which is situated outside of Philadelphia. Founded in 1910, the team was cultivated by owner Ed Bolden into one of the true standouts of Negro League baseball. Hilldale won the first pennant of the Eastern Colored League in 1923, and repeated the feat in 1924 (however, they dropped the first Negro League World Series to the Kansas City Monarchs, five games to four). The next year, the Hilldales won their third straight ECL pennant, then earned a revenge victory against the Monarchs, taking the World Series five games to one. Bolden, frustrated with the lack of organization in the league, took his club out of the ECL prior to the 1928 season. When the American Negro League was organized in 1929, Hilldale joined, but that particular league lasted only one season. Bolden was soon forced out of the team, and a man named Lloyd Thompson took control of the club in 1930. After just one season, John Drew purchased the team, but during the 1932 season, he had the club disbanded because the Great Depression all but killed attendance. Among the many legendary players to appear on Hilldale's noted roster were Louis Santop, Biz Mackey, Judy Johnson, Chaney White, Jesse "Nip" Winters, Jud Wilson, Oscar Charleston, and Phil Cockrell. A marker here reads: "This baseball team, whose home was here at Hilldale Park, won the Eastern Colored League championship three times and the 1925 Negro League World Series. Darby fielded Negro League teams from 1910 to 1932. Notable players included baseball hall of fame members Pop Lloyd, Judy Johnson, Martin Dihigo, Joe Williams, Oscar Charleston, Ben Taylor, Biz Mackey, and Louis Santop. Owner Ed Bolden helped form the Eastern Colored League."

Brooks Robinson Statue

City: York
Location: Sovereign Bank Stadium
5 Brooks Robinson Way
717-801-HITS

Sovereign Bank Stadium opened on June 16, 2007, with the York Revolution beating the Newark Bears, 9–6. The scenic park features the Brooks Robinson Plaza at the home plate entrance of the ballpark, which includes a statue of the famed Oriole third baseman, along with information related to his illustrious 23-year career in professional baseball. Why do they honor him here? Well, in 1955, Brooks played with York's previous team, the White Roses, and it was at the end of the season that he was first signed by Baltimore. Interestingly, the ballpark itself resembles Oriole Park at Camden Yards, which is in tribute to the former Oriole. Also, the dimensions of the park are identical to those of the former Memorial Stadium, the Orioles' previous home. In addition to the Brooks Robinson Plaza, the official postal address of Sovereign Bank Stadium was changed to 5 Brooks Robinson Way in the fall of 2007. The change was made to honor Robinson's baseball career, which started in the city of York.

Brooks Robinson is honored in York.

So far, the park has been a huge hit with fans. The Atlantic League of Professional Baseball, at the conclusion of its 2008 regular season, honored Sovereign Bank Stadium as the "Ballpark of the Year." According to the stadium Web site, the award recognizes "the efforts of the Revolution staff and groundskeepers, judging such criteria as field conditions, stadium operations, cleanliness, and atmosphere."

Hall of Famers Buried in Pennsylvania

Richie Ashburn
Gladwyne Methodist Church Cemetery
Gladwyne

Chief Bender
Hillside Cemetery
Roslyn

Chief Bender

George Davis

Herb Pennock

Nestor Chylak
St. Cyril and Methodist
Church Cemetery
Peckville

George Davis
Fernwood Cemetery
Philadelphia

Pud Galvin
Calvary Cemetery
Pittsburgh

Bucky Harris
St. Peter's Lutheran Church
Cemetery
Hughestown

Hugh Jennings
St. Catherine's Cemetery
Moscow

Herb Pennock
Union Hill Cemetery
Kennett Square

Pie Traynor
Homewood Cemetery
Pittsburgh

Harry Wright
West Laurel Hills Cemetery
Bala Cynwyd

Rhode Island

Historic Cardines Field
City: Newport
Location: 20 America's Cup Avenue
401-862-4494

It might be America's oldest ballpark. No one is sure when this stadium was built, but a substantial portion of its existing grandstand might date back as far as 1889. If so, that would make Cardines the only surviving example of 1800s-era baseball stadium architecture in the world. (Labatt Park in London, Ontario, is an older ball field, but its structure has been rebuilt over the years.) Cardines was home for the Newport Colts of the New England League from

Cardines Field is believed to be America's oldest ballpark.

1897 to 1899. In 1919, the George Donnelly Sunset League began playing at Cardines and various Negro League teams made frequent barnstorming stops in the 1930s and '40s. Cardines Field was almost torn down in the 1980s, but a local group raised funds and made overdue repairs on the aging facility. Today, the Friends of Cardines Foundation works hard to improve the historic landmark, which now is home to the Newport Gulls of the New England Collegiate Baseball League. Over the years, many baseball legends have played at Cardines, including Jimmie Foxx, Larry Doby and Satchel Paige, who would sit in his rocking chair between the dugouts thinking up colorful names for his many pitches.

Future Indians teammates Satchel Paige (left) and Larry Doby (right) played at Cardines.

McCoy Stadium
City: Pawtucket
Location: 1 Ben Mondor Way

This cozy minor-league park, built in 1942 and renovated in 1998–1999, is home to the Class AAA Pawtucket Red Sox. Many great games have been played here, but none more memorable than the one that began on the night of April 18, 1981, and continued until 4 AM—at which time the game, tied at 2–2, was suspended after Rochester and the hometown "PawSox" had played 32 innings. The game was resumed on June 23, and it ended in the 33rd inning when Pawtucket's Dave Koza delivered a bases-loaded single.

Among the participants in the longest game in professional baseball history were Rochester third baseman Cal Ripken Jr., Pawtucket third baseman Wade Boggs and Sox pitcher Bob Ojeda. Ripken went 2 for 13 at the plate and Boggs was 4 for 12. Ojeda pitched one inning and got the victory in the 8-hour, 25-minute game.

Vermont

Centennial Field

City: Burlington
Location: University of Vermont

Centennial Field, which dates back to 1906, is used today by the Vermont Expos of the Class A New York-Penn League.

The University of Vermont's baseball team has played at Centennial Field since 1906. Though many renovations were made to the park in the 1990s—the Vermont Expos of the short-season Class A New York-Penn League began playing here in 1994 and remain a tenant—the existing grandstand was put in place in 1922. Tris Speaker is one of many great stars of yesteryear who visited Centennial Field for exhibition games. And Barry Larkin, Ken Griffey Jr. and Omar Vizquel are among those who called the park home when they played for the Vermont team in the Class AA Eastern League in the 1980s.

Birthplace of Larry Gardner

City: Enosburg Falls
Location: 14 School Street

A marker reveals that third baseman Larry Gardner, a member of four World Series championship teams, was born here on May 13, 1886. A local high school star and a standout at the University of Vermont, Gardner joined the Boston Red Sox in 1908 and was a regular on Sox teams that won the Fall Classic in 1912, 1915 and 1916. In 1920, he was a key player on Cleveland's Series champions. It was Gardner's fly ball that drove home the Series-winning run against the New York Giants in 1912. In 1916, Gardner managed only three hits in the Series (against the Dodgers)—but two of them were home runs. He later served two decades as University of Vermont baseball coach.

Virginia

Ron Necciai's 27 Strikeout Game

City: Bristol
Location: DeVault Memorial Stadium
1501 Euclid Avenue

On May 13, 1952, 19-year-old Bristol right-
hander Ron Necciai struck out 27 Welch
hitters in a nine-inning no-hitter that put
the Appalachian League on the baseball
map. Necciai, a Pirates farmhand, faced
31 batters—walking one, hitting another
and losing two outs when his catcher
dropped a third strike and a fielder committed an error. One out was recorded on
a ground ball. Necciai's remarkable feat
gained national attention and prompted

Ron Necciai, a hard-throwing right-
hander for Pittsburgh's Bristol farm
team in the Appalachian League,
gained national prominence when
he struck out 27 batters in a nine-
inning 1952 no-hitter.

Branch Rickey to say, "There have been only two young pitchers I was certain were destined for greatness. . . . One of those boys was Dizzy Dean. The
other is Ron Necciai." Rickey was only half right. Necciai was 4-0 at Bristol
with 109 strikeouts and allowed only 10 hits in 43 innings. He was 7-9 with
172 strikeouts in 126 innings when he moved up to Burlington of the Carolina League before finishing his 1952 season at Pittsburgh, where he struggled to a 1-6 record and 7.08 ERA in 54 innings. After that 1952 season,
physical problems took a toll on Necciai and his stock tumbled quickly. But

a baseball that Necciai threw in his
memorable 1952 game remains on
display at the Baseball Hall of Fame
in Cooperstown, and a commemorative marker at DeVault Memorial
Stadium honors his monumental
pitching performance. DeVault
is the current home of the Bristol
White Sox, a Chicago affiliate in
the Appalachian League, but the
original park where Necciai tossed
his no-hitter is gone. The original
ballpark, located about a mile from

A marker in honor of Ron Necciai's
remarkable pitching accomplishment.

the current park at Gate City Highway and Catherine Streets, was torn down
in the 1960s and is now the current location of a dairy.

Bing Crosby Stadium

City: Front Royal
Location: 8th Street behind the Youth Center

In 1948, while serving as Grand Marshall of the Apple Blossom Festival in Winchester, Bing Crosby came to the small town of Front Royal at the invitation of Senator Raymond R. Guest to help with a fund-raising campaign for a new ballpark. The actor/crooner contributed $1,000 to the effort. In 1950, Crosby returned for the premiere of his movie, *Riding High*, and he made another contribution of $3,572.92, which completed the fund-raising campaign. Now, after more than five decades of athletic activity at the park and numerous renovations, Bing Crosby Stadium stands as a tribute to the man and the citizens who worked hard to create recreational facilities in Front Royal and Warren County. Today, the field is used by the local high school and the Front Royal Cardinals, who play in the Valley League. The Valley League is one of only eight summer collegiate baseball leagues certified by the National Collegiate Athletic Association and endorsed by Major League Baseball. The eight leagues are members of the National Alliance of College Summer Baseball. A plaque within the stadium pays tribute to Bing Crosby.

The stadium in Front Royal that's named for Bing Crosby.

Virginia Sports Hall of Fame and Museum

City: Portsmouth
Location: 206 High Street
757-393-8031

Established in 1972, the Virginia Sports Hall of Fame and Museum is the Commonwealth's official sports hall of fame, honoring champions from every region of Virginia. The museum houses one of the country's largest collections of sports artifacts and memorabilia, including a tennis racket used by Arthur Ashe, the signature straw hat of legendary golfer Sam Snead and the game ball from

The Virginia Sports Hall of Fame and Museum has a quaint feel and an impressive collection of artifacts and memorabilia.

a 1903 football battle between Virginia Tech and Navy. But baseball is well-represented, too. More than 20 local players from the major leagues and Negro Leagues are honored, including such performers as Al Bumbry, Ray Dandridge, Leon Day, George Lacy and Jim Lemon.

Calfee Park
City: Pulaski
Location: 700 South Washington Avenue

This cozy historic ballpark is where the Seattle Mariners' Appalachian League affiliate, the Pulaski Mariners, play. Constructed in 1935 as a Works Progress Administration (WPA) project, Calfee Park is listed on the National Register of Historic Places. It was named after the mayor of Pulaski in 1935, Ernest W. Calfee, and holds approximately 2,500 people. The park's locale is unique, as it is set off of US Route 11 in a valley within a residential neighborhood. Because of this, some of the houses that surround the park have good views of games. The park had major renovations just before the 1999 season, including the addition of a new grandstand behind the plate. Also, a new scoreboard was installed. What can I say but hats off to another classic WPA ballpark?

West Virginia

Bowen Field
City: Bluefield
Location: Route 460 at Westgate

Located on the state line that divides Virginia and West Virginia, historic Bowen Field has a charming, tree-shaded "country" feel. The park was built in 1939 and has undergone numerous renovations. But fans still flock through the turnstiles to experience its throwback environment. Bowen Field today is home to the Bluefield Orioles in the Appalachian League.

Watt Powell Park
City: Charleston
Location: 3403 MacCorkle Avenue SE

Another of the great old minor-league parks in the Appalachian League was Watt Powell Park. At the time of the first edition of this book, it was home to the Class A Charleston Alley Cats of the South Atlantic League. It was named for Watt Powell, the man who financed part of its construction, which started in August of 1948. Powell's efforts were aided by a $350,000 government bond issue. The park was needed because Kanawha Park, the former home of professional baseball in Charleston, had burned to the ground in 1944. Sadly, Powell died just two months before the park opened, so he never got to experience a game at the place that was fittingly named for his efforts. Torn down in 2005, all that remain standing today from Watt Powell Park are the light standards.

Hometown of George Brett

City: Glen Dale
Signs north and south of town proclaim it to be the "Birthplace of George Brett–Baseball Hall of Fame."

The tough-as-nails Kansas City third baseman was born in Glen Dale, which is located in north-central West Virginia. Brett's major-league career started in 1973 and lasted 21 years, all with the Kansas City Royals. Brett was the American League MVP in 1980, when he hit .390, the highest batting average since Boston's Ted Williams hit .406 in 1941. He played in two World Series, contrib-

George Brett earned Hall of Fame distinction in Kansas City, but his roots can be traced to Glen Dale in north-central West Virginia.

uting to the Royals' first championship in 1985. A participant in 10 All-Star Games, Brett was named to the Hall of Fame in 1999.

Hall of Famers Buried in West Virginia

Lewis "Hack" Wilson
Rosedale Cemetery
2060 Rosedale Road
Martinsburg

Hack Wilson's 190 RBIs in 1930 is still a major-league record.

ROADSIDE BASEBALL

THE SOUTH

Alabama

Alabama Sports Hall of Fame

City: Birmingham
Location: 2150 Civic Center Boulevard
205-323-6665

Founded in 1967, this world-class sports museum boasts three floors of memorabilia focusing on state athletes, interactive kiosks, a film room, a gift shop and other displays and exhibits. Baseball fans will get a great feel for the history of the game in Alabama. Willie Mays, Satchel Paige, Cleon Jones, Hank Aaron, Don Sutton—many enthusiasts do not realize what a major-league breeding ground the state has been over the years.

The impressive Alabama Sports Hall of Fame chronicles the considerable baseball history of the state that produced home run king Hank Aaron.

Rickwood Field, modeled after Pittsburgh's Forbes Field when it was built in 1910, has been the playground of such Hall of Famers as Ty Cobb, Christy Mathewson, Babe Ruth, Honus Wagner and Rogers Hornsby.

Rickwood Field

City: Birmingham
Location: 1137 Second Avenue West
205-458-8161

Built in 1910, Rickwood Field was the vision of a young Birmingham industrialist named Rick Woodward. While still in his 20s, Woodward bought controlling interest in the city's professional baseball team, the Coal Barons, and sought help from legendary baseball star and Philadelphia Athletics manager Connie Mack in designing "the finest minor-league ballpark ever." Woodward's passion was contagious and, fueled by fervent publicity, the entire city of Birmingham turned baseball-crazy and many businesses closed to celebrate the facility's grand opening. Modeled primarily after Pittsburgh's Forbes Field, Rickwood lived up to its owner's wildest dreams. Over the years, local fans were dazzled by some of baseball's greatest stars.

Standing-room-only crowds watched such future Hall of Famers as Ty Cobb, Christy Mathewson, Honus Wagner and home team sensation Burleigh Grimes—the last legal spitball pitcher in the major leagues.

By the 1920s, the newly formed Black Barons of the Negro League were also drawing overflow crowds, most of whom were mesmerized by the considerable talents of such black immortals as Mule Suttles, Satchel

Attending a game at Rickwood Field, one of baseball's oldest fields, is like stepping back into another era.

Paige, Jimmie Crutchfield, Piper Davis and Willie Mays, who would go on to greater glory in the major leagues. The New York Yankees and Babe Ruth were also frequent visitors to Rickwood; occasional stops were made by such stars as Rogers Hornsby, Shoeless Joe Jackson and Dizzy Dean. Old Diz, the St. Louis Cardinals' ace right-hander, lost 1-0 to the Barons after guaranteeing a victory— one of the most famous games in Rickwood history.

Today's Rickwood Field, technically "the oldest stadium in America," is on the National Register of Historic Places and the Class AA Birmingham Barons come back once a year to play in the Rickwood Classic. In addition, this park is used frequently by Birmingham city schools, men's amateur leagues, junior colleges and other groups.

Optimist Park
City: Huntsville
Location: Corner of Oakwood Avenue and Andrew Jackson Way

Built in 1928 and originally called Dallas Park, this was home to Dallas Mill baseball teams coached by H.E. "Hub" Myhand, who came to Huntsville in 1927 as physical director for Dallas Manufacturing Co. Until the 1940s, Myhand was a local Huntsville legend who spearheaded the rise of semipro baseball featuring local mill teams that drew loyal crowds of 6,000-plus fans. In 1935, the Lincoln and Dallas Mill teams merged to form the Redcaps. The Huntsville Dr. Peppers (1937–43), a women's semipro softball team coached by Cecil Fain, also played here. This also was one of the few early ballparks open to all races and was used during the 1950s and '60s for exhibition games by the Birmingham Black Barons and other Negro League teams. Jackie Robinson, Willie Mays and other African-American baseball legends were routine visitors to Huntsville. The park was renovated and re-opened for baseball in 1994 by the city. Known today as Optimist Park, there is a historical marker that celebrates its colorful past.

Hank Aaron Stadium

City: Mobile
Location: 755 Bolling Bros.
Boulevard
334-479-2327

Officially opened on April 17, 1997, beautiful Hank Aaron Stadium is the home of the Mobile Bay Bears in the Southern League. It is also the annual site for the Hank Aaron High School Baseball Classic featuring Mobile County and Baldwin County high school baseball teams; the Satchel Paige Invitational, an event featuring area independent schools; and the Willie McCovey Challenge and Billy Williams Showdown, classics featuring local college teams. The ballpark is named after baseball's all-time

Mobile native Hank Aaron lends his name to a stadium that has become a hub of baseball activity in southern Alabama.

home run king and Alabama native Hank Aaron, who was born in Mobile on February 5, 1934. Aaron grew up in an area called "Toulminville," which was also home to Paige, McCovey, Williams, Cleon Jones, Tommie Agee, Amos Otis and Hank's brother, Tommie Aaron. A nearby street is called Hank Aaron Loop.

Walt Cruise Field

City: Sylacauga

In May 1973, the local Babe Ruth Field was renamed for Walton "Walt" Cruise, who grew up in Sylacauga. The 82-year-old Cruise was presented with a plaque (he played for the Cardinals and Braves, 1914-24).

Keep Your Eyes Peeled for . . .

★ A highway sign and community center touting Titus as "Home of Joe Sewell."

★ A water tank with the words "Home of Don Sutton" on its side in Clio—where there's also a Don Sutton Street.

★ A sign reading "Hometown of Don Kessinger" in Forrest City.

★ Early Wynn Field in Hartford.

Hall of Famers Joe Sewell (top left), Don Sutton (top right) and Early Wynn (right) are Alabama natives who are honored in their hometowns.

Arkansas

Lamar Porter Field
City: Little Rock
Location: 7th and Johnson Streets

Completed in 1936 as part of the Works Progress Administration, this charming, classic piece of baseball history has played host to thousands of Arkansas-born athletes, including Hall of Fame third baseman Brooks Robinson. Still used by Boys Club and other youth leagues, Lamar Porter Field has also been the location for several films shot in Arkansas, including 1984's *A Soldier's Story*.

Ray Winder Field

City: Little Rock
Location: War Memorial Park
Jonesboro Drive at I-630

This historic stadium was home to the state's only professional baseball team, the Arkansas Travelers of the Class AA Texas League (affiliated with the Anaheim Angels). Built for the Travelers in 1932, the stadium originally was called Travelers Field

Ray Winder Field is a cozy experience for fans who want a throwback aura while watching the Arkansas Travelers.

and also served as home for a team in the Negro Southern League that debut season. The Travelers previously had played their games at Kavanaugh Field, which is now the site of Little Rock's Central High School football stadium. Travelers Field was renamed in honor of the late Ray Winder, a man who dedicated himself for more than a half-century to the promotion of professional baseball for the Little Rock and Arkansas Travelers. When the stadium closed in 2006, it was one of the five oldest stadiums still in use in professional baseball, but today, it sits empty and its future as of this writing is unclear. The ballpark is recognized as a historic site by the city and it has been proposed by some that the park be restored as a functional baseball field for city and college teams. Other groups have proposed demolishing the historic ballpark in order to utilize the area as a parking lot for the adjacent Little Rock Zoo.

George Kell Park

City: Newport
Location: Off Highway 367, about five miles from downtown Newport

During World War II, when many players had gone off to serve their country, third baseman George Kell emerged as one of the best players in the major leagues. Long after the war was over, Kell remained as a mainstay hot-corner specialist for five American League teams. His best seasons were with the Detroit Tigers, where he earned All-Star stature and national prominence by dramatically edging Ted Williams for the 1949 AL batting crown (.343). The hard-working, hard-throwing Kell topped the .300 plateau nine times and topped AL third basemen in fielding percentage seven times. Kell was elected to the Hall of Fame by the Committee on Veterans in 1983. The park dedicated to Kell is not far from Swifton, where he was born in 1922. The American Legion and Newport High School baseball teams play at the park, which also plays host to several state tournaments. The complex has baseball and softball fields as well as the Newport city pool, tennis courts and a volleyball playing area.

The memory of third baseman George Kell's Hall of Fame exploits live on at the Newport-area ballpark named in his honor.

Travelers Baseball Museum
City: North Little Rock
Location: Dickey-Stephens Park
400 West Broadway

As one of the oldest and most popular Minor League franchises in the United States, it only made sense that the Arkansas Travelers would showcase their history, hence the opening of the Travelers Baseball Museum. The collection of memorabilia the team assembled is located in the main concourse at Dickey-Stephens Park, and it contains many interesting artifacts ranging from the Travelers' original 1901 charter into the Southern Association to all team photos from the years as an affiliate of the St. Louis Cardinals (1966–2000) and Los Angeles Angels (2001–present). The museum is sponsored by Arkansas Specialty Orthopaedics and St. Vincent Orthopedic Center and was built by Southwest Display and Design of North Little Rock. Inside the museum, fans can relive great moments in team history and recall some of the more colorful players and fans like R. C. Otey, "Hookslide" Bradshaw and Willie Bunch are also profiled. Photos of ex-Travs turned Hall of Famers Travis Jackson, Jim Bunning and Ferguson Jenkins are displayed. There are also many baseballs used in historic games, authentic uniforms and game equipment plus photos of the Travelers' two previous home ballparks: Kavanaugh Field and Ray Winder Field. A must-visit when you're in the area.

Hall of Famers Buried in Arkansas

Bill Dickey
Roselawn Memorial Park
2801 Asher Avenue
Little Rock

Travis Jackson
Waldo Cemetery
Columbia County Road 27 and US Highway 82
Waldo

Bill Dickey, an eight-time All-Star, had a career batting average of .313.

Travis Jackson, an excellent defensive shortstop, batted over .300 six times.

Florida

Jackie Robinson Ballpark
(formerly called City Island Ballpark)
City: Daytona Beach
Location: 105 East Orange Avenue
386-258-3106

This historic ballpark can claim a milestone moment in American history. City Island Ballpark was the place where Jackie Robinson, on March 17,

1946, began his professional career as a member of the Montreal Royals, a Brooklyn Dodgers Class AAA farm team that trained in Daytona Beach. The spring training game between the Royals and the Dodgers was the first integrated major-league game of the 20th century and a preview of Robinson's major-league debut in 1947. The ballpark was renamed in Robinson's honor in 1990 and a statue bearing his likeness is located at the entrance. Jackie Robinson Park was built in 1930 and has served as temporary home to many Hall of Famers. In November 1998, the ballpark was listed on the National Register of Historic Places for its status and contributions to the civil rights movement. Today, the ballpark is home of the Daytona Cubs, a Chicago Cubs Class A farm team that plays in the Florida State League.

A statue honoring Jackie Robinson stands at the entrance to the Daytona Beach ballpark named in his honor.

Tate High School
City: Gonzalez
Location: 1771 Tate Road
850-937-2300

Since 1954, 45 players from Tate High School have been drafted by major-league teams, including Hall of Famer Don Sutton, who pitched in the major leagues for 23 years, earned four All-Star Game selections and pitched in four World Series. Other Tate High School products include Jay Bell and Travis Fryman. A nearby billboard touts the major-leaguers the school has produced and there's an exhibit within the school.

Henley Field
City: Lakeland
Location: 1049 North Florida Avenue

Opened in 1922 and named for Clare Henley, a local merchant and baseball supporter in Lakeland, Henley Field was spring home to the Cleveland Indians (1924–27) and the Detroit Tigers (1934–1966). It was also home field for the Florida State League Lakeland Tigers for the 2002 season, while Tigertown underwent a yearlong renovation project. It is now home to the nine-time national champion Florida Southern College Moccasins. Located just off downtown Lakeland, the park is listed on the National Register of Historic Places.

Joe Tinker Building

City: Orlando
Location: 16–18 West Pine Street

Joe Tinker

Joe Tinker, the original owner of the building, was best known as a professional shortstop for the Chicago Cubs. He was also a baseball manager and a member of the Baseball Hall of Fame. Tinker is perhaps most famous as the shortstop in the "Tinker to Evers to Chance" double-play combination immortalized in the fabled poem "Baseball's Sad Lexicon," by New York newspaper columnist Franklin Pierce Adams. Yet on September 14, 1905, Tinker and Evers ended up in fisticuffs on the field all because Evers took a cab and left his teammates behind in the hotel lobby. The men didn't speak to one another for 33 years until they were both asked to help broadcast at the 1938 World Series between the Cubs and Yankees. Tinker moved to Orlando in December of 1920 to manage the Orlando baseball team. Tinker had this building built to house his real estate business. The style of the building is 20th Century Commercial. It is a brick structure covered in terracotta and glazed tile. Many businesses have called the Tinker Building home, starting with Joe Tinker's real estate business, a pool hall and a Singer Sewing Machine Company store (1928), and Balfour Hardware Store (1930-1941). It was owned by the Massachusetts Mutual Life Insurance Company (1941) and then sold to Carey Hand. It currently houses a law firm.

Tinker Field

City: Orlando
Location: 287 South Tampa Avenue
407-849-2001

Though the current ballpark was built in 1963, pro baseball has been played on this field since 1914. It served as the spring training facility for several major-league teams as well as the home for Florida State League and Southern League teams until being abandoned in 2000. The stadium is named for Hall of Famer Joe Tinker (of "Tinker-to-Evers-to-Chance" fame), who lived in Orlando after retiring and managed Orlando's first semiprofes-

Tinker Field is dwarfed by the Citrus Bowl football stadium that was built perilously close to its right field fence.

sional team. Interestingly, several hundred grandstand seats from Washington's Griffith Stadium are used at Tinker Field and a monument to Senators owner Clark Griffith stands out front. (The Senators used to train here.) The Citrus Bowl football stadium is built ridiculously close to Tinker, almost touching the right field exterior wall. In the late 1980s, Boston's Sam Horn hit a monster shot that cleared the exterior of Tinker Field and landed in the football stadium.

The Hometown of Chipper Jones
City: Pierson

"Fern Capital of the World and Hometown of Chipper Jones." (There is also a street and ballpark named after Jones in Pierson.)

Ripley Plaque
City: St. Augustine
Location: Original Ripley's Believe It or Not Museum 19 San Marco Avenue

Pierson, Florida, has honored favorite son Chipper Jones with a sign, a street and a ballpark.

Believe it or not, the world famous cartoonist, LeRoy Ripley, has some baseball history. He was born in Santa Rosa, California, in 1890. Even though he was socially awkward as a young person, Roy, as he was called, was a great artist as well as a competitive athlete. Ripley pitched semipro baseball when he was just 13 and actually designed the posters advertising the games. Sadly, in his first serious outing, he broke his arm, thus ending his pitching career. But the pen proved mightier than the bat. One year later, Ripley sold a cartoon to *LIFE* magazine for eight dollars. The artwork showed several young women washing clothes and it was called *The Village Belles Were Slowly Ringing*. After a friend of the family saw his work, she went ahead and shared his drawings with several newspapers. As a result of this, incredibly, Ripley landed a job with the *San Francisco Bulletin* at the age of just 15. In 1912, he moved to New York and added Robert to his name. Soon after, Ripley was hired by the *New York Globe* to create a sports cartoons series called

Champs and Chumps. It was while he worked at the *Globe* that on a slow sports day, he created the cartoon *Believe It or Not!* A plaque here at the original Believe It or Not Museum was placed in his honor.

Ted Williams Museum and Hitters Hall of Fame
City: St. Petersburg
Location: Tropicana Field
1 Tropicana Drive
727-825-3250

The Ted Williams Museum and Hitters Hall of Fame brings a special element to Tropicana Field for fans of all ages. When you go to catch a game, why not arrive a bit early to take in the vast array of different artifacts and pictures of the "greatest hitter that ever lived." These intriguing displays span from Ted Williams's days in the military to his professional playing career. This museum is dedicated to some of the greatest players to ever suit up, including Willie Mays, Joe DiMaggio, Mickey Mantle, Roger Maris, and the Japanese legend Sadaharu Oh. The museum is located just past the rotunda on the right-hand side. And the good news is that admission to the museum is free to fans attending Devil Rays home games. Previously located in Hernando, Florida, in Citrus County, a few blocks from where Ted Williams himself lived during his later years, the Ted Williams Museum and Hitters Hall of Fame was the first museum ever dedicated, at the time, to a living athlete. As it was then, the museum's goal is to preserve and build on the rich tradition and heritage of our national pastime—baseball.

The Swain Apartments
City: St. Petersburg
Location: 1511 22nd Street S

In the 1950s and '60s, Dr. Robert James Swain Jr., a prominent African-American dentist in St. Petersburg, helped lead the struggle against segregation in the city. This area was the heart of the African-American community during the civil rights era and the apartments on 22nd Street housed many of the black major-league players of the St. Louis Cardinals and New York Yankees when they arrived in St. Petersburg for spring training. African Americans in that period were often denied housing in areas where their white teammates would stay. Built in 1956, the apartments offered a sanctuary while Swain and other leaders fought through the system to expose the racial injustice. Attitudes started to change after 1961 and the Cardinals eventually made an effort to integrate their housing. The Yankees had already relocated their spring facilities to Fort Lauderdale. The former Swain apartment building is still used for commercial purposes and was recently granted landmark status for its significant role in the American civil rights era.

St. Petersburg's Al Lang Field has served as a spring training base since 1916, thanks to the inspired thinking of the city's former mayor.

Progress Energy Park

City: St. Petersburg
Location: Al Lang Field
230 First Street S
727-825-3284

Al Lang Field is named after St. Petersburg's former mayor, the local "father of baseball" who provided the impetus for bringing spring training to this Gulf Coast community. For more than 80 years, Al Lang has been a spring training home. The Philadelphia Phillies played here from 1916 to 1921; the Boston Braves from 1922 to 1924; the New York Yankees (Babe Ruth, Lou Gehrig, Joe DiMaggio) from 1925 to 1937; the St. Louis Cardinals (Stan Musial, Bob Gibson, Lou Brock) from 1938 to 1997; and currently, the Tampa Bay Devil Rays. During the summer, the field serves as home to the St. Petersburg Devil Rays, a Class A farm team for Tampa Bay. A marker in the shape of home plate stands just north of the stadium, detailing some of the field's rich history.

One of Babe Ruth's Longest Home Runs

City: Tampa
Location: Pepin-Rood Stadium
University of Tampa
401 West Kennedy Boulevard
813-253-3333

In 1919, during an April 4th spring training game between the defending World Series-champion Red Sox and the New York Giants, young Babe Ruth hit one of his most memorable home runs out of Plant Field. George Smith, pitching for the Giants, fired a fastball that the Red Sox pitcher-turned-slugger

In Tampa, a sign marks one of Babe Ruth's longest home runs.

crushed an estimated 587 feet–purported by some to be the longest ball ever hit in baseball history. Ruth's home run was not the only significant moment or event that occurred here. One of the most memorable was a barnstorming football game between Red Grange's Chicago Bears and a pickup team led by Jim Thorpe called the Tampa Cardinals. More recently, hurdler Roger Kingdom won a national championship at reconfigured Pepin-Rood Stadium on his way to winning a second Olympic gold medal. The stadium has also been used by the Tampa Smokers of the International League and the Cincinnati Reds as a spring training site. Pepin-Rood Stadium, now considered the finest collegiate soccer venue in NCAA Division II, has been the site of two national championship finals.

Dodgertown
City: Vero Beach
Location: 3901 26th Street

This was easily the most historic spring training site in Major League Baseball. The Dodgers were lured to the area in 1948 by Bud Holman, director of Eastern Airlines, who persuaded Brooklyn farm director Buzzy Bavasi to economize and bring together all 30-plus Dodgers farm teams to one central facility. In 1952, the current Dodgertown,

Dodgers players (from left) Steve Garvey, Bill Russell, Ted Sizemore, Don Sutton and Ron Cey look up to manager Walt Alston in this 1976 photo.

featuring Holman Stadium, was constructed in the city of Vero Beach. Dodgertown was a former naval air base and Brooklyn players were originally housed in former Navy barracks. When Holman Stadium opened in 1953, 1,500 of its steel chairs were former seats used at Brooklyn's Ebbets Field. The original barracks were eventually replaced by more comfortable villas (90 of them), along with a golf course and Safari Pines Estates, a residential development. The Dodgers played their last game at Holman Stadium here in March of 2008, opting to move their spring training facilities to Glendale, Arizona, at the start of the 2009 spring season. As of this writing, it is unclear if another team will be moving in to Dodgertown.

Hall of Famers Buried in Florida

Nap Lajoie
Bellevue Cedar Hill Memory
1425 Bellevue Avenue
Daytona Beach
904-253-7603

Dazzy Vance
Stage Stand Cemetery
(East Side of US Highway 19,
a quarter mile south of Yulee Road)
Homosassa Springs

Nap Lajoie batted .338 lifetime.

Bill Terry
Evergreen Cemetery
4535 North Main Street
Jacksonville
904-353-3649

Bill Klem
Graceland Memorial Park
4580 SW 8th Street
Coral Gables
305-446-2922

Jimmie Foxx
Flagler Memorial Park
5301 West Flagler Street
Miami
305-446-7625

Bill Terry's career batting average was .341.

Max Carey
Woodlawn Park North Cemetery
and Mausoleum
3216 SW 8th Street
Miami
305-445-5425

Max Carey

Bill McKechnie

Paul Waner

Heinie Manush had a .330 career batting average.

Ed Walsh
Forest Lawn North
200 West Copans Road
Pompano Beach
954-523-6700

Joe Tinker
Greenwood Cemetery
1603 Greenwood Street
Orlando
407-246-2616

Ray Dandridge
Fountainhead Memorial
7303 Babcock Street SE
Palm Bay
407-727-3977

Bill McKechnie and Paul Waner
Manasota Memorial Cemetery
1221 53rd Avenue East
Bradenton
941-755-2688

Hoyt Wilhelm
Palms Memorial Park
170 Honore Avenue
Sarasota
941-371-4962

Heinie Manush
Sarasota Memorial Park
5833 South Tamiami Trail
Sarasota
941-924-1993

Billy Herman
Riverside Memorial Park
4534 County Line Road
Tequesta
561-747-1100

Georgia

Hank Aaron Statue

City: Atlanta
Location: Turner Field
755 Hank Aaron Drive SE
404-577-9100

On the north side of the Braves' current home ballpark, facing downtown Atlanta, is a 10-foot bronze statue of Hank Aaron. Hammerin' Hank hit a major league-record 755 home runs, drove in a record 2,297 runs and collected a record 6,856 total bases in his storied 23-year career with the Braves and Milwaukee Brewers. Aaron became a first-ballot Hall of Famer in 1982.

Ty Cobb Statue

City: Atlanta
Location: Turner Field

Located outside the northern entrance to Turner Field is a bronze statue of Ty Cobb sliding into a base. The plaque under the statue reads:

Tyrus Raymond Cobb
1886–1961
Known as the Georgia Peach
Charter member of Baseball
Hall of Fame
Leading Batsman of all
Major League History
.367 Average, 4,191 Hits

Ty Cobb, executing his distinctive fadeaway slide, is a fixture outside the entrance of Atlanta's Turner Field.

Phil Niekro Statue

City: Atlanta
Location: Turner Field

The famed knuckleballer has also been immortalized with a bronze statue outside the northern entrance of Turner Field. The plaque under it reads: "Five times an All-Star, Phil was always an All-Star to Atlanta and baseball fans everywhere. He won 318 games in a 24-year Major League career, including a 9-0 no-hit victory in Atlanta-Fulton County Stadium on August 5,

1973. He struck out 3,342 batters in 864 games. Led N.L. in games started 4 times, in complete games 4 times and in victories twice. Phil and brother Joe, the winningest brothers in Major League history, won a combined record total 539 M.L. games."

Knuckleballer Phil Niekro, a longtime fan favorite in Atlanta, has been immortalized by a bronze statue outside Turner Field.

Ivan Allen Jr. Braves Museum and Hall of Fame
City: Atlanta
Location: Turner Field
755 Hank Aaron Drive SE
404-614-2311

This great in-stadium museum and hall of fame contains more than 500 franchise artifacts from its history in Boston, Milwaukee and Atlanta—including the bat and ball from Hank Aaron's record-breaking 715th home run. Through the museum, you can also arrange a guided tour of Turner Field and behind-the-scenes looks at the press box, broadcast booth, clubhouse, dugout and other areas not generally open to the public. A tour of the Hall of Fame triggers memories of special moments and provides inside looks at such Braves legends as Aaron, Eddie Mathews, Dale Murphy, Phil Niekro, Warren Spahn, Greg Maddux and owner Ted Turner. Walk-up tickets can be purchased and free parking is available in the north lot.

The Braves Museum is filled with memorabilia celebrating the long history of a franchise that has been located in Boston, Milwaukee and Atlanta.

Spot Where No. 715 Landed
City: Atlanta
Location: Fulton County Stadium
Parking lot at Turner Field

When Fulton County Stadium was demolished to make way for Turner Field, Braves officials were careful to preserve the landing spot of one of baseball's most historic home runs. In the large reserved parking lot (the green lot) at

Turner Field, a portion of the original Atlanta Stadium fence still stands— the section where the ball left the park— with a big sign proclaiming "715." The original outer wall from Fulton County also remains, serving as a barrier between the green and the blue lots. Aaron's record-breaking homer was hit on April 8, 1974, in a dramatic season home opener against the Los Angeles Dodgers. The image of Aaron trium-

Where Hank Aaron's famous homer landed in 1974.

phantly circling the bases remains imbedded in the city's baseball history.

Ponce de Leon Park
City: Atlanta
Location: 650 Ponce de Leon Road

Baseball was played on this site as far back as 1907. Home of the legendary Atlanta Crackers, the wooden park burned to the ground in 1923 and was rebuilt with concrete and steel. Originally called Spiller Park in honor of Rell J. Spiller, the club's president, Ponce de Leon served as primary home for Atlanta baseball through 1964, at which point the Crackers (a Braves' farm team) moved over to new Atlanta-Fulton County Stadium. The Crackers played their last season there in 1965. Ponce de Leon was especially busy during the 1930s when Georgia Tech used the park and the Atlanta Black Crackers called it home for a period. Ponce de Leon provided proving grounds for such future Hall of Famers as Eddie Mathews and Luke Appling while entertaining numerous legendary stars in both exhibitions and minor-league games. In April of 1949, Jackie Robinson and the Brooklyn Dodgers played a three-game exhibition against the Crackers, marking the first time in Atlanta history that blacks and whites competed against each other in a professional sports event. The only reminder of Ponce de Leon Park today is a magnolia tree that stands in the parking lot of a Home Depot store.

Birthplace of Jackie Robinson
City: Cairo
Location: Hadley Perry Road

The tin-roofed wooden house in this small southwest Georgia town burned down in 1996, leaving only the brick chimney and double fireplace as a physical reminder of Jackie Robinson's birthplace. Born on January 31, 1919, to sharecropper parents on what was once a slave-worked plantation,

Robinson was two years old when his mother packed up their belongings and headed to California with Jackie and his four siblings. A recently unveiled marker, placed by the Georgia Historical Society, identifies the exact spot where the house was located.

A recently placed marker identifies the location of the wooden house where Cairo native Jackie Robinson was born in 1919.

Other Jackie Robinson Tributes in Cairo

★ A 10-mile stretch of State Highway 93 between Cairo and Beachton is now called the Jackie Robinson Memorial Highway. And Cairo High School recently renamed its baseball grounds Jackie Robinson Field.

Golden Park

City: Columbus
Location: 100 4th Street
706-571-8866

Golden Park, built in 1926, was named for T.E. Golden, the man who led the drive to land the town's first South Atlantic League team. In the 1940s, a minor-league club called the Cardinals played here; through the 1960s, it was home to a Yankees farm club. In 1994, the remodeled stadium was chosen to play host to the softball competition in the 1996 Summer Olympic Games. Golden Park today is a historic landmark, featuring a wall of fame honoring Babe Ruth, Hank Aaron, Willie Mays, Ernie Banks and other legends who played there over the years.

Golden Park, built in 1926, was named for T. E. Golden.

Home of Johnny Mize

City: Demorest
Location: Corner of Georgia and
Oak Streets, 1 block east of
US 441 Bus.

A historical marker (right) is placed
here to commemorate the "Home
of Johnny Mize, 'The Big Cat.'"

Johnny Mize Monument

City: Demorest
Location: Demorest Springs Park
Between Georgia Street and Massachusetts Boulevard

Johnny Mize, "The Big Cat," was born in Demorest on January 7, 1913. The
big, burly first baseman played for the St. Louis Cardinals, New York Giants
and New York Yankees during a storied career that lasted from 1936 to 1953.
He either led the National League or tied for the NL lead in home runs four
times while winning three RBI crowns and one batting championship. The
Yankees were unstoppable during Mize's five-year stay, winning five straight
World Series championships (1949–53). In the 1952 classic against Brooklyn, he hit three homers and drove in six runs. Mize finished his career with
359 home runs and a .312 average, earning induction into the Hall of Fame
in 1981. He died in his hometown of Demorest in 1993. The park where the
monument stands is just down the street from city hall.

Piedmont College
named its 51,000-
square-foot athletic
center after Johnny
Mize, who was born and
raised in Demorest.

Johnny Mize Athletic Center
and Baseball Museum

City: Demorest
Location: Piedmont College
165 Central Avenue
1-800-277-7020

While attending high school at the former Piedmont Academy, Johnny Mize played for the varsity
baseball team. When Piedmont College opened a
51,000-square-foot facility with gymnasium, fitness
center, classrooms and training rooms in November of 2000, officials decided to name it the Johnny
Mize Athletic Center. The center also houses the
Johnny Mize Baseball Museum, a collection of
Mize memorabilia from his major-league playing

days (1936–53) with the Cardinals, Giants and Yankees.

Mize is buried at Yonah View Memorial Gardens, 441 Historic Highway S in Demorest, 706-778-8599.

Historic Luther Williams Field
City: Macon
Location: Central City Park
Riverside Drive

Luther Williams Field, which dates back to 1929, has served as home to several South Atlantic League minor-league teams as well as a team in the Negro American League in the 1940s. As current home of the Macon Braves, Luther Williams Field has provided proving grounds for such future Atlanta players as Chipper Jones, Andruw Jones, Kevin Millwood and Rafael Furcal. The field also achieved status in 1976 when it was used to film the movie *The Bingo Long Traveling All-Stars and Motor Kings* starring Billy Dee Williams, Richard Pryor and James Earl Jones.

Georgia Sports Hall of Fame
City: Macon
Location: 301 Cherry Street
478-752-1585

Among the many historic baseball items on display at this excellent museum are a book autographed by Hank Aaron while in the minor leagues, a Thomasville Orioles uniform from the Georgia-Florida League, 1915–17 Cracker Jack cards of selected Georgia baseball players, the Boston Red

The Georgia Sports Hall of Fame is a worthwhile stopover for baseball fans traveling through Macon.

Sox uniform of Willard Nixon, images and reproductions from the Atlanta Black Crackers and a 1962 opening day ticket to an Atlanta Crackers game at Ponce de Leon Park. There are even some items on display in actual lockers from Fulton County Stadium, former home of the Atlanta Braves. More than 30 players have been inducted into the Georgia Sports Hall of Fame, including Hank Aaron, Luke Appling, Ty Cobb, Josh Gibson and Jackie Robinson.

Sherry Smith Historical Marker

City: Mansfield
Location: GA 11, just south of the
railroad tracks

"Mansfield's Famous Southpaw" was
honored with a historical marker bearing that inscription in 1994. Sherrod
Malone "Sherry" Smith (1891-1949)
was born in Monticello and played
town ball in Mansfield, Madison, Elber-
ton and Newborn before turning pro
in 1910. Babe Ruth called Smith "the
greatest pickoff artist who ever lived."
Smith played 14 major-league seasons

The memory of Sherry Smith, a former big-league pitcher and Georgia
baseball legend, is honored by a
prominent marker in Mansfield.

with Pittsburgh, Brooklyn and Cleveland, posting a 114-118 record. But his
remarkable legacy is the pickoff move that baffled runners and resulted in
only two stolen bases against him in 2,0522/3 innings. Smith appeared in
two World Series and worked 301/3 innings in three games, compiling an
0.89 ERA. In a 1916 thriller against Boston, the Dodgers lefty pitched 14
innings before losing, 2-1, to Red Sox lefty Babe Ruth. Ruth failed to get a
hit and struck out twice against Smith, who doubled once in his five trips
against the Babe. Smith managed the Macon Peaches in his last professional
season (1932) and served in the Army during World War I. He later served
as chief of police in Porterdale and Madison. Smith, who is buried in Mansfield, was inducted into the Georgia Sports Hall of Fame in 1980.

Ty Cobb Museum

City: Royston
Location: 461 Cook Street, in the Joe A. Adams Professional Building of
the Ty Cobb Healthcare System
706-245-1825

Ty Cobb, who moved to Royston as a young boy, remains a celebrated figure
in this small Georgia city. The museum is an outgrowth of a major donation
Cobb made in 1949. Royston, in need of a hospital, received $100,000 from
the Georgia Peach and began building what would become the Cobb Memorial Hospital—a facility dedicated to the memory of Cobb's parents, William
and Amanda Cobb. The hospital has grown into the Ty Cobb Healthcare
System, which now includes two hospitals, two long-term care facilities, a
personal care unit and an elderly housing complex. The museum, dedicated
in 1998, features an impressive collection of Cobb artifacts and memorabilia, including a Detroit Tigers uniform, one of Cobb's gloves, his childhood

Bible, a Shriners' cap, his shotgun and much more. An audio-visual presentation spans the life of the man considered by many to be the greatest player in baseball history. Cobb became a charter member of the Hall of Fame in 1936 and he built an off-field reputation as an astute businessman, an investment-savvy operator who was dubbed "baseball's first millionaire athlete." Cobb died at Atlanta's Emory hospital on July 17, 1961.

This is one of many displays that attract visitors to Royston's Ty Cobb Museum, a fitting memorial to one of baseball's greatest players.

Other Ty Cobb-Related Sites in Royston

★ Ty Cobb Memorial Statue
Royston City Hall
634 Franklin Springs Street
706-245-7232

★ The Royston "Welcome" sign coming into town features Cobb.

★ Ty Cobb's ornate family mausoleum is visited by many who come to Royston. It is located at Rosehill Cemetery, Route 17, Royston.

A sign in Royston celebrates local legend Ty Cobb.

William L. Grayson Stadium

City: Savannah
Location: Daffin Park on Victory Drive between Bee Road and Waters
Avenue
912-351-9150

The Class A Savannah Sand Gnats play their games at Grayson Stadium, a beautiful, old-fashioned brick ballpark that dates back to 1941. Located in picturesque Daffin Park, Grayson has been the stomping grounds for numerous future major-leaguers on teams affiliated with the Los Angeles Dodgers, Atlanta Braves, St. Louis Cardinals, Texas Rangers and currently, the Montreal Expos. The stadium is named for Savannah native and Spanish American War hero William Grayson, who spearheaded the drive to build the stadium, which has long existed as one of the true baseball gems of the south.

Historic Grayson Stadium, home to the Savannah Sand Gnats, is a beautiful Southern baseball gem that has been playing host to Minor League Baseball teams since 1941.

Hall of Famers Buried in Georgia

Luke Appling
Sawnee View Gardens
1390 Dahlonega Highway
(Highway 306)
Cumming
770-887-2387

Luke Appling was a 16-time .300 hitter.

Kentucky

Jackie Robinson Marker

City: County of Union
Location: 2¼ miles from Morganfield at entrance to Earle C. Clements
Job Corps Academy, US 60

There is a marker here stating that Jackie Robinson began his professional career in 1944 while he was a lieutenant at Camp Breckinridge. The next year, Brooklyn general manager Branch Rickey signed the four-sport letterman from UCLA to a minor-league contract with the Montreal Royals, a Class AAA team in the Dodgers' chain. In 1947, Robinson was promoted to the major-league roster and went on to lasting fame as the man who broke baseball's color barrier.

Marker for Governor Albert B. Chandler

City: County of Woodford
Location: Junction of Pisgah Pike and US 60

Better known as Happy Chandler, this Henderson County native was a state senator and lieutenant governor before winning election as governor in 1935 and '55. (He also served as a US senator from 1939 to 1945.) As baseball commissioner, it was Chandler who approved Jackie Robinson's contract, giving him the go-ahead to become the first black player in modern major-league history. Chandler, who was elected to the Hall of Fame in 1982, is buried at Pisgah Presbyterian Church, 710 Pisgah Road, Versailles.

Kentuckian Happy Chandler took time away from his political career to serve as commissioner of baseball.

There is another historic marker for Happy Chandler at Park Field Atkinson Park, off Elm Street, Henderson, County of Henderson.

Birthplace of Pee Wee Reese
City: Ekron
Location: Corner of Third Street and
Broadway
County of Meade

Born July 23, 1918, in Ekron, Reese was one
of six children. He made his major-league
debut in 1940 and spent 16 years with the
Brooklyn and Los Angeles Dodgers. One
of the premier shortstops of his era, "Pee
Wee" (his nickname comes from his mar-
ble-shooting prowess as a youngster) captained the dominating Dodgers teams of
the 1950s. An outstanding defensive player
and inspirational leader, he led the Dodgers to seven National League pennants and
one World Series championship in his 16
seasons and is credited with providing an
emotional lift to teammate Jackie Robinson

Former Brooklyn shortstop
Pee Wee Reese still holds a
special place in the hearts of
Ekron residents.

during his efforts to integrate Major League
Baseball. Reese and Robinson formed one of the game's top double-play
combinations for a decade. Reese, who lost three prime years to military
service during World War II, played in 44 World Series games and collected
46 hits, which ranks fifth of all time. He retired after the 1958 season (the
Dodgers' first in Los Angeles) with a .269 career average and was elected to
the Hall of Fame by the Committee on Veterans in 1984.

"Pee Wee" Reese died August 14, 1999, and is buried at Resthaven
Memorial Park, 4400 Bardstown Road, Louisville.

Louisville Slugger Museum & Factory
City: Louisville
Location: 800 West Main Street
877-775-8443

The 120-foot bat that stands at the front of the museum suggests something
special. And few visitors are disappointed. The legacy of Hillerich & Bradsby dates back to 1884, when the company started making Louisville Slugger
bats in its family woodworking shop. The legend goes like this: The owner's
son, Bud Hillerich, attended a local baseball game and, noticing that local
star Pete Browning was in a hitting slump, brought him to the shop to have a
new bat made. With his new weapon, Browning clubbed three hits the next
day, and soon word spread of the effective new bat manufactured by Hiller-

ich & Bradsby. Today, visitors to the factory and museum in downtown Louisville watch bats being made and experience a baseball history museum that is rivaled only by Cooperstown. Everyone, from Honus Wagner and Ty Cobb to Babe Ruth, have sworn by the famous bats made from Pennsylvania white ash.

The Hillerich name is still prominent in the business; the Bradsbys have been gone since the late 1930s. The company has always been located in Louisville, except for a few years when it moved across the Ohio River to Indiana. The company produces 2,000 wooden bats per workday, using high-speed lathes. Some go to young players, but 60–70 percent of all major-league players have contracts with Hillerich & Bradsby. The bats crafted for professionals match precise computer specifications for each player. The company also makes golf clubs, hockey sticks and aluminum bats

The 120-foot Louisville Slugger bat guards a baseball museum that hosts 300,000 visitors a year.

at other facilities, but wooden baseball bats are made exclusively at the Louisville plant.

Tours end at the gift shop, appropriately named A League of Your Own. Every person who takes a tour also receives a miniature Louisville Slugger as a souvenir. The Louisville Slugger Museum & Factory, which entertains 300,000 visitors a year, is open Monday through Saturday, with limited hours on Sunday.

Parkway Field

City: Louisville
Location: University of Louisville
Brook Street just south of Eastern Parkway, edge of the Belknap Campus

Historic Parkway Field opened in 1923 and was quickly recognized as one of the finest minor-league ballparks in the nation. Over the years, Parkway also served as home to several Negro League teams, including the Colonels, the Black Caps and the Buckeyes. Many area baseball fans remember Parkway best for memorable barnstorming games and exhibitions that featured such stars as Babe Ruth, Lou Gehrig, Honus Wagner, Grover Cleveland Alexander, Satchel Paige, Pee Wee Reese and Jackie Robinson. In 1961, the permanent stands were torn down, but the diamond remained intact, as did part of its original brick outfield wall. Until recently, Parkway Field served as home field for the Louisville Cardinals. Since the first edition of this book, which came out in 2003, the stadium has been razed, but some of the original brick walls remain.

Earle Combs was a key member of the 1927 Yankees, considered by many the greatest team of all time.

Birthplace of Earle Combs
City: Pebworth
Location: County of Owsley

A historic marker identifies Pebworth as the birthplace of the former Yankees center fielder (1899-1976). Combs played for the Bronx Bombers from 1924 to 1935 and served as a Yankees coach from 1936 to 1943. As a player, Combs contributed to four American League pennants and three World Series championships, retiring with a lifetime average of .325. Combs, the outstanding leadoff hitter for teams that featured Babe Ruth, Lou Gehrig, Tony Lazzeri and Lefty Gomez, was elected to the Kentucky Athletic Hall of Fame in 1963 and to the Baseball Hall of Fame by the Committee on Veterans in 1970. When he died in 1976, he was buried at Richmond Cemetery, 606 East Main Street, Richmond.

Louisiana

Alex Box Stadium
City: Baton Rouge
Location: Louisiana State University
South Stadium Drive

Alex Box Stadium is a Works Progress Administration (WPA) project that was finished in 1938. The concrete-and-steel stadium on the LSU campus was designed with 2,500 seats and became the spring training home for the New York Giants in 1938 and 1939. It was named for Alex Box in 1943, an athlete who lettered on the 1942 LSU baseball team. Sadly, Box was killed while fighting in North Africa during World War II. Consistently ranked above all collegiate baseball facilities in attendance, Alex Box has had over three million fans watch the Tigers play at "The Box" since 1984. Renovated multiple times over the years, the capacity at the stadium is now 7,760. Another great old ballpark, courtesy of the WPA.

Delhi Municipal Baseball Park
City: Delhi
Location: Chicago and Louisiana Streets
(Also known as Billy Bryan Memorial Park)

This quaint little field with the old wooden grandstand is the first sporting facility in Louisiana to be placed on the National Register. Built in 1948, it was the community's first permanent baseball facility and the first to provide lighting for night games. In its early years, amateur baseball competition was fierce among town teams and the acquisition of a permanent baseball facility with bleachers and lighting in 1948 was an event of considerable magnitude in the life of a town. It was built especially for the Delhi Oilers, who were in a six-team amateur league and played two games per week—40 per season. The park was paid for by a local stock drive and its first game was played in May of 1948. The first night game at Delhi was later than planned because of a delay in getting all the lighting equipment in place. But its "first night game in history" (as it was described in the local paper) occurred on July 15, 1948, and was accompanied by a local celebration. Baseball parks with covered wooden grandstands, once typical in towns throughout rural America, are now scarce, which is why this charming slice of history has earned its place on the National Register. Today, the field is used by various local groups.

The wooden grandstand at Delhi Municipal Baseball Park gives it an ambience long forgotten in most American cities.

Mel Ott Park

City: Gretna
Location: Belle Chase Highway (Highway 23)

Dedicated to "Master Melvin" Ott, this ballpark (and the monument within) shows the undying pride of a city for a player who ended his major-league career in 1947. Born in Gretna, Ott was only 16 when New York Giants manager John McGraw spot-

ted him in a tryout. McGraw, intrigued by the Louisiana kid with the odd batting stance and impressive left-handed power stroke, signed him straight out of high school and kept him on the big-league roster in 1926 and '27, watching and learning at the side of the master. By the end of Ott's 22-year career, he had compiled Hall of Fame numbers. He

The monument to Gretna native Mel Ott has its own quiet section in Mel Ott Park, which is dedicated to the former New York Giants slugger.

was a .304 hitter whose stroke was tailor-made for the Polo Grounds' short right field fence. His 511 home runs ranked third on the all-time list and he had driven in 1,860 runs. He topped .300 10 times, played in three World Series and was the National League home run leader six times. Ott is best

remembered for his "foot in the bucket" batting stance—he would step high and shift his weight into the pitch with his bat swooping low and nearly upright. Ott played his entire career with the Giants and managed the team from 1942 to 1948, all but one of those years as a player/manager. He was the toast of the town, the "favorite ballplayer" of actress Tallulah Bankhead and restaurateur Toots Shor, and a New York personality dwarfed only during his playing days by Babe Ruth, Lou Gehrig and Joe DiMaggio. After retiring as a player, Ott managed the Oakland Oaks of the Pacific Coast League in 1951 and '52, and then opted for a second

career as a Detroit broadcaster. On November 21, 1958, Ott was tragically killed in an automobile accident while returning home from dinner with his wife. The car driven by Ott was slammed head-on by a drunk driver. In addition to Mel Ott Park and the accompanying monument, Gretna also honors its favorite son with a photo exhibit at city hall on Huey P. Long Avenue and 2nd Street.

Hall of Famers Buried in Louisiana

Mel Ott
Metairie Cemetery
5100 Pontchartrain Boulevard
New Orleans

Ted Lyons
Big Woods Cemetery
Highway 388 and
Big Woods Cemetery Road
Edgerly

Ted Lyons won 260 games.

Mississippi

Mississippi Sports Hall of Fame & Museum
City: Jackson
Location: 1152 Lakeland Drive
601-982-8264

This 22,000-square-foot museum, which was opened in the early 1990s, has become one of the state's exceptional sports facilities and a vital part of its sports heritage. What makes it particularly special to a baseball history fan are the artifacts it inherited from the former Dizzy Dean Museum. On the second floor, visitors will discover the best collection of Dizzy Dean memorabilia in America—items that make the legendary St. Louis Cardinals pitcher come alive. There are personal items donated by Dean's family, including his 1934 World Series and Hall of Fame rings, many photos, vintage newsreel clips, an original uniform and much more. Among the other Mississippi-born former baseball stars honored at the museum are James "Cool Papa" Bell and Guy Bush, a pitcher best remembered for giving up Babe Ruth's last two major-league home runs.

Cool Papa Bell Marker

City: Starkville
Location: McKee Park
Cool Papa Bell Drive
Directions: As you enter Starkville from the south on Highway 25, turn left at the traffic light marking the intersection of Lynn Lane and Highway 25. Go approximately one mile on Lynn Lane and turn right on Cool Papa Bell Road, which is the entrance to McKee Park. The historic marker is across from the concession stand between the two largest baseball fields. McKee Park is to the right of Lynn Lane and not to be confused with the Starkville Sportsplex, which is on the left just before the entrance to McKee Park.

James "Cool Papa" Bell, born in Starkville, enjoyed his reputation as the fastest man in baseball. Rumor had it that Bell, who starred as a Negro League outfielder, could hit the light switch in his bedroom and hop into bed before the light went out. Bell was an offensive and defensive force for almost three decades with such teams as the St. Louis Stars, Detroit Wolves, Kansas City Monarchs, Homestead Grays, Memphis Red Sox, Chicago American Giants and the legendary Pittsburgh Crawfords—a team that boasted a lineup with Josh Gibson, Judy Johnson and Buck Leonard, three future

"Cool Papa" Bell's Hall of Fame career is saluted by a marker in McKee Park, a sports facility in his hometown of Starkville.

Hall of Famers. While Bell never got a chance to play in the majors, there's little doubt he would have succeeded. He was a consistent .300-plus hitter, a speedy Tris Speaker-caliber center fielder and one of the best base stealers at any professional level. The tales of Bell's speed have been greatly exaggerated over the years, but there was little doubt he deserved a place in the Hall of Fame when a special committee announced his selection in 1974.

Hall of Famers Buried in Mississippi

Dizzy Dean
Bond Cemetery
Bond (in town to the east side of US
Highway 49)

Bill Foster (unmarked)
Carbondale Cemetery
S. R. 552, 3 miles northwest of
Alcorn and 2 miles southeast of
the Windsor Ruins, Claiborne
County

Dizzy Dean led the league
in strikeouts four times and
posted a 30–7 record in
1934.

North Carolina

Historic McCormick Field
City: Asheville
Location: 30 Buchanan Place

Babe Ruth called it
"the prettiest ballpark
in America." Over the
years, that opinion
has been seconded
many times. Built into
a scenic hillside, Mc-
Cormick Field opened
in 1924 and remained
largely intact until it
was rebuilt in 1992.
Throughout its exis-
tence, the park has
served as home for the

McCormick Field, once called "the prettiest ballpark in
America" by Babe Ruth, is still the home of the Class A
Asheville Tourists.

minor-league Asheville Tourists. Willie Stargell played for the Tourists in 1961 and his monumental home runs here are still the stuff of legend. For a while, the Ebbets Field clock sat over the scoreboard in center field, reportedly because Dodgers boss Branch Rickey loved the smell of the honeysuckle in the outfield and felt it would provide a fitting home for the former Brooklyn relic. McCormick played a small part in the so-called "Bellyache Heard 'Round the World" in 1925 when Ruth, who was scheduled to play an exhibition there with the Yankees, collapsed at an Asheville train station and was rushed to a hospital. Rumors quickly circulated that the Bambino had died in Asheville. Ruth returned to the city for an exhibition game in 1926, but it was rained out. He finally played at McCormick on April 8, 1931, in a game that also featured Yankees teammate Lou Gehrig.

Today's McCormick Field is still the home of the Asheville Tourists Professional Baseball Club, a Class A team in the South Atlantic League now affiliated with the Colorado Rockies.

Historic Durham Athletic Park
City: Durham
Location: 409 Blackwell Street
919-956-2855

Though many notable major-leaguers, including Chipper Jones, David Justice, Mickey Lolich, Rusty Staub and Joe Morgan, have played at this little gem of a ballpark in Durham, the stadium is probably best known as the setting for the 1988 movie *Bull Durham*. Built in 1940 on the same site as El Toro Park, which had burned to the ground, Durham served as

Durham Athletic Park is best remembered by baseball fans as the setting for the popular 1988 movie *Bull Durham*.

home for minor-league teams in both the Piedmont League and Carolina League. But its professional association ended in 1995, when nearby Durham Bulls Athletic Park played host to its first game. Today, Durham Athletic Park is used primarily by college summer and high school leagues.

Hicks Field

City: Edenton
Location: 111 East Freemason

Historic Hicks Field is home to the John A. Holmes High School Aces as well as the Edenton Steamers of the Coastal Plain League. This venerable park was built as a WPA project in 1939.

The main structure is comprised of a wooden grandstand, which can hold approximately 500 people. The main grandstand, which still exists, is the oldest remaining wooden grandstand of its kind in North Carolina. Up until 1952, Hicks Field was home primarily to Minor League Baseball and semipro teams. The Edenton Colonials of the original Coastal Plain League, the Albemarle League, and the Virginia League were the primary tenants.

In addition, Hicks Field served as a spring training facility for several minor-league teams during the 1940s. These teams included Binghamton, New York, and Reading, Pennsylvania. In honor of all that's taken place here, Hicks Field was also added to the National Register of Historic Places in 1995.

In 1997, Hicks Field underwent a near-complete renovation. The main grandstand behind home plate was redone and two new grandstands were added; one down the first baseline and one down the third baseline. A manual wooden scoreboard was placed in right field, and the double decking of the outfield fence in left field gave Hicks a "Fenway Park" atmosphere that was an instant hit with fans. After all of the remodeling was finished, Hicks Field grew in capacity to seat 1,200 fans. In 1998, the Edenton Steamers were formed in the new Coastal Plain League summer collegiate baseball league and they became the newest tenants at Hicks, which continues to host the Steamers, Edenton Holmes High School baseball, American Legion Post 40 contests, and various tournaments in the summer. In 2004, the well-respected publication *Baseball America* rated Historic Hicks Field the number two summer collegiate venue in the country. It's a very pleasant ballpark environment, and yet another old WPA baseball project that has stood the test of time.

Babe Ruth's First Professional Home Run

City: Fayetteville
Location: Gillespie Street (near the North Carolina Department of Transportation building)
Cumberland County

The historic marker here commemorates Babe Ruth's first home run in professional baseball. In March of 1914, the Baltimore Orioles, offered free lodging by the Baltimore-born owner of the Lafayette Hotel, traveled to Fay-

A plaque marks the Babe's famous homer in North Carolina.

etteville for spring training. That season's Orioles team featured an 18-year-old phenom pitcher named George Herman Ruth. During an Orioles intrasquad game at the old Cape Fear Fairgrounds, Ruth clobbered a ball out of the park and into a lake, marking his "unofficial" first home run as a professional player. The ballpark has long been gone and replaced by a local Department of Transportation building. But the marker was erected in 1951, thanks to the persistence of Maurice Fleishman, a 1914 bat boy who witnessed the historic blow. The ceremony at the marker's dedication was attended by former Philadelphia A's manager Connie Mack and Babe Ruth's wife, among other notables.

Fuquay Mineral Spring Inn and Garden
City: Fuquay Varina
Location: 333 South Main Street
866-552-3782

The owner of this cozy bed and breakfast is John Byrne, whose father, Tommy Byrne, pitched for the New York Yankees in the 1940s and '50s—for teams that included Joe DiMaggio and Mickey Mantle. Byrne led the American League in winning percentage in 1955, when

A bed and breakfast at Fuquay Varina keeps alive the memory of pitcher Tommy Byrne, a former teammate of Joe DiMaggio with the Yankees.

he went 16-5. One of the game's better hitting pitchers, he belted 15 career homers and was used as a pinch hitter 80 times. John, who has entertained many of his father's former teammates, honors his legacy by displaying some of his Yankees memorabilia. If you visit Byrne, be sure to check out his finger—he still wears his father's 1950 World Series ring.

Greensboro Red Wings Marker
City: Greensboro
Location: 3300 Randleman Road

In the 1930's, the Goshen Red Wings were organized on this site as a community Negro baseball team. The team was organized by F. B. Morris, principal of Goshen School. The original school and ball field are located here. In 1947, the Goshen Red Wings became the Greensboro Red Wings and joined the Carolina League, playing other Negro baseball teams in North Carolina and Virginia. Organizers of the team were A. Crump, S. Kelly, F. B. Morris, E. Alexander and M. Watkins. Several members of the Red Wings played with National Negro League baseball teams. In 1954, Thomas E. Alston, first baseman for the Red Wings, became the first black man to play with the St. Louis Cardinals. He is buried on this site. The contributions made by these men helped to shape baseball in Greensboro and nationally. A marker was erected here in 1997 by a group called the Friends of the Goshen Community (and the current use for the site is for the New Goshen United Methodist Church).

Historic World War Memorial Stadium
City: Greensboro
Location: Yanceyville and Lindsay Streets

Built in 1926 as a memorial to Greensboro casualties of World War I, War Memorial currently ranks as the fourth-oldest minor-league ballpark still in use. Originally built for football and track, it became a baseball facility in 1930. Amazingly, night games were played here four years before the first major-league game was played under the lights. War Memorial played its first night game on July 28, 1930, and an overflow crowd watched as the local Patriots lost to the Raleigh Caps, 22–6. In that game, playing for the Caps, was future Hall of Famer Hank Greenberg. Later that season, another Hall of Famer joined the Patriots—Johnny Mize. Ted Williams, making a stopover during World War II, blasted a famous ninth-inning bomb into the trees in right field while playing for the Carolina Pre-Flight team of Chapel Hill. In 1950, throngs turned out to see Jackie Robinson's Dodgers play an exhibition game at War Memorial. Carl Yastrzemski played here when he was in the Carolina League, Bob Hope once staged a benefit here and, more recently, Don Mattingly, Derek Jeter, Otis Nixon, Mariano Rivera and Curt Schilling all spent time at War Memorial. The minor-league Greensboro Bats (now called the Grasshoppers) played here through 2004. The stadium is still used for other minor-league and semipro games. One of the stadium's notable features is an ornate, triple-arched entrance, which made a cameo appearance during the "road trip" segment of the 1988 movie *Bull Durham*. The stadium also has a pair of bronze plaques framing the archway and listing the area's war dead during the years 1917 to 1919. Close examination of the right-side plaque reveals that there were actually *two* alphabetical lists. Some sources say that this was a separation of white from "colored" in the conventional apartheid practice of that era. The marker between the two lists was later roughly chiseled away.

"Shoeless Joe" Jackson Memorial Park

City: Greenville
Location: West Avenue

After his banishment from baseball, Shoeless Joe Jackson lived a quiet life in Greenville.

This ballpark, which contains a memorial to Jackson, is on the original field where, in 1903, at the age of 13, Shoeless Joe began his baseball career. He started here in the old textile league for the Brandon Mill team in Greenville and went on to become one of the outstanding—and controversial—players in baseball history. Initially brought to the majors by Connie Mack in 1908, Jackson was sent to Cleveland, where his career took off. Jackson starred for the Indians from 1910 to 1915, batting .408 in 1911 with a near-perfect swing that was copied by a young Babe Ruth. An outstanding outfielder as well as one of the game's most dangerous hitters, Jackson was traded to Chicago in 1916 and helped the White Sox win a 1917 World Series championship. But in 1919, after playing in a World Series loss to Cincinnati, he was caught up in one of the most infamous gambling scandals in sports history—the "Black Sox" incident that resulted in his lifetime banishment from baseball. Jackson returned to Greenville's West End and quietly resumed his life. Until his death in 1951, he operated a liquor store on Pendleton Street. Near the park today is a life-size bronze statue at Shoeless Joe Jackson Plaza, located at the intersection of Augusta, South Main and Pendleton Streets. This area is in the middle of the West End District, where Shoeless Joe spent much of his life.

Joe Jackson is buried beside his wife in Woodlawn Memorial Park on Wade Hampton Boulevard in Greenville.

Jim "Catfish" Hunter Statue

City: Hertford
Location: Perquimans County Courthouse lawn
Church Street

Jim "Catfish" Hunter was a beloved figure in Hertford, the rural town where he was born on April 8, 1946. Hunter, one of the top right-handers in the game from 1965 to 1979, earned five World Series championships—three with the Oakland Athletics in the early 1970s and two more with the New York

Yankees. The unassuming Hunter won 224 games over his 15-year career, topping the 20-win plateau five times, earning a 1974 Cy Young and pitching a perfect game in 1968. Arm trouble finally ended his career at age 33, setting the stage for his Hall of Fame induction in 1987. Hunter died tragically in his hometown at age 53 of amyotrophic lateral sclerosis (ALS), the same disease that claimed the life of former Yankee great Lou Gehrig in 1941.

Catfish Hunter, a "country boy" from Hertford, was a championship-winning machine for the Oakland A's and New York Yankees.

     "Catfish" Hunter is buried at Cedarwood Cemetery, Hyde Park Road, Hertford.

Jim Thorpe's Professional Baseball Debut
City: Rocky Mount
Location: US 301 Business (Church Street)
Nash County

A state historic marker commemorates the area where legendary multiple-sport athlete Jim Thorpe made his professional baseball debut with the Rocky Mount Railroaders in 1909. It was because of his role as a pitcher on this Eastern Carolina League team in 1909 and '10, as well as the time he spent playing for the Fayetteville Highlanders, that Thorpe was stripped of his 1912 Olympic gold medals—a punishment for violating the amateur status rules of that era. In his Class D career, Thorpe batted only .250 in 89 games.

Enos Slaughter Museum Exhibit
City: Roxboro
Location: Person County Museum of History
309 North Main

Located in historic uptown Roxboro, the Person County Museum of History opened in 1992. Operated over its first few years out of the old post office building on Main Street, it is located today in the lovely and historic "Kitchin House," the onetime residence of the former North Carolina governor W.W. Kitchin. One of the museum's permanent exhibits is a tribute to local legend Enos "Country" Slaughter, who was born at Roxboro in 1916. The hard-nosed Hall of Fame outfielder, best remembered for his 1946 "Mad Dash" that gave the St. Louis Cardinals a seven-game World Series win over the Boston Red Sox, was a career .300 hitter who never stopped hustling over a 19-year career that also included stints with the New York Yankees, Kansas

City Athletics and Milwaukee Braves. Slaughter, who was devastated by his shocking 1954 trade from the Cardinals to the Yankees, helped the New Yorkers win three American League pennants and two World Series before ending his career in 1959 at Milwaukee. The museum's Slaughter exhibit offers an impressive collection of trophies, news articles, baseballs, pictures and other interesting items. Slaughter, who was named to the Hall of Fame in 1985 by the Committee on Veterans, died in 2002 at age 86 and is buried at Allensville United Methodist Church Cemetery, 80 Dirgie Mine Road, Roxboro.

Enos Slaughter is remembered as a Cardinal and a Yankee, but his baseball roots were in North Carolina.

North Carolina Baseball Museum

City: Wilson
Location: Fleming Stadium
300 Stadium Street
252-399-2261

Located at pretty Fleming Stadium, the North Carolina Baseball Museum has over 3,328 square feet and showcases baseball memorabilia of many aspects from across North Carolina. Memorabilia is from ballplayers who played in North Carolina, such as Catfish Hunter, Hoyt Wilhelm, Gaylord Perry, Enos Slaughter, Rick Ferrell and Buck Leonard. Athletes who have played at Fleming Stadium include Ted Williams, Richie Ashburn, and Robin Roberts. The museum features a "Walk of Fame," a collection of bricks to honor and recognize the NC's baseball players. Fleming Stadium, originally known as Wilson Municipal Stadium, was erected in 1938 as a WPA project. The stadium was officially dedicated on June 29, 1939, and the Wilson Tobs played here during the inaugural season. In 1952, the stadium was renamed Fleming Stadium in memory of Allie W. Fleming, a local businessman who also happened to be president of the Wilson Baseball Club in 1939. Professional teams playing in Wilson's Fleming Stadium have been the Coastal Plain League Class D, 1939–1941; Bi-State League Class D, 1942; the Coastal Plain League Class D, 1946–1956; the Carolina League Class B, 1956–1968; and the Carolina League Class A, 1973. Another classic WPA project that has outlasted many other ballparks.

Hall of Famers Buried in North Carolina

Rick Ferrell
New Garden Friends Cemetery
801 New Garden Road
Greensboro

Walter "Buck" Leonard
Gardens of Gethsemane
3020 North Raleigh Street
Rocky Mount

Willie Stargell
Oleander Memorial Gardens
306 Bradley Drive
Wilmington

Rick Ferrell hit over .300 four times and caught all nine innings of baseball's first All-Star Game in 1933.

Buck Leonard was a home run leader in the Negro Leagues.

South Carolina

Riley Park
City: Charleston
Location: Fishburne Street near Lockwood Drive

Riley Park, affectionately called "The Joe," is named for Joseph P. Riley Jr., the mayor of Charleston. While The Citadel plays its home games here (the park is located near campus), the fun really starts when the Charleston RiverDogs square off against an opponent in a South Atlantic League game. Anything goes because the RiverDogs' president is none other than Mike Veeck, son of immortal baseball innovator Bill Veeck. In his father's unpredictable

Riley Park is home to the Charleston RiverDogs and plenty of fan-friendly promotions, thanks to team president Mike Veeck.

and sometimes-zany tradition, Mike works overtime to dream up the most fan-friendly, off-the-wall promotions in sports, making a RiverDogs game a once-in-a-lifetime experience. Actor Bill Murray is part owner of the River-Dogs, who are also a Class A affiliate of the Tampa Bay Devil Rays.

Historic Duncan Park
City: Spartanburg
Location: On Duncan Street off Union Street

It is billed as "the oldest minor-league stadium in the nation." Opened in 1925, Duncan Park served for decades as home to the Spartanburg Phillies, the South Atlantic League's affiliate of the Philadelphia Phillies. Duncan is one of those cozy, small-town parks that feels blissfully trapped in another,

Duncan Park, a ballpark from a simpler era, is now the stomping grounds for college, high school and American Legion teams.

simpler era. Given its longtime association with the Phillies, Duncan Park was fortunate to have inherited some of the box seats from Philadelphia's Connie Mack Stadium when that park was torn down. Today, though no longer associated with Minor League Baseball, Duncan Park is home to Wofford College, the University of South Carolina at Spartanburg and the American Legion in addition to high school and summer league games.

Tennessee

Historic Joe Engel Stadium
City: Chattanooga
Location: 1130 East 3rd Street

Built in 1930, this venerable old park was the longtime home of the Lookouts, initially a Washington-affiliated franchise that played in the Southern Association. Senators owner Clark Griffith built the franchise from scratch with the help of scout and former pitcher Joe Engel, who was dispatched to Chattanooga to get things organized. It didn't take long for Engel to become the Southern version of Bill Veeck, a brainstorming promoter whose crazy promotions made every visit to the park an event to remember. Engel gave away a house at one game and swapped a player for a turkey at another. But it was his Jackie Mitchell stunt that gained the most publicity and shocked the baseball world.

In 1931, Mitchell was a 17-year-old southpaw, honing her skill as a pitcher in Atlanta, when Engel offered her a minor-league contract. His plan was to have the young lady pitch in an exhibition game against the New York Yankees. One New York newspaper reporter snidely remarked: "The Yankees will meet a club here that has a girl pitcher named Jackie Mitchell, who has a swell change of pace and swings a mean lipstick. I suppose that in the next town they will find a squad that has a female impersonator in left field, a sword swallower at short and a trained seal behind the plate." The game went off as planned on April 2, 1931, and 4,000 fans turned out, including dozens of reporters and other media—just the kind of response Engel had anticipated.

The first batter Mitchell faced was Babe Ruth, who gamely swung at and missed her first pitch—a sinker. At 2-1, Ruth missed on another swing. At 2-2, the Babe was called out looking, a borderline pitch that prompted a futile protest before Ruth sulked back to the dugout. Next up was Lou Gehrig. Like Ruth, Gehrig missed the first pitch. But he also missed the second and third, giving the teenager strikeouts against the two most feared hitters in baseball. Mitchell walked the next hitter, Tony Lazzeri, before being pulled from the game. The story was huge, splashed across the top of major newspapers throughout the country; film of the event played in theaters everywhere. Whether or not the players were merely going along with the stunt has been debated for years, but many in attendance believe Mitchell's nasty sinker was, indeed, effective and that the strikeouts were legitimate.

Within days, baseball commissioner Kenesaw Mountain Landis came down hard on the stunt, voiding Mitchell's contract on the grounds that professional baseball was too strenuous to be played by a woman. By

1937, tired of the publicity that followed her everywhere, Mitchell retired and went to work in her father's optometry office. In 1982, she returned to Joe Engel Stadium to throw out the first pitch for the Lookouts on opening day. Mitchell died in 1987. The Lookouts have since moved to a new park, but Joe Engel Stadium proudly remains, a host for high school and college games.

Lindsey Nelson Stadium

City: Knoxville
Location: University of Tennessee

Lindsey Nelson was a sportscaster best known for his broadcasts of college football and New York Mets baseball. Opened in 1993, Lindsey Nelson Stadium is named after the Tennessee alum and sports broadcasting legend. Both the National Baseball Hall of Fame and the Pro Football Hall of Fame have honored Nelson with its highest honors for broadcasters. As good as Nelson was behind the mic, he was just as famous for his sartorial splendor. TV broadcasts featuring Nelson were widely watched for his wildly colored, plaid sports jackets. He supposedly owned 335 of them! The crazy jackets became a trademark for Nelson and he's still remembered for them today. After he retired, Lindsey Nelson moved to Knoxville and lived in an apartment across the Tennessee River from the University of Tennessee campus. Nelson died at age 76 on June 10, 1995, in Atlanta, Georgia.

Martin Park

City: Memphis
Location: 494 E. H. Crump Boulevard

The Memphis Red Sox were a professional Negro League baseball team that played in Memphis from the 1920s until the end of segregated baseball. They participated in the Negro National League for most of the league's existence, although they also played independently and in the Negro Southern League before becoming charter members of the new Negro American League in 1937. The team did not perform as well in the new league as its roster would suggest.

For the greater part of the team's history, J. B. Martin and B. B. Martin of Memphis, brothers who both maintained dental practices and other business enterprises, owned the team. The brothers built Martin Park on Crump Boulevard for their team, making the Red Sox one of the few clubs in the Negro Leagues with their own ballpark. Today. The site is currently the site of a trucking company. There is a historical marker on the site noting it was the former site of Martin Park.

Russwood Park

City: Memphis
Location: Jefferson and Madison Avenues

Russwood Park was the home of the Memphis Chicks Minor League Baseball team until the spring of 1960, when the park burnt to the ground. Originally constructed in 1896, it was known then as
Elm Wood Park. Prior to its demise, Russwood
was revered as one of the uniquely shaped
fields in the country. It was crafted on a six-sided, asymmetrical block, with the deepest parts
of left and right fields being substantially farther from home plate than straightaway center.
Some of the park's boundary streets included
Pauline Street (east, right field), Madison Avenue (south, home plate), and Hospital Street
(west, left field). In addition to baseball, there's
some rock and roll history at the site, too: Elvis Presley performed a memorable show here
on July 4, 1956. The last event at the ballpark
was a preseason exhibition game between the

A fire destroyed Russwood
Park in Memphis. Today the
site is marked with a plaque.

Chicago White Sox and the Cleveland Indians on Easter Sunday, April 17,
1960. That night, after the game, a fire broke out and completely destroyed
the ballpark. It was so fierce that Baptist Hospital, located across the street,
evacuated many patients. Today, a historic marker can be found at the site.

Tennessee Sports Hall of Fame & Museum

City: Nashville
Location: 501 Broadway
615-242-4750

Located inside the Gaylord Entertainment Center, this relatively new museum, while dedicated primarily to college football, does contain some memorabilia related to local baseball history (including some Negro League uniforms worn by teams that played at Sulphur Dell).

Sulphur Dell

City: North Nashville
Location: Marker located on Fourth Avenue between Jackson Street and
the railroad tracks (Farmer's Market area of downtown)

Today, it's a parking lot used by state workers. But one of the minor leagues'
most historic stadiums once sat here. Baseball was reportedly played on this

site as far back as 1876–the reputed first-ever game in Nashville. When the Southern League was organized in 1885, Nashville was a charter city and the state capital fielded several different teams that played in the league over the next 10 years, including the Americans, the Blues, the Tigers and the Seraphs. When the Southern Association was formed in 1901, Sulphur Dell, then known as Sulphur Spring Bottom (it was the site of a historic sulphur spring), became the permanent home to the Nashville Volunteers. In time, legendary writer Grantland Rice, while working as a newspaper reporter in Nashville, nicknamed the park "Sulphur Dell" and the name stuck. One of the park's more interesting quirks was its right field area, which was defined by irregular-shaped hills. One incline rose to 25 feet, forming a "shelf" that forced fielders to position themselves at its top. Right fielders at Sulphur Dell became known as "mountain goats," a reference to the unusual hill climbing they had to do during a typical game. The Vols called Sulphur Dell home for 61 years, until the Southern Association disbanded. In addition to the Vols, the Negro American League Elite Giants called the park home in 1933 and '34. Sulphur Dell was torn down in 1963 and the only reminder of its colorful past is a historic marker at its former site.

A parking lot and marker stand at the site of Sulphur Dell, a former minor-league landmark.

Texas

Nolan Ryan Center
City: Alvin
Location: On the campus of Alvin Community College
2925 South Bypass 35
281-388-1134

This is Nolan Ryan country, pure and simple, and you can get a full appreciation of the "Ryan Express" at Alvin Community College's Nolan Ryan Center for Continuing Education. The center was built by the Nolan Ryan Foundation and donated to the college in the summer of 1996. About one-third of the building functions as a museum dedicated to Ryan. This area chronicles the life and baseball career of Alvin's favorite son in many state-of-the-art displays, including an interactive pitch-catch exhibit where the visitor "feels" a Nolan Ryan fastball in a catcher's mitt. There are video clips of Ryan's career with the Mets, Angels, Astros and Rangers, the full chronology of his 27 major-league seasons and much more. The Rawlings Hall of Records sells replica

It's difficult to visit Alvin without encountering Nolan Ryan, either physically or in spirit.

strikeout balls depicting each of Ryan's 5,714 strikeouts with "owners" listed in a computer database. Outside Alvin city hall you'll find a statue of Nolan Ryan at 216 West Sealy.

Alvin High School

City: Alvin
Location: 802 South Johnson

Ryan graduated from Alvin High School in 1965. His wife, Ruth, followed in 1967 and their two sons and daughter attended school there. The baseball diamond has been named Nolan Ryan Field and a trophy case there includes Ryan's high school jersey. Also, look for signs proclaiming Alvin as the "Hometown of Nolan Ryan" and the Nolan Ryan statue that stands beyond the center field seats at The Ballpark in Arlington (now called Rangers Ballpark in Arlington).

Potter County Memorial Stadium

City: Amarillo
Location: 801 South Pol Street

Potter County Memorial Stadium is the home field of the Amarillo Dillas minor-league baseball club of United League Baseball. It opened way back in 1949 and is nicknamed "Dilla Villa," dating back prior to Amarillo National Bank's purchase of naming rights when the Dillas made their first appearance in Amarillo in 1994. The ballpark underwent a serious renovation in the winter of 2005, replacing many of the badly needed renovations.

Meadowbrook Park
City: Arlington
Location: East Abram Street

Built in 1921 by the "Optimist Club," Meadowbrook was Arlington's first ballpark. Donkey baseball was once played on a diamond in the area, where the recreation center is now located, and a Texas sandstone building on the knoll inside the loop road once housed a small monkey zoo.

Legends of the Game Museum
City: Arlington
Location: Rangers Ballpark in Arlington
1000 Ballpark Way
817-273-5600

This museum and learning center, opened with the new Texas Rangers' ballpark in 1994, features the largest collection of baseball-related artifacts outside Cooperstown. With more than 140 items from the Hall of Fame (and more than 1,000 objects from private donors and the Rangers), the story of baseball's greatest legends is told through jerseys, bats, gloves, words and much more. The Legends of the Game features outstanding exhibits about Arlington's own "boys of summer," the Texas Rangers. You can trace the roots of the Rangers back to their previous life as the Washington Senators and learn about the top players throughout the club's history.

> You'll also find exhibits on:
> • Texas League—Fort Worth Cats, Dallas Spurs and more
> • Heroes of the Negro Leagues
> • Women in professional baseball

The center field complex at Rangers Ballpark in Arlington is home to Rangers offices as well as the Legends of the Game Museum.

- A replica of the KLIF radio broadcast booth
- Famous ballparks

Along with the permanent exhibits, the museum offers outstanding temporary exhibits as well as a display dedicated to "Baseball's 25 Greatest Moments," selected by The Sporting News and including historic photographs and interpretive text. The three-story, 24,000-square-foot museum also features an interactive learning center, designed for all those fans curious about the history and science of baseball. Visitors can examine the insides of a four-foot baseball, predict the trajectory of a pitch on a windy day and stand in for former Rangers catcher Ivan Rodriguez while catching a curveball from Nolan Ryan.

Arlington Stadium
City: Arlington
Location: Next to Rangers Ballpark in Arlington
1000 Ballpark Way

Now a parking lot, the area immediately adjacent to Rangers Ballpark in Arlington was where Arlington Stadium once stood. Turnpike Stadium opened in 1965 as home for the local Texas League club and eventually was expanded to accommodate Major League Baseball. The Washington Senators relocated to renamed Arlington Stadium in 1972. Arguably, the park's most memorable moment occurred on May 1, 1991, when 44-year-old Rangers right-hander Nolan Ryan fired his record seventh no-hitter while beating the Toronto Blue Jays on Arlington Appreciation Night. The final score was 3-0 and Ryan struck out 16 batters with a fastball that averaged 93 mph. The final game at Arlington Stadium was played October 3, 1993, and the ballpark was demolished a year later. There is nothing to mark the former site of the historic ballpark.

Stuart Stadium
City: Beaumont
Location: 3330 Avenue A
The stadium shopping center

The site today is covered by a parking lot and small shopping center, but a plaque in front of the post office reminds visitors that this was once the home of the Texas League's Beaumont Exporters. The plaque reads, "Home plate—On this spot the Beaumont Exporters took their final swing. Rube Stuart's contribution is fondly remembered and appreciated." Stuart Stadium, which opened in 1923, was a baseball hotbed for more than 30 years. The former Detroit Tigers farm team featured such stars as Hank Greenberg,

Dizzy Trout and Rip Sewell. By the mid-1940s, the team was known as the Roughnecks and it was here that Rogers Hornsby ended his career in 1950 as a manager. The ballpark was torn down in 1955.

Reagan County High School Baseball—Home of The Rookie
City: Big Lake
Location: 1111 12th Street

This is where Jim Morris, a high school science teacher and baseball coach of the Owls, made a bargain with his players: If they made the playoffs, he would try out for the majors. His team delivered and Morris, a left-handed pitcher, began an amazing journey that ended in the major leagues. Morris pitched as a 35-year-old rookie for the Tampa Bay Devil Rays in 1999. A movie starring Dennis Quaid told Morris's improbable story in 2002.

Jack Lummus Marker
City: Ennis
Location: Ennis Public Library
501 West Ennis Avenue

In 1999, a Texas historical marker was placed near this library to honor athlete and war hero Jack Lummus. A standout athlete as a youth in Ennis, Lummus attended Baylor University on scholarship and played Minor League Baseball in Texas and one season of pro football for the NFL's New York Giants. He joined the Marines in 1942 and landed in 1945 with the Fifth Marine Division in the first wave of assault troops on Iwo Jima. After fighting without rest for two days and nights, Lummus single-handedly destroyed three enemy placements before stepping on a land mine and getting killed. There is also a small exhibit on Lummus inside the library.

Former athlete and war hero Jack Lummus is honored with a historical marker in Ennis.

LaGrave Field
City: Fort Worth
Location: 301 NE 6th Street

This is a story of two ballparks. The first, built in 1926, was used by the Fort Worth Cats until 1964. The second was built on the exact same site in 2001 and remains in use today. Suffice it to say LaGrave Field has enjoyed a "Texas-size" history.

Spring exhibitions over the years brought Ty Cobb, Babe Ruth, Lou Gehrig, Rogers Hornsby and many other great players to the Fort Worth ballpark. Because Branch Rickey chose Fort Worth as a pillar of the Brooklyn Dodgers farm system, the Dodgers made frequent spring stops there with such players as Jackie Robinson, Gil Hodges,

New LaGrave Field is built on the exact site of the old ballpark, where the legendary Fort Worth Cats once played.

Duke Snider, Don Newcombe and Pee Wee Reese. But the Cats also made a little of their own history. Five future Hall of Famers called Fort Worth home—Carl Hubbell, Hornsby, Snider, Sparky Anderson and Billy Williams. (Anderson earned his nickname at LaGrave in 1955 when Cats broadcaster Bill Hightower remarked on his fiery demeanor following a loud argument with an umpire.) In 1949, the first Texas League game was televised from LaGrave and, later that year, the park's grandstands caught fire and were destroyed. (The Cats played San Antonio the next day with the stands still smoldering.) The Dodgers rebuilt in 1950 and, at the urging of Rickey, dedicated the ballpark to Paul LaGrave, who spearheaded the modern baseball era in Fort Worth. But expansion eventually pushed baseball out of LaGrave and the park hosted its final game on September 4, 1964; the historic home of the Cats was torn down in 1967. With the Cats gone, the site sat vacant for years with bits and pieces of the old stadium buried beneath the weeds.

Then came the rebirth. The Central League's Fort Worth Cats, an independent professional team, came to town and, fittingly, set up operations at new LaGrave Field. The old dugouts have been restored as suites, the view of downtown is perfect and the Cats have succeeded in breathing new life into one of the great baseball fields of all time.

Majors Stadium
City: Greenville
Location: 1807 Church Street

A walking tour of this historic northeast Texas town puts visitors in touch with former actor and war hero Audie Murphy, a native of Greenville, and a former ballpark that claimed some significant history of its own. At 2714 Washington Street, a plaque describes a baseball game that took place about six blocks away at Majors Stadium—an event described enthusiastically by Judy Woods of the Hunt County Historical Commission: "Greenville's baseball team belonged to the East Texas Baseball League in the 1930s and '40s. In 1947, the Greenville Majors became a Class B team in the Big Texas League. They also became famous that year. Our minor league team beat the celebrated New York Yankees, with Joe DiMaggio in center field, in a preseason exhibition game!"

It happened on April 10, 1949, as documented by historian John Mark Dempsey. It was common in those days for major-league teams to barnstorm through the South near the end of spring training. Because no major-league teams were stationed farther south than St. Louis at the time, Majors owner George Schepps, the owner of several minor-league teams, had to pull strings to bring the Yankees to Greenville. DiMaggio started in center that day and wound up with a single and a run scored in two at bats. Righthander Allie Reynolds started for the Yankees, who also posted a lineup with second baseman Snuffy Stirnweiss, shortstop Jerry Coleman, third baseman Bobby Brown and right fielder Gene Woodling. The Yankees committed four errors and the winning run was scored by aging former St. Louis "Gas House Gang" shortstop Pepper Martin, who ended his career in the minors. The game was costly for the Yankees, who lost DiMaggio with a heel injury that would plague him the rest of the season.

Majors Stadium is gone, its former location now occupied by the Greenville Transformer Co. But there are some reminders. A building that stands on the corner of Houston and Church Streets is part of the old stadium locker rooms. The old brick arch through which fans entered the stadium still stands, with the words "Majors Stadium" in welded metal letters across the top. Also in Greenville is a Little League park named after former major-league pitcher Monty Stratton, who grew up in the city. Stratton, who played for the Chicago White Sox, lost his leg in a tragic 1938 hunting accident and returned to play Minor League Baseball with an artificial leg. Hollywood made a movie (*The Stratton Story*) about his life, starring James Stewart and June Allyson, both of whom came to Greenville for the film's 1949 premiere.

The old brick arch entryway is a physical reminder of Majors Stadium, where the Greenville minor-league team once defeated the Yankees.

Buff Stadium

City: Houston
Location: Finger Furniture Center
4001 Gulf Freeway

A furniture store occupies the former site of Buff Stadium, the only reminder a marker that sits on the floor in the exact spot where home plate used to sit. Buff Stadium, built in 1928, opened as home of the Texas League's Houston Buffaloes. The Spanish-style park was renamed Busch Stadium for a period when the Buffs were part of the St. Louis Cardinals farm system. Red Schoendienst, Joe Garagiola and Solly Hemus all played at Buff Stadium,

Buff Stadium's home plate lies in state—on the floor of a Houston furniture store.

as did numerous other major-league stars in exhibition games. The ballpark, damaged in 1961 by Hurricane Carla, was sold at auction for $19,750 and demolished in 1963. When the Finger Furniture Center was built, a plaque was imbedded to mark home plate and from that seed grew the Houston Sports Museum, which is also located in the store. In addition to chronicling Houston baseball from its Texas League beginnings, the museum celebrates the major-league Astros as well as professional teams from other sports.

Houston Astrodome

City: Houston
Location: 8400 Kirby Drive

Dubbed the "Eighth Wonder of the World" by Astros owner Judge Roy Hofheinz, the Harris County Domed Stadium became the world's first air-conditioned, domed, all-purpose stadium when it opened in 1965. The Astrodome, as it came to be known, was home of the Houston Astros through 1999. In addition to introducing the world to indoor baseball and

The Astrodome, baseball's renowned former Eighth Wonder of the World, remains intact, though mostly unused.

cookie-cutter ballparks, the stadium spawned the use of synthetic playing surfaces. After experimenting with a natural grass field, Houston officials turned to an artificial surface that became known as AstroTurf. As new multi-purpose ballparks sprang up in other cities, artificial carpets were installed to safeguard against wear and tear—a trend that proved offensive to baseball purists. Today's Astrodome is used sporadically, no longer associated with Major League Baseball.

Some Memorable Moments in Astrodome History

★ APRIL 28, 1965: New York Mets announcer Lindsey Nelson broadcasted a game from a hanging gondola, 208 feet above the infield.

★ JUNE 10, 1974: Phillies slugger Mike Schmidt crushed a ball that bounced off the public address speaker hanging from the Astrodome roof, 117 feet up and 300 feet from the plate. It was ruled a single.

★ SEPTEMBER 25, 1986: Mike Scott's no-hitter beat the Giants and clinched a West Division title for the Astros.

Colt Stadium
City: Houston
Location: Parking lot of Astrodome

Colt Stadium was located a few yards northwest of the Astrodome, in the area now occupied by its north parking lot. Used by the Houston Colt .45s from 1962 to 1964, the 32,000-seat ballpark was home to the expansion Houston franchise until the Astrodome opened in 1965. Colt Stadium, famous for its heat and huge mosquitoes, played host to its final game on September 27, 1964. It remained standing for five more years, used primarily as a storage facility. But it became such an eyesore that Astros owner Roy Hofheinz painted its exterior gray so that it wouldn't be visible in aerial photos of his sparkling new Astrodome. Colt Stadium, after being sold to a minor-league team in the late 1960s, was taken apart, moved to Torreón, Mexico, and moved again to Tampico, Mexico. It exists today as part of a public playground.

Tris Speaker Exhibit
City: Hubbard
Location: Hubbard Museum
304 NW 6th

This small museum, which is housed in a restored high school, contains an exhibit dedicated to Tris Speaker, who was born and buried in Hubbard. Speaker's incredible numbers sometimes get overshadowed because he played in the same era as Ty Cobb. The Grey Eagle, who spent 20 of his 22 big-league seasons with the Indians and Red Sox, hit .380 or better five times, but won only one American League batting title (1916). He compiled a .345 lifetime

Tris Speaker remains popular in his hometown of Hubbard.

average, struck out only 220 times and was considered one of the great defensive center fielders of all time. The first Texan inducted into the Hall of Fame, Speaker always returned to Hubbard in the off-season and was a lifelong Hubbard volunteer firefighter.

Tris Speaker is buried at Fairview Cemetery, 201 West 3rd, Hubbard.

Tris Speaker Historic Plaque
City: Hubbard
Location: Hubbard City Hall
118 Magnolia Street (Route 171)

In addition to the museum exhibit, Hubbard also placed a historic marker that chronicles Speaker's major-league career.

Driller Park
City: Kilgore
Location: Hunter Street, one block east of Commerce

One of the few landmarks still standing from the town's oil boom days is Driller Park, former home of the Kilgore Drillers of the Texas Lone Star League. Built in 1946 from oil field pipe, tank steel and concrete, Driller Park may be one of the stur-

Driller Park is a vivid reminder of Kilgore's oil boom days.

diest little parks ever constructed. The stadium bears a Texas Historical Marker and today is home to the Kilgore High School baseball team. Driller Park is also the site of numerous postseason high school playoff games.

Zychlinski Park
City: Pearland
Location: 2319 Grand Boulevard

Captain Wilhelm Zychlinski, a Polish nobleman, arrived in the Pearland area in the late 1880s and fell in love with its flowering pear trees. He bought 5,991 acres of land, including the Zychlinski Park site, completed his town plot and then sold most of his holdings before disappearing. In 1911, two land developers, in an attempt to promote the Pearland area, created a baseball team called the Suburban Gardens. For nearly two generations, the team (as well as the people of Pearland) played baseball in Zychlinski Park, a particularly popular activity during the Depression era. Until the late 1990s, Zychlinski Park was the playground for the C.J. Harris Elementary School. Today a historic marker documents the "town baseball" that was played here for so many years.

Babe Didrikson Zaharias Birthplace
City: Port Arthur
Location: 2232 7th Street

Mildred Ella ("Babe") Didrikson Zaharias was named by the *Guinness Book of Records*, along with Lottie Dod, as the most versatile female competitor of all time. She achieved outstanding success in golf, basketball, track and field, and baseball. To honor her, a marker to the great female athlete here at her birthplace sits. It reads:

> Babe Didrikson Zaharias
> (June 26, 1911–September 27, 1956)
> One of seven children, Mildred Ella "Babe" Didrikson was the daughter of Norwegian immigrants Hannah Marie (d.1945) and Ole Didrikson (d.1943). For the first several years of her life, the family occupied a frame house at this location. Later they moved to Beaumont. The Didriksons encouraged their children to develop their natural athletic abilities. Called "Baby" by her family, Mildred was later nicknamed "Babe" for baseball star Babe Ruth.
> Babe first demonstrated her athletic skill as a high school basketball star. After training in track and field events, she won two gold medals at the 1932 Olym-

pic games in Los Angeles. An exceptionally versatile athlete, Babe excelled in baseball, bowling, tennis, and other
sports. Eventually she concentrated her efforts on golf and
won many tournaments as both an amateur and a professional. The Associated Press named her the "Woman Athlete of the First Half of the 20th Century."

In 1938 Babe married George Zaharias. Popu-
lar with sports fans for her skill and personality, she won
further admiration during a long and courageous battle
against cancer. She died in Galveston and was buried in
Beaumont.

Plymouth Oil Company and Plymouth Oilers Baseball Team
City: Sinton
Location: 301 North Rachal Street

A plaque here reads:

> Pennsylvania-based Plymouth Oil Company was founded
> in 1923 by M.L. "Mike" Benedum. With operations head-
> quarters in Sinton, the company profoundly affected the
> city's development by creating jobs, building company
> housing, and providing health and retirement benefits for
> many local workers. In 1933 Plymouth began leasing vast
> amounts of property in the area and in 1935 discovered oil
> on the Welder Ranch with completion of Welder Well C-1.
> In 1937 the company's second major discovery in San Patri-
> cio County was the Brigham Well No. 1 in the East White
> Point Field South of Taft. In 1949 company executive W.M.
> "Mike" Griffith (d.1954) organized the semi-professional
> Plymouth Oilers baseball team, providing a tremendous
> boost to the Sinton area. The company hired proven players
> as permanent employees and employed college athletes
> during the summers. The team's games at company-built
> Oiler Park were major community events. The team won
> state, national, and world semi-pro championships in 1951.
> The baseball team played until 1957, and the company op-
> erated until 1962, when it was purchased by Ohio Oil Com-
> pany, later known as Marathon Oil.

It's becoming more commonplace for companies to place markers
where their baseball teams played as the company teams came to mean a lot
both to the places of business as well as to the communities. In this case, the
team actually became semipro!

Texas Sports Hall of Fame
City: Waco
Location: 1108 South University Parks Drive
254-756-1633

Tris Speaker was the first Texas Sports Hall of Fame inductee in 1951. Over the years, he has been joined by Ernie Banks, Norm Cash and Roger Clemens, among others. The museum was established to celebrate and preserve Texas's sports history. It boasts an impressive array of classic baseball memorabilia, including Speaker's Cleveland Indians jersey, a complete Rogers Hornsby Cardinals uniform, Silver

The Texas Sports Hall of Fame honors such Texas-born stars as Tris Speaker, Ernie Banks, Norm Cash and Roger Clemens.

Slugger Awards from Norm Cash and Pete Reynolds, a Nolan Ryan jersey and, amazingly, the last-out ball from the 1920 World Series when Cleveland beat the Brooklyn Dodgers.

Rogers Hornsby Field
City: Winters
Location: In Ted Meyers Park off Main Street, on Novice Road
310 South Main

Rogers Hornsby had roots in this small Texas town. His ancestors settled there in 1830, in an area now known as Hornsby Bend. Hornsby was born in 1896 on his father's Hereford ranch and played Minor League Baseball with Texas teams based in Hugo, Dallas and Denison

One of baseball's greatest players, Rogers Hornsby is also one of Texas's favorite sons.

before moving up to the St. Louis Cardinals in 1915. He went on to make legitimate claim as the greatest right-handed hitter in baseball history. Hornsby led the National League in batting seven times, topped the magical .400 plateau three times and posted one of the most incredible five-year stretches in major-league history. From 1921 to 1925, Hornsby batted .397, .401, .384, .424 and .403 while compiling 1,078 hits. His six consecutive batting titles were unprecedented and he won two League MVP citations. As manager, Hornsby also led the St. Louis Cardinals to their first World Series cham-

pionship in 1926. Ra-
jah, who was elected
to the Hall of Fame
in 1942, finished his
long baseball associ-
ation as a manager in
the Mexican League.
Hornsby died in 1963
from a heart attack
following an opera-
tion for cataracts. The
field named in his
honor also features a
plaque and monument.

A sign commemorates local Texas legend Rogers Hornsby.

Rogers Hornsby is buried at Hornsby Bend Cemetery, Highway 969, Hornsby Bend.

Hall of Famers Buried in Texas

Willie Wells
Evergreen Cemetery
3304 East 12th Street
Austin

Mickey Mantle
Hillcrest Memorial Park
7403 West Northwest Highway
Dallas

Ross Youngs and Rube Waddell
Mission Park Cemetery
1700 SE Military Drive
San Antonio

Rube Waddell led the AL in strikeouts six times and had a lifetime ERA of 2.16.

ROADSIDE BASEBALL

BASEBALL

THE MIDWEST

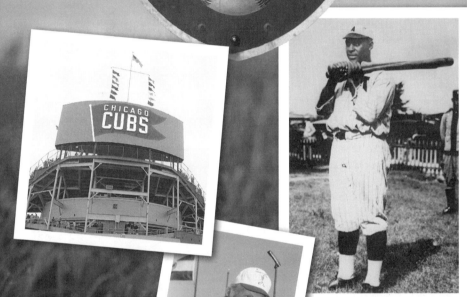

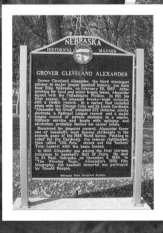

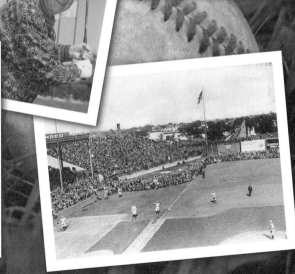

Illinois

Bob Groom Marker

City: Belleville
Location: Whitey Herzog Legion Field
Citizen's Park
317 South 44th Street

Bob Groom was born in Belleville. He hurled in two Midwest minor leagues and the Pacific Coast League from 1904 to 1908, and then in the major leagues from 1909 to 1918. He threw for the Washington Senators (1909-1913), St. Louis Terriers (Federal League, 1914-1915), St. Louis Browns (1916-1917) and Cleveland Indians (1918). On May 6, 1917, he pitched a 3-0 no-hit game against the Chicago White Sox, the team that would go on to win the World Series that year. The no-no came in Game 2 of a Sunday doubleheader, after Groom sealed the win in the first game, pitching the last two innings without allowing a hit. His best major-league season was with the 1912 Senators, when Groom won an outstanding 24 games and Washington finished second in the American League.

The Bob Groom marker placed by David Stalker.

At the end of the 1918 season, Bob Groom came home to Belleville. He would go on to manage the family coal mining business. During the summers, he pitched for and managed local teams into the 1920s, the best of which was Belleville's White Rose team. Throughout the '20s and '30s, Groom was involved with the St. Louis Trolley League as a mentor, and in 1938, the George E. Hilgard American Legion Post 58 asked that he form Belleville's first tournament team. He did, and even coached them to the state and regional championships in their initial season. Groom managed the "Hilgards" through 1944, and in honor of all he did for the team, was inducted into the Hilgard Hall of Fame in February 2008. This marker, part of the wonderful series that grew out of the Society for American Baseball Research (SABR) *Deadball Stars* books, was presented on June 5, 2008, at the Belleville Hilgards' home ballpark, Whitey Herzog Field. Thanks again to the remarkable Mr. David Stalker for spearheading this precious Deadball Era marker project. Incidentally, he shared this story about the marker: "An interesting story goes along with the Bob Groom monument. The Belleville American Legion Hilgrads (a team Groom started) play their home games at the location of the monument, which went up at their home opener last season. The team considers it a good luck talisman. At the opener and before every home game, and before going on a road trip the players touch the ball for good luck. Last year they ended up winning the state championship."

Albert Spalding Birthplace
City: Byron
Location: 133 East 2nd Street

One of the premier pitchers of the 1870s, Albert Spalding is described on his Hall of Fame plaque as an "organizational genius of baseball's pioneer days." His 47 wins in 1876 led the Chicago White Stockings to the first-ever National League championship. Spalding, who helped draft the NL's first constitution, retired as a player to join the White Stockings' front office in 1882, a move that also allowed him to tend to the thriving sporting goods business he had founded with his brother. A plaque marking the house where Spalding was born on September 2, 1850, is located about 80 miles west-northwest of Chicago.

The memory of Albert Spalding, a 19th-century baseball pioneer, is preserved throughout his hometown of Byron.

Albert Spalding Exhibit
City: Byron
Location: Byron Public Library
109 North Franklin Street
815-234-5107

The Byron Public Library houses two large display cases of Albert Spalding memorabilia, including signed baseballs, photos, awards and more.

Albert Spalding

Harry Caray's Italian Steakhouse
City: Chicago
Location: 33 West Kinzie Street
312-828-0966

Harry Caray, of course, was the legendary broadcaster who, over the length
of his career, announced for four Major League Baseball teams. He started
with a long tenure doing the games of the St. Louis Cardinals and ended
as the announcer for the Chicago Cubs, both of the National League. In
between that, he also did a stint for the Oakland Athletics (for one year)
and the Chicago White Sox (for 11 years). And beyond broadcasting, Caray
also had a thing for good restaurants. On October 23, 1987, Harry Caray's
Italian Steakhouse opened in the Chicago Varnish Company Building; a
Chicago Landmark building that is also listed on the National Register of
Historic Places. Today, there are six eateries, a 10-pin bowling lounge, and
even an off-premises catering division that bear the Harry Caray name. Over
the years, the original restaurant has received numerous awards for its food
and service, and features many items of famed sports memorabilia, even a
statue of a "Holey Cow" (complete with holes) wearing the trademark Harry
Caray eyeglasses. Harry may be gone, but his legend lives on today, through
his famous steakhouses.

Historic Wrigley Field
City: Chicago
Location: 1060 West Addison
773-404-CUBS

Being a Cubs fan is a challenge. But being a fan of Wrigley Field is easy. The
brick, the ivy, the neighborhood—all combine to make this one of baseball's
most beloved environments. Originally known as Weeghman Park, Wrigley
originally was home to Chicago's entry in the short-lived Federal League.
The first major-league game at the ballpark took place in 1914 with the hometown Federals defeating Kansas City, 9-1. When the Federal League folded
in 1916, team owner Weeghman headed a group that bought the Cubs, who
defeated Cincinnati in the first National League game at renamed Cubs
Park. William Wrigley Jr. bought the team in 1918 and the stadium became
Wrigley Field in 1926. The bleachers, the scoreboard on its center field
perch and many of the other nuances that contribute to Wrigley's lore came
during a 1937 renovation. Baseball at Clark and Addison Streets remains
refreshingly simple, from the hand-updated scoreboard to the quaint, earthy
atmosphere. One longstanding tradition is the flying of a flag bearing either
a "W" or "L" atop the scoreboard after each game—a signal to fans whether
the Cubs won or lost. The original ivy vines that cover the outfield walls were

Wrigley Field remains true to its early century heritage, a ballpark that charms even the most hard-core baseball fan.

planted by then-owner Bill Veeck in 1937. He strung bittersweet from the top of the wall to the bottom, then planted ivy at the base of the wall. And if you look up at the flags atop the foul poles, Ernie Banks's uniform number (14) is on the left field foul pole and Billy Williams's No. 26 adorns the right field pole. For many years, the Cubs resisted the temptation to install lights, preferring to keep Wrigley as the lone bastion of daytime baseball. But they finally gave in, installing the standards in 1988 and agreeing to a limited number of night games. Wrigley Field exists today as the second oldest ballpark in the major leagues, second only to Boston's Fenway Park.

Some Memorable Moments at Wrigley Field

★ OCTOBER 1, 1932: During Game 3 of the 1932 World Series, Babe Ruth executed his famous "called shot." Allegedly, Ruth pointed to the bleachers in center field, then hit Charlie Root's next pitch for a homer. (Root always denied Ruth was calling his shot.)

★ SEPTEMBER 28, 1938: Gabby Hartnett hit his famous "Homer in the Gloamin'" against the Pittsburgh Pirates.

★ MAY 12, 1970: Ernie Banks hit his 500th career home run off Atlanta's Pat Jarvis.

★ SEPTEMBER 8, 1985: Pete Rose collected career hit 4,191 off Chicago's Reggie Patterson, tying him with Ty Cobb for the all-time hits record.

Murphy's Bleachers
City: Chicago
Location: 3655 North Sheffield Avenue

This legendary open-air bar/restaurant, located just across the street from Wrigley Field, features the famous Murphy's roof where you can sit and watch Cubs games while knocking back one of their many available brews. Bill Veeck used to greet fans here, and it's not uncommon for a player or two to stop in after a game. The walls are covered with Chicago-related sports memorabilia in what might be the most perfectly located sports bar in the country.

"Black Sox" Courthouse
City: Chicago
Location: 54 West Hubbard Street

"Say it ain't so, Joe" were the words allegedly uttered by a devastated kid as the disgraced Joe Jackson entered this former courthouse. Whether that really happened is anybody's guess. But what did happen here was a trial involving the eight members of the Chicago White Sox who conspired to fix the 1919 World Series against the Cincinnati Reds. Despite their acquittal in the so-called "Black Sox" scandal, the players received a lifetime baseball ban from commissioner Kenesaw Mountain Landis, a ruling that still stands today despite repeated efforts to get Jackson reinstated for election to the Hall of Fame. Shoeless Joe compiled a Series average of .375 and played error-free defense, but he was implicated in the scandal. The trial attracted huge headlines and made a nation of fans feel betrayed. This building, which housed the Cook County Criminal Courts for 35 years, was also the site of other legendary trials, including the Leopold and Loeb murder case.

National Italian American Sports Hall of Fame
City: Chicago
Location: 1431 West Taylor Street
312-226-5566

When businessman George Randazzo decided to raise money for a struggling local Catholic youth program in 1977, he organized a dinner featuring 21 former Italian boxing champions. The event was so successful that another local businessman, Don Ponte, encouraged Randazzo to start an entire hall of fame to honor all Italian-American athletes. Just one year later, the first National Italian American Sports Hall of Fame banquet was held honoring Lou Ambers, Eddie Arcaro, Charlie Trippi, Gino Marchetti, Joe and Dom DiMaggio and (posthumously) Vince Lombardi. In 1978, the National

Italian American Sports Hall of Fame officially opened in Elmwood Park, Illinois, and over the years it grew into one of the most impressive sports memorabilia collections in the world. Among the baseball inductees are Roy Campanella, Dolph Camilli, Tony Conigliaro, Joe and Dom DiMaggio, Tony Lazzeri, Tommy Lasorda and Tony LaRussa. The National Italian American Sports Hall of Fame relocated from Elmwood to its new address in the fall of 2003. Located in Chicago's historic Little Italy neighborhood, the expansive 40,000-square-foot limestone building features two spacious exhibition halls with special exhibit galleries on each of the four floors. An elegant staircase leads visitors from a 150-seat theater in the lower level to a third-floor banquet hall that seats as many as 300 dinner guests.

Piazza DiMaggio

City: Chicago
Location: On Taylor Street, just across from the National Italian American Sports Hall of Fame

Piazza DiMaggio, a small Romanesque park in Chicago's Little Italy, is dedicated to New York Yankee legend Joe DiMaggio. The centerpiece is a nine-foot statue of DiMaggio that was dedicated in 1991 to commemorate the 50th anniversary of the Yankee Clipper's 56-game hitting streak and re-dedicated in 1998. DiMaggio was present at both ceremonies.

A nine-foot Joe DiMaggio still swings freely in Chicago's "Little Italy."

Comiskey Park

City: Chicago
Location: Parking lot of "new" Comiskey Park

When it was closed after the 1990 season, old Comiskey Park had survived 81 seasons and was baseball's oldest major-league ballpark. It opened on July 1, 1910, replacing the 39th Street Grounds where the White Sox had played from 1901 to 1910. After the 1926 season, a $1 million renovation replaced the original wooden bleachers with seats and totally enclosing the stadium grandstand. The seating capacity was increased from 32,000 to 52,000. In addition to the White Sox, Comiskey was home to the National Football League's Chicago Cardinals for 35 seasons and it played host to the Negro Leagues' yearly east-west All-Star Game from 1933 to 1950. The inven-

Old Comiskey Park, site of baseball's first All-Star Game in 1933, is now a parking lot adjacent to new Comiskey Park.

tive Bill Veeck bought the White Sox in 1959 and had the red brick façade painted white. He also created a picnic area in left field and installed the first electric scoreboard behind the center field bleachers. In 1960, Veeck took his scoreboard fascination a step further, installing baseball's first exploding board complete with fireworks, aerial bombs and sound effects. In 1969, AstroTurf was installed to save money, but it was removed in 1976. By the 1980s, with Comiskey showing signs of wear and tear, the White Sox threatened to leave town if a new park wasn't built. Comiskey Park's days were numbered.

New Comiskey was built next door to its predecessor and the final old Comiskey game was played on September 30, 1990–the team's 3,024th regular-season victory at the ancient park. A parking lot now covers the former site with a home plate area marked by a plaque.

The exact spot of old Comiskey Park's batter's box is preserved outside of new Comiskey Park.

Some Memorable Moments at Comiskey Park

★ SEPTEMBER 5, 1918: Babe Ruth pitched the Red Sox to a 1-0 Game 1 victory over the Cubs in the World Series. The Cubs played the classic at Comiskey because of its larger capacity.

★ OCTOBER 9, 1919: The Cincinnati Reds ended the World Series by beating the White Sox, 10-5. It was later learned the Series was thrown by the infamous "Black Sox."

★ JULY 6, 1933: The first All-Star Game was played at Comiskey with Babe Ruth's home run leading the American League to a 4-2 victory.

★ JULY 5, 1947: Cleveland Indians pinch hitter Larry Doby became the first black player in the American League.

★ JULY 12, 1979: Disco Demolition Night, a Bill Veeck promotion, went awry when a fan riot broke out between games of a doubleheader, forcing the White Sox to forfeit the nightcap to Detroit.

Chicago White Sox Hall of Fame
City: Chicago
Location: Comiskey Park (Now US Cellular Field)
333 West 35th Street
312-674-1000

A good selection of White Sox history is on display in this Hall of Fame, located in the stadium gift shop on the main concourse behind home plate. You can see Shoeless Joe Jackson's original White Sox contract.

Andrew "Rube" Foster Home
City: Chicago
Location: 39th Street and Wentworth Avenue

Rube Foster is considered by many historians to be the "Father of Negro League Baseball." Although the former player founded the Negro National League in Kansas City in 1920 (at the Paseo YMCA), he lived near this corner, where a historical marker has been placed.

Birth of Softball
City: Chicago

The game of softball originated in Chicago on Thanksgiving Day, 1887. The story goes like this: A group of about 20 young men had gotten together in the gymnasium of the Farragut Boat Club for the purpose of hearing the outcome of the Harvard-Yale football game. After Yale's victory was announced and all of the bets were paid off, a man picked up a stray boxing glove and supposedly threw it at someone, who hit it with a pole they were holding.

A man named George Hancock, today considered by many to be the inventor of softball, shouted, "Let's play ball!" He tied the boxing glove in a tight formation so that it resembled a ball, chalked out a diamond on the floor (which included smaller dimensions than those of a baseball field in order to fit the gym) and broke off a broom handle to serve as a bat. What then took place was a unique, smaller version of baseball. That game is now considered to be the first true version of what we know as softball. A week later, Hancock created an oversized ball and an undersized rubber-tipped bat and went back to the gym to paint permanent white foul lines on the floor. After he wrote new rules and named the sport indoor baseball, a more organized, yet still new, game was played. Its popularity was immediate.

Hancock's original game of indoor baseball quickly caught on in popularity, becoming international with the formation of a league in Toronto. That year, 1897, was also the premiere publication of the Indoor Baseball Guide. This was the first nationally distributed publication on the new game and it lasted a decade.

Cracker Jack Is Born
City: Chicago

Given the sweet snack's place in the song "Take Me Out to the Ballgame," it only seemed fitting to include the origin of Cracker Jack in this book. It goes back to 1893, when a man named Frederick William Rueckheim and his brother Louis started mass-producing the soon-to-be-famous snack and selling it at the first Chicago World's Fair in 1893. At the time, it was a mixture of popcorn, molasses, and peanuts and was called "Candied Popcorn and Peanuts." In 1896, Louis developed a way to keep the popcorn kernels separate. As each batch was mixed in a spinning drum, a small quantity of oil was added—a closely guarded trade secret. Before this shift in preparation, the mixture had been difficult to process and manipulate as it clung together in large pieces. In 1896, the first large amount of Cracker Jack was produced. It was named by an enthusiastic taster who remarked, "That's a Cracker Jack!" In 1899, a man named Henry Gottlieb Eckstein created the "waxed sealed package" for freshness, known then as the Eckstein Triple

Proof Package, which was a revolutionary protective wrapping. In 1902, the company was reorganized into Rueckheim Bros. & Eckstein and 10 years later, small prizes were inserted in Cracker Jack boxes for the first time. Since then, the toy and trinket prizes have been replaced with paper pieces displaying riddles and jokes. As far as the now-familiar mascots, Sailor Jack and his dog, Bingo, they were created in 1918. In 1964, Borden purchased the Cracker Jack Company after a fierce bidding war between Borden and Frito-Lay and then finally, in 1997, Borden sold the Cracker Jack brand to Frito-Lay.

West Side Grounds

City: Chicago
Location: 912 South Wood Street

This comes from a group called the Way Out In Left Field Society in Chicago. I got to know their founder, Mike Reischl, after the first edition of *Roadside Baseball* came out in 2003. It seems the former site of old West Side Grounds in Chicago was not included in the book (it didn't make the final edit) and so Mike made me aware of the fact. But he didn't stop there. He actually spent years raising funds and getting permission (no small feat in Chicago) to have a marker placed

The West Side Grounds marker in Chicago placed by Mike Reischl, seen here at the marker with his kids.

at the site. Some background from the man himself:

> The phrase "way out in left field" has evolved to mean an eccentric, odd, misguided or peculiar statement or act. Although the origin of the phrase has been challenged and debated over the years, the most logical and realistic explanation comes from an extinct baseball park called West Side Grounds that the Chicago Cubs called home from 1893 to 1915. As legend has it, a mental hospital called the Neuropsychiatric Institute was located directly behind the left field wall. The Institute housed mental patients who could be heard making strange and bizarre comments within listening distance of players and fans. Thus, if someone said that you were "way out in left field," the person was questioning your sanity and comparing you with a mental patient.

The Way Out In Left Field Society was formed to place a historical marker in front of 912 S Wood Street in Chicago to commemorate the history of West Side Grounds. The Chicago Cubs were a very successful organization in the early part of the 20th Century at West Side Grounds where they won four National League Pennants, became the first Major League franchise to win back-to-back World Series titles, and in 1906 hosted the first intra-urban World Series game against their cross-town rivals the Chicago White Sox. Our society is committed to honoring the location of West Side Grounds as a historical site so that all citizens as well as baseball fans can take civic pride in the rich history of Chicago baseball. The Way Out In Left Field Society will continue its effort to preserve the legacy of baseball in Chicago and to establish tribute markers for any other unusual or out of the ordinary places that have had a historical significance to the game of baseball. Our organization is dedicated to supporting the interests and activities of other baseball fans throughout America who promote the unique and obscure aspects of baseball and display the same enthusiasm and fervor as the people who cheered from the grandstands of West Side Grounds as well as the ones who screamed and hollered from "way out in left field."

Well, the marker was placed in the fall of 2008. Well done, Mike. And thanks for having me as a (proud) member of the Way Out In Left Field Society.

Bottomley-Ruffing-Schalk Baseball Museum

City: Nokomis
Location: 121 West State Street
217-563-2516

This small museum honors three players from the Nokomis area. Jim Bottomley, a standout first baseman and two-time RBI champion for the St. Louis Cardinals, Cincinnati Reds and St. Louis Browns, was voted

A small Nokomis museum is primarily dedicated to three Hall of Famers—Jim Bottomley, Red Ruffing and Ray Schalk.

League MVP in 1928. Right-hander Red Ruffing posted 273 victories, four 20-win seasons and seven World Series wins with the New York Yankees from 1930 to 1946. Ray Schalk was a top defensive catcher for the White Sox from 1912 to 1928 and the first catcher to routinely back up plays at first and third base. The museum has many more honorees, including umpire Al Barlick, Hall of Fame right-hander Robin Roberts and former slugging first baseman Mark McGwire. The museum's displays include baseballs, bats, hats, books, articles, personal letters, scrapbooks and uniforms.

Abe Lincoln Played Baseball Here
City: Postville
Location: Postville Park
5th and Washington

In 1965, a marker was erected to acknowledge a Baltimore adventurer named Russell Post, who laid out the town of Postville in 1835. The marker also notes that Abraham Lincoln and his friends played town ball, a predecessor to baseball, in the park in addition to throwing the maul, a heavy wooden hammer, and pitching horseshoes. While in his 30s, the future US president visited Postville as part of his circuit law practice. His athletic endeavors took place during his free time.

Billy and Ma Sunday Historical Marker
City: Sleepy Hollow
Location: Route 72 at Sleepy Hollow Road

Erected in the early 1970s, the marker indicates the area where former Chicago Cubs outfielder William Ashley "Billy" Sunday held a month-long religious revival from May to June 1900, in West Dundee Park. Billy Sunday owned the farm with his wife, Helen "Ma" Sunday, from the end of the 19th century to the mid-1910s.

Robin Roberts Stadium at Lanphier Park
City: Springfield
Location: North Grand near 11th Street

Opened in 1928, Lanphier has at different times been home to minor-league teams serving the Browns, Tigers, Giants and Cardinals organizations. It also briefly played host to games in the All-American Girls Professional Baseball League.

Robin Roberts is still remembered in his hometown of Springfield.

Situated several blocks from old Route 66, the stadium is named for local hero Robin Roberts, the former Phillies Hall of Fame pitcher. Lanphier today is used primarily for college baseball.

Hall of Famers Buried in Illinois

William Hulbert

Cap Anson

Kenesaw Mountain Landis

Charles "Old Hoss" Radbourne
Evergreen Memorial Cemetery
302 East Miller Street
Bloomington
309-827-6950

CHICAGO METROPOLITAN AREA

Andrew "Rube" Foster
Lincoln Cemetery
12300 Kedzie Avenue
Blue Island
773-445-5400

Urban "Red" Faber
Acacia Park Cemetery
7800 West Irving Park Road
Chicago
773-625-7800

William Hulbert
Graceland Cemetery
4001 North Clark Street
Chicago
773-525-1105

Cap Anson and Kenesaw Mountain Landis
Oak Woods Cemetery
1035 East 67th Street
Chicago
773-288-3800

Gabby Hartnett and Fred Lindstrom
All Saints Cemetery
700 North River Road
Des Plaines
847-298-0450

Charles Comiskey
Calvary Catholic Cemetery
301 Chicago Avenue
Chicago
847-864-3050

Gabby Hartnett

Ray Schalk
Evergreen Cemetery
8700 South Kedzie Avenue
Evergreen Park
773-776-8434

Lou Boudreau
Pleasant Hill Cemetery
East side of Elsner Road, 1.5 miles
south of US Highway 30
Frankfort

William Harridge
Memorial Park Cemetery
9900 Gross Point Road
Skokie

Lou Boudreau

Warren Giles
Riverside Cemetery
6th Avenue and 29th Street
Moline

William Harridge

Indiana

Historic Grandstand
City: Brookville
Location: 8th and Mill Streets

Baseball has been played in Brookville since at least 1867, when local amateur teams competed against out-of-town teams. A local team joined the semipro Southern Indiana Baseball Association in 1922 and other regional leagues in later years. This grandstand was built in 1922 to seat 1,000 and serve fans of the new Brookville semipro team. The structure, renovated in 1992 for use by the community, is recognized today with a historic marker.

A historic marker salutes the grandstand that seated 1,000 fans when it was built in 1922.

Big Sam Thompson gave new meaning to the term "power hitter" in the 19th century.

Sam Thompson Plaque at Sam Thompson Field
City: Danville
Location: In Ellis Park, right off Highway 36

Born in Danville on March 5, 1860, Sam Thompson went on to fame as one of the game's first true power hitters. Playing for National League teams in Detroit and Philadelphia, Thompson hit 126 home runs and collected 200-plus hits three times while compiling a .335 career average. Big Sam was elected to the Hall of Fame in 1974. This Danville plaque and field were dedicated to Thompson in 1998.

Bosse Field
City: Evansville
Location: 1701 North Main Street

Built in 1915, legendary Bosse Field is the third oldest ballpark in the country used for professional baseball on a regular basis, surpassed only by Fenway

Park (1912) in Boston and Wrigley Field (1914) in Chicago. It is currently where the Frontier League Evansville Otters, a minor-league franchise, play their home games. The Otters franchise came to Evansville in 1995 and has attracted a record number of fans for the league.

In 1991, Columbia Pictures used the historic stadium for shooting game scenes in the hit movie *A League of Their Own*, which starred Madonna and Rosie O'Donnell. Bosse Field opened on July 17, 1915 and was named in honor of Benjamin Bosse, Evansville's mayor from 1914 to 1922. He was the man who helped to build the stadium. Over the years, no less than 10 baseball teams other than the Otters have called Bosse Field home. Some of the most famous are the Evansville Triplets (1970–84),

Bosse Field in Evansville is where the film *A League of Their Own* was filmed.

Evansville Braves (1946–57), Evas/Pocketeers/Hubs (1919–1931) and the Evansville River Rats (1914–15, the River Rats had played in Evansville previously from 1903 to 1910 and 1901 to 1902). The Triplets won the American Association titles in 1972, 1975, and 1979. The River Rats won the Central League title in 1908 and 1915. The Braves won the Three-I League title in 1946, 1948, 1956, and 1957. From 1921 to 1922, Bosse Field was used as a football stadium and was home to the Evansville Crimson Giants of the NFL. But it's the baseball stars who played here that have made the place famous, including Hall of Fame members Hank Greenberg, Chuck Klein, Edd Roush, Warren Spahn, and Sam Thompson.

Huntingburg League Stadium—*A League of Their Own*
City: Huntingburg
Location: 1st and Cherry Streets

This stadium, originally built in 1894, was used for the filming of the 1992 hit movie, *A League of Their Own*, starring Tom Hanks, Geena Davis, Madonna and Rosie O'Donnell, among others. When Columbia Pictures decided to film here in 1991, they expanded and renovated the old park to give it a more nostalgic feel and make it more true to the 1940s time period in which the film took place. That look and atmosphere has been maintained ever since and, thanks to the movie, this has the feel of a true throwback park. (Except for the orange and red plastic box seats salvaged from Atlanta-Fulton County Stadium.) During the spring months, the field is home to the Southridge Raiders and it also hosts the high school sectional and regional playoffs. The Dubois County Dragons, a Class A professional team of the Independent Frontier League, play their home games here as well.

Oscar Charleston Park
City: Indianapolis
Location: 2800 East 30th Street

Oscar Charleston was the first Indianapolis-born player to get a plaque at Cooperstown. The former Negro League star, who was elected to the Hall of Fame in 1976, was considered by many of his peers the greatest player ever—black or white. As a youth he served as batboy for the local ABCs. After a short stint in the Army, he came home and played with that team, helping lead the ABCs to a 1916 victory in the Black World Series. After playing 30 seasons for the ABCs, Chicago American Giants, Hilldale Daisies and other Negro League teams, the outstanding defensive center fielder returned to Indianapolis as manager of the Clowns. In 1998, this park, less than a mile from where he was born and raised, was dedicated. Oscar

Few players, black or white, could match Oscar Charleston's incredible skills.

Charleston, "The Hoosier Comet," died in 1954 and is buried at Floral Park Cemetery, 3659 Cossell Road, Indianapolis.

Indiana Baseball Hall of Fame
City: Jasper
Location: Highway 162 S and College Avenue
Campus of Vincennes University Jasper
Ruxer Student Center

The first inductions to this hall were made in 1979 with Mickey Mantle serving as guest speaker. Over the years, other speakers have included Ernie Banks, Johnny Bench and Lefty Gomez. There are 114 inductees in the Hall of Fame covering four categories: pro player, coach-manager (high school, college, pro), contributor and veteran. In addition to plaques honoring the inductees, memorabilia includes an impressive selection of bats and jerseys dating from the early 1900s as well as photos, autographed baseballs and more.

Mordecai "Three-Finger" Brown Farm Site

City: Nyesville
Location: Nyesville Road
Travel east of Rockville on US 36 to Billy Creek Village, then head north about two miles on Nyesville Road until you reach the plaque.

Mordecai Brown was born October 19, 1876, in Nyesville, a tiny farming community just north of Terre Haute. At age five, Brown's right hand was mangled when he stuck it into a running feed-cutter machine. Missing an index finger, he learned to throw a baseball with a peculiar spin, a "handicap" that gave him what Ty Cobb called "the best curveball in the game." Over Brown's 14-year career, 11 with the Chicago Cubs, he compiled a 239-130 record, a 2.06 ERA and a 5-4 mark in World Series play. He is best remembered for his stirring pitching duels against Giants ace Christy Mathewson. The historical marker placed here by family and friends in 1994 is on the land where the Brown family farm existed, approximately 50 yards from where the family house stood. Brown died in 1948 at Terre Haute and was inducted into the Hall of Fame in 1949. He is buried at Roselawn Memorial Park, 7500 North Clinton Street, Terre Haute.

Edd Roush Hometown Marker

City: Oakland City
Location: Main Street

Born in Oakland City in 1893, Edd Roush played for the Chicago White Sox, New York Giants and Cincinnati Reds over a major-league career that spanned 18 seasons. The center fielder, a career .323 hitter, won batting crowns in 1917 and '19, the latter while leading the Reds to a World Series victory over the infamous Chicago "Black Sox." Roush, who was known for his breathtaking outfield catches, was elected to the Hall of Fame in 1962, the same year his plaque was mounted on the wall of a bank on Main Street in his hometown.

Edd Roush was a member of the Reds team that won the 1919 World Series.

Roush died in 1988 and is buried at Montgomery Cemetery, 200 South, one-fifth mile east of 1200 East, Oakland City.

Gil Hodges Statue
City: Petersburg
Location: Pike County Courthouse
801 Main Street

In the rotunda of the county courthouse is a large bronze bust of Gil Hodges, who was born in Princeton, Indiana, and grew up and attended school in Petersburg. There is also the Gil Hodges Memorial Bridge, located just north of Petersburg on SR 57 at White River.

Gil Hodges Memorial Field/
Rueth-Fitzgibbon Baseball Facility
City: Rensselaer
Location: Saint Joseph's College
US Highway 23

In 1994, Saint Joseph's College named its baseball field in honor of former Brooklyn Dodgers first baseman Gil Hodges, who attended school there. Each year, the college also presents a "Gil Hodges Award" to its outstanding senior player.

Billy Sunday made his name as an evangelist, but his roots were in baseball.

Billy Sunday Home and Visitor Center
City: Winona Lake
Location: 1101 Park Avenue
574-268-0660

Billy Sunday, one of the 20th century's best-known evangelists, was a major-league outfielder for Chicago, Pittsburgh and Philadelphia before pursuing a more spiritual career. Born in Ames, Iowa, in 1862, the aptly named Sunday went straight from semipro baseball in Marshalltown, Iowa, to the majors in Chicago. He was converted to Christ in 1886 through the street preaching of Harry Monroe of the Pacific Garden Mission in Chicago and gave up his baseball career in 1891, after eight seasons. Sunday, ordained to the ministry in 1903 by the Presbytery of Chicago, eventually began preaching at his own services. He preached in the army camps during World War I and later held citywide meetings across the United States. In one celebrated meeting in Philadelphia, more than 2.3 million people attended his eight-week crusade. Sunday held campaigns for more than 20 years—a practice called "hitting the sawdust trail" because the tabernacle floors were covered with saw-dust—and at the close of each service, throngs of people came forward to grasp the evangelist's hand, signifying their conversion. Sunday was also known for wild acrobatic feats on the platform while he preached. Sunday and wife Helen settled in Winona Lake, Indiana, home of the Winona Lake Bible Conference and famed Chautauqua meetings, in 1911. He died in Chicago in 1935. Today at this museum, near the home where the Sunday family lived until 1957, the Billy Sunday legacy is alive and well.

Hall of Famers Buried in Indiana

Chuck Klein
Holy Cross/St. Joseph Cemeteries
Meridian Street and Pleasant Run Parkway
Indianapolis

Stan Coveleski
St. Joseph Polish Roman Catholic Cemetery
24980 State Road 2
South Bend

Ban Johnson
Riverside Cemetery
West Wayne Street and South West Street
Spencer

Chuck Klein

Iowa

Breda Memorial Park
City: Breda

Breda Memorial Park is the wonderful former home stadium of the Breda Eagles, semipro team of the 1940s and the 1975 St. Bernard High School State Baseball Champions. This ballpark features one of the last remaining wooden covered grandstands in the Midwest. Built way back in 1947 (totally restored in 2001 for $15,000), it was described as "one of the best baseball parks in the state" with grandstand seating 600 and "lighting facilities equal to any in Iowa." It's truly a step back in time to a simpler era of baseball.

Community Field
City: Burlington
Location: Mount Pleasant Avenue, east of Route 61

Community Field was built in 1947 as home for Burlington's professional team in the Central Association of Professional Baseball. Burlington joined the Class A Midwest League in 1962 and the franchise has been competing in that circuit ever since. Over the years, Community Field has been home to many outstanding teams and future major-leaguers. Chicago Cubs legend Billy Williams started his Hall of Fame journey at Burlington in 1958. Sal Bando, who would gain World Series fame with the Oakland Athletics and later serve as Milwaukee's general manager, led the team to its first Midwest League championship in 1965. In 1968, young Oakland farmhand Vida Blue struck out a Midwest League-high 231 batters—a mark that still stands as the Burlington single-season record. On June 8, 1971, Community Field's original grandstand burned to the ground. Although the rebuilding process wasn't completed until 1973, play continued with temporary bleachers, and community volunteers, demonstrating their dedication to professional baseball, spent countless hours returning the stadium to working order. Today, the Burlington Bees, a Kansas City Royals affiliate, call this historic field home.

Alliant Energy Field
City: Clinton
Location: Riverview Park
6th Avenue N and 1st Street

The former Riverview Stadium, built in 1937, has played host to Clinton professional baseball since the original Owls were affiliated with the Brooklyn

Dodgers. The historic ballpark sits in Clinton's Riverview Park, a 65-acre city recreational area on the Mississippi River. Over the years, Clinton teams have been affiliated with the Chicago Cubs and White Sox, Seattle Pilots, Milwaukee Brewers, Pittsburgh Pirates, Detroit Tigers, San Francisco Giants, Los Angeles Dodgers, San Diego Padres, Cincinnati Reds and, today, the Texas Rangers—as the Clinton Lumber Kings. The Mount St. Clare College baseball team also uses the field for games and the historic stadium hosts activities in conjunction with Clinton Riverboat Days, an annual Fourth of July festival.

Modern Woodmen Park (formerly John O'Donnell Stadium)
City: Davenport
Location: 209 South Gaines Street

The current home of the Midwest League's Quad City River Bandits (Twins) was built in 1931, just yards from the Mississippi River. The stadium has experienced three major floods—1965, 1993, 2001—and has been rebuilt several times, but it retains a nostalgic charm. Originally called Municipal Stadium, the historic ballpark was renamed for

Davenport's John O'Donnell Stadium, located on the banks of the Mississippi River, has survived three major floods.

John O'Donnell, the sports editor of the *Quad-City Times* during the 1940s and '50s. After 2007, it became Modern Woodmen Park. The stadium is nothing if not picturesque. The Centennial Bridge creates a scenic view beyond first base foul territory; a railroad line runs along the third-base side. Fans get a spectacular view of downtown Davenport beyond the outfield walls.

Field of Dreams
City: Dyersville
Location: 28963 Lansing Road
Located on two farms, 3.3 miles northeast of Dyersville.

"If you build it, they will come," the voice in the movie promises. And they still do, in droves, to see, experience, dream and play on the very field where the 1989 movie starring Kevin Costner, Amy Madigan and James Earl Jones was filmed. One of the ultimate baseball landmarks in the country exists on two Iowa farms near a small east-central Iowa community. Tourists are allowed to run bases, play catch and bat on the Field of Dreams, or they can simply sit in the bleachers and enjoy its considerable aura. The house, part of the Lansing family farm, is also open to visitors. And so, of course, is the cornfield. Great efforts have been taken to not over-commercialize the field and surrounding area. It is pristine and simple. Since the movie, more than 60,000 people have flocked to Dyersville. Though privately owned, the attraction is open daily, 10 AM–6 PM, April through November.

Bill Zuber's Dugout Restaurant
City: Homestead
Location: 2206 44th Avenue

The restaurant is located in the historic Amana Colonies, a religion-inspired commune that was founded by German immigrant members of the Community of True Inspiration in 1854. Even though sports were frowned on by the church, colony native Bill "Goober" Zuber crafted an 11-year major-league pitching career (1936-47) with the Indians, Senators, Yankees and Red Sox. Zuber, a right-hander, retired with a 43–42 record. After baseball, he returned to Homestead and bought the commune-run eatery and operated it until his death in 1982. The restaurant still serves up the same rich, authentic German meals that made it popular in 1862.

Bob Feller Museum
City: Van Meter
Location: 310 Mill Street
515-996-2806

This small-town museum was opened in 1995 as a tribute to Van Meter's native son, Hall of Famer Bob Feller. "Rapid Robert" compiled a 266–162 record over 18 major-league seasons (1936-56) with the Indians while

A large sign urges travelers to stop in Van Meter, where a worthwhile Bob Feller Museum pays tribute to one of the game's great pitchers.

pitching three no-hitters and setting numerous strikeout records. Although Feller lives in retirement near Cleveland, he has retained an active interest in the museum and donated many of its displays. He also shows up occasionally to meet visitors and autograph balls and photos. Among the artifacts are Feller's uniforms, trophies he earned, newspapers trumpeting his victories and photos of him on the field and in the presence of US presidents. One display case features the bat Babe Ruth carried on June 13, 1948, when he made his final Yankee Stadium appearance. The Indians were playing the Yankees that day and the bat belonged to Feller. The museum also has an outstanding gift shop with many autographed and collectible items.

Kansas

Mickey Mantle Is Discovered

City: Baxter Springs
Location: Kiwanis Park
Located on Highway 166, one block from the Spring River Bridge

It was one of those mythical stories that color baseball history. Just 10 miles up the road from Commerce, Oklahoma, Mantle's hometown, is Baxter Springs—a small town tucked into the southeastern corner of Kansas. A teenage Mantle played for the Baxter Springs Whiz Kids in 1948, the same year Yankees scout Tom Greenwade traveled to Baxter Springs to scout a third baseman named Billy Johnson. The young Mantle blasted two homers into the nearby river that day, one from the

Mickey Mantle is an Oklahoma kid, but baseball fans in Kansas remember him well.

right side and another from the left, and Greenwade immediately targeted the speedy youngster. Since Mantle was only 16, Greenwade promised to return with a Yankees contract on his high school graduation day in 1949, which he did. Mantle signed a minor-league contract with the Yankees' Class D team in Independence, Kansas. The ballpark where Mantle performed his impromptu audition no longer exists. The grandstand is gone and kids now play mostly soccer where baseball was once king. But the river is a physical reminder of where a 16-year-old future star hit two gigantic home runs so many years ago, the day he was discovered by the New York Yankees.

Baxter Springs Little League Museum

City: Baxter Springs
Location: 14th and Grant Avenue

Baxter Springs has one of the most successful Little League programs in the country. The small Kansas community has long been the state's Little League power, the winner of 15 state titles from 1976 to 2000. The city also has an impressive ballpark with a Little League Museum that features awards and memorabilia from such local sports heroes as Mickey Mantle, Hale Irwin and Bill Russell in addition to collectibles from such other stars as Yogi Berra and Whitey Ford.

Mickey Mantle Exhibit

City: Baxter Springs
Location: Baxter Springs Heritage Center and Museum
740 East Avenue
620-856-2385

This impressive local museum, which celebrates the rich history of Baxter Springs, "The First Cowtown in Kansas," is a small display featuring artifacts from Mickey Mantle's brief time spent in Baxter Springs and other Baxter Springs Whiz Kids memorabilia and photographs.

Site of Historic Baseball Game

City: Blue Rapids
Location: Baseball diamond located at West 5th at Riverside Park
785-363-7736
(Blue Rapids is located in southwest Marshall County at the junction of the Little Blue River and the Big Blue River, about 46 miles north of Manhattan, Kansas.)

On October 24, 1913, Blue Rapids was the proud host of an exhibition game between the Chicago White Sox and New York Giants. The stopover was a prelude to a 1913 worldwide barnstorming tour. More than 3,000 fans watched the game at the Riverside Park field that is still in use today. (Advance tickets sold for $1.00; tickets were $1.50 at the gate.) Sam Crawford, John McGraw, Bill Klem, Christy Mathewson and Jim Thorpe were all part of the contest, which the White Sox won, 8-5. After leaving Blue Rapids, the teams traveled through the Southwest and up the Pacific Coast to Vancouver, where they caught a ship for Japan. They played games along the Pacific Rim, passing through Ceylon, India and the Suez Canal all the way to Egypt. They also played several games in Europe, the last of which was witnessed by King George V in England. The teams arrived back in New York on March 6, 1914.

Walter Johnson Park

City: Coffeyville
Location: 8th and Park

Walter Johnson Park in Coffeyville, Kansas.

The Coffeyville Red Ravens play their home games at Walter Johnson Field, located in Walter Johnson Park. Construction of the field began in the summer of 1998 and was completed almost a year later with the installation of tournament lighting and grandstand seating. The field is named for Johnson because he lived in Coffeyville for several years during his heyday as a star pitcher for the Washington Senators. (His house, a private residence, is located at 1701 East 8th Street.) Guarding the field is an exact replica of the monument that was posthumously dedicated to Johnson and which originally stood at Griffith Stadium in Washington. The original now stands outside Walter Johnson High School in Bethesda, Maryland.

Walter Johnson Exhibit

City: Coffeyville
Location: Dalton Museum
113 East 8th Street
620-251-5944

The Walter Johnson mural in Coffeyville, Kansas.

This museum, dedicated to local history, contains an exhibit of memorable Walter Johnson moments. There's also a mural of Johnson in Coffeyville, one of many murals featuring various subjects painted by Don Sprague. They are visible throughout the city.

Walter Johnson Birth Site

City: Humboldt
Location: Two miles north on old Highway 169 to sign (west) and two miles west to the intersection of 900 Road and Iowa Street.
Allen County

Walter Johnson was born November 6, 1887, to Swedish emigrants on a rural farm four miles west of Humboldt in Allen County—about an hour drive

from Coffeyville. His family left
the Humboldt area for the oil
fields of California in 1901, six
years before the 19-year-old
fireballing right-hander began
his phenomenal major-league
career with the Washington
Senators. Over 21 seasons,
the "Big Train" carved out 417
wins, second of all time only to
Cy Young, and recorded two
30-win seasons and 12 more

A simple marker alerts visitors to the location
of Walter Johnson's birth site in Humboldt.

of 20 or more victories while pitching for generally weak Senators teams.
His fastball was legendary and the 3,509 strikeouts he recorded stood as
a record for many years. The Johnson birth site marker resulted from the
dedicated efforts of local baseball historian Richard Davis, who has worked
for more than 30 years to preserve the Johnson legacy throughout Humboldt.
In 2001, Davis staged a banquet for the third annual Walter Johnson-George
Sweatt World Series Classic that was attended by Negro League legend
Buck O'Neil, and Johnson's daughter Carolyn and grandson Hank Thomas.
Davis and wife Gloria even hand-painted the sign that directs people to the
Johnson birthplace and the sign at the marker. He also runs the Walter John-
son Fan Club and is a driving force for all of the annual baseball events that
take place in Humboldt.

Walter Johnson carved out his Hall of Fame career in Washington DC, but it is
obvious his roots were in rural Kansas.

Walter Johnson Athletic Field

City: Humboldt
Location: 6th and Pine

Here are excerpts from the October 27, 1921, edition of the *Humboldt Union* newspaper that described the dedication of Walter Johnson Athletic Field:

Well, it was a great and glorious day. Humboldt closed up shop at 1:30 on this Wednesday, October 26th, 1921, and drilled out to Walter Johnson Athletic Field to see the great Walter Johnson pitch and the Monarch Cement Plant ball team win a ten inning game 5 to 4.

Walter Johnson's autographed ball is embedded in the cornerstone at the field bearing his name.

The crowd was the best ever, packing the grandstand and bleachers while an immense fringe of occupied automobiles and pedestrians hugged the foul lines on either side.

The Field was formally and officially dedicated as Walter Johnson Athletic Field. Mr. Charles L. McKnight, acting for Mayor J. W. Braucher and in well chosen words, explained the motive that actuated the planning and naming of the ground, on behalf of the citizen of Humboldt. Mr. McKnight also had a half dozen league base balls upon which Walter Johnson had written his name and were for sale at $2 each.

Walter Johnson pitched the first ball and Mr. Gilliland caught it. The ball was then given to C. M. Hilleary, who explained that it had on it the name of Walter Johnson, October 26, 1921, and was to be placed in the cornerstone of the new high school building in honor of the man who is an exponent of clean sport, true manhood and right living. There are Sporting men and Sportsmen. Walter Johnson never confounded them. A

Walter Johnson pitched the first ball in the inaugural game at this athletic field named in his honor in Humboldt.

Sportsman every inch. A more Sporting man he does not know. He is one of the cleanest and most respected men in his calling of the day and age. We speak not by the book but have lived where we could see and judge for ourselves.

This was the last of eight times Walter Johnson traveled to Humboldt for exhibition games that raised money to buy the land for the field that is still in use today. And that first ball he signed? It is still in the cornerstone at Humboldt High School, 1011 Bridge Street, Humboldt.

George A. Sweatt Park
City: Humboldt
Location: 12th Street and Wulf Drive

Walter Johnson is not the only professional player from Humboldt. George Sweatt, a former Negro League star, was also born there in 1893. Sweatt, an outstanding athlete, attended Pittsburg (Kansas) Normal College on scholarship and excelled in baseball, football, basketball and track. After college, he taught in Coffeyville while playing semipro baseball. When World War I erupted, Sweatt enlisted in the 816th Pioneer Infantry Division, which arrived in France only two weeks before the armistice, and he returned to teaching and semipro ball after his discharge. Sweatt got his big break when the owner of the Negro National League's Kansas City Monarchs saw him play in a Pittsburg game. Sweatt signed his first professional contract and played for Kansas City in 1921, a second baseman, third baseman and outfielder who helped the Monarchs win the 1924 Negro League World Series—the same year Johnson and the Washington Senators won the major-league World Series. Sweatt retired from professional baseball in 1928 but remained involved with youth leagues and semipro teams for the rest of his life. He died in 1983 in Los Angeles. In honor of Sweatt, and with the heartfelt persistence and leadership of Richard Davis, Humboldt dedicated this baseball field, Sweatt Park, to him. It plays host every summer to the Johnson-Sweatt Classic baseball tournament.

The George A. Sweatt Memorial can be found one block away from the park at 11th and Wulf Drive.

Exhibit Featuring Walter Johnson and George Sweatt
City: Humboldt
Location: Humboldt Historical Society Museum
Corner of Second and Neosho Streets

The Humboldt Museum is divided into five buildings. The first opened to the public as a museum in October of 1967. In building number five, several very special displays, featuring many rare artifacts, are dedicated to both major-league great Walter Johnson and Negro League star George Sweatt. The museum is open from Memorial Day through the second weekend of October. Interestingly, these two Humboldt-born ballplayers lived near each other in the tiny town at the turn of the century. Sweatt's home was just across from the site where the Walter Johnson Field was built, in the block between 6th and 7th Streets. The Johnson home was located at 3rd and Cherokee.

Walter Johnson Information Center
City: Humboldt
Location: *Humboldt Union* Newspaper
8th and Bridge Street

Baseball historian Dick Davis has created a display with some of his Walter Johnson and George Sweatt memorabilia, photos and information. A visit here also provides visitors with all of the location information they might need to catch the interesting baseball-related sites in Humboldt. Davis's displays also include information about and photographs of other legendary stars who have played in the area—Hall of Famers like Lou Gehrig and Christy Mathewson who made off-season exhibition visits to Blue Rapids, Kansas. This is a good starting point before touring the town.

The First Night Game in Organized Baseball
City: Independence
Location: Shulthis Stadium
Riverside Park

A historic marker at the former Producer Park identifies the stadium as the location of the first lighted night game ever played in organized baseball. The game took place on April 28, 1930, and 1,000 fans saw the Class C Western Association Muskogee Chiefs defeat the Independence Producers, 13–3. By the end of the 1930 season, 38 minor-league teams had lights—five years before major-league baseball took its first night-game plunge at Cincinnati.
    Independence was also the city where Mickey Mantle played his first minor-league season in 1949—for the Independence Yankees in New York's minor-league system. Other notables who played at Independence are Bill Virdon and Lou Skizas. The current stadium hosts high school football, track and other local events.

Charley Faust Marker

City: Marion
Location: Marion Baseball Complex
308 Eisenhower Drive

Another project from David Stalker,
who has worked tirelessly to place
markers in relevant places dedicated
to Deadball Era players, here's how he
described the Charles Faust marker:

> After reading Gabriel
> Schechter's book, *Victory
> Faust: The Rube Who Saved
> McGraw's Giants*, I became
> very inspired to help Char-
> ley's legend to live on.
>
> The most heart-
> warming, intriguing and
> mysterious story from the
> Deadball Era is recorded in
> depth by Gabriel. The story

The Charles Faust marker placed by
David Stalker.

> represents how our country
> and baseball once was, and simply could not take place
> today. On the other hand, did Charley Faust have the deter-
> mination, along with the right blend of innocence that no
> one before or after him has had?
>
> Many of us dream of playing in the big leagues
> someday, including those with more talent than Charley,
> but have only seen those dreams slip away. Charley focused
> on pitching for the New York Giants, and he did just that
> and more. He traveled with the team, brought them good
> luck, while entertaining many fans at the ballpark, and
> leaving a wonderful story behind for us to enjoy today.
>
> I collected funds from Gabriel, and other fellow
> members from SABR's Deadball Era committee who had a
> special place in their heart for Charley Faust, and donated
> a beautiful plaque to a baseball field in Charley's home-
> town of Marion, KS.

Another job well done, David. Seriously, Faust truly is one of baseball's great mysteries, and the fact Mr. Stalker worked so hard to commemorate his life is something that we as fans should be very thankful for. Are
you aware of Faust's peculiar history? He first won a spring tryout with the
Giants back in 1911, after telling manager John McGraw that a fortune-teller

back home in Kansas had told him he needed to go pitch for the Giants and help them win the pennant. In reality, Faust had no legitimate pitching ability, but McGraw, being superstitious, decided to bring Faust along just in case what he was saying was true. Incredibly, McGraw even put Faust in to pitch a couple of innings in different games, late in the 1911 season.

According to Giants great Fred Snodgrass, Faust remained with the Giants for three seasons, mostly as an oddball mascot as opposed to being a roster player, and during that time the Giants won three pennants, although they failed to win a World Series (Snodgrass himself made an infamous error in the final game of the 1912 Series). After the 1913 season ended, Faust relayed to McGraw that he was not a well man, and would be unable to help the team during the 1914 campaign. Faust was committed to an institution in 1914 and died in the late spring of 1915, at the age of 34. A strange, tragic end to a unique, real-life baseball fable.

Kansas Sports Hall of Fame
City: Old Town Wichita
Location: 238 North Mead Street

Slated to open in the fall of 2003, this museum dedicated to Kansas sports will include substantial baseball displays honoring such noteworthy Kansans as Walter Johnson, Fred Clarke, Ralph Houk, Joe Tinker, Elden Auker, Darren Daulton, Mike Torrez, Ralph Terry, Joe Rogan and Dummy Taylor. A display for the National Baseball Congress will also be included, as will a tribute to the Wichita State University national championship team.

National Baseball Congress (NBC) Hall of Fame
City: Wichita
Location: Lawrence-Dumont Stadium
Corners of Sycamore and Maple
316-267-3372

The National Baseball Congress and its NBC World Series were the brainchildren of a Wichita sporting goods salesman named Hap Dumont. During the Depression, Dumont hatched the idea after watching a Sunday baseball game between circus clowns, who were in Wichita for the week, and local firemen. The circus wasn't allowed

Lawrence-Dumont Stadium, the brainchild of sporting goods salesman Hap Dumont, is home to the National Baseball Congress World Series. Satchel Paige headlined the first tournament.

to perform on Sunday because of the blue laws still in effect, but the base-ball-playing clowns drew a large crowd, triggering Dumont's brainchild. He created the National Semipro Baseball Congress Kansas State Tournament, which premiered in 1931 on Island Park in the middle of the Arkansas River. Over the years, as the event grew more popular, Dumont approached Wichita about building him a new stadium so he could expand his tournament and include teams from all over the country. The city built his stadium on the west bank of the river, just south of the old park, and named it after Wichita pioneer Robert Lawrence. In a brilliant public relations move in 1935, Du-mont paid Satchel Paige $1,000 to bring his touring team to town for the first NBC tournament. The idea paid off. Paige struck out 60 batters and won four games, thrilling the local crowds. The national tournament was a hit. Since then, thousands of young prospects and former major-leaguers have played here. Today's tournament features mostly college players with a few former professionals and some outstanding former college or high school players who were never drafted by a professional team. The museum outside the cen-ter field wall is dedicated to the NBC and memories of its long-running tour-nament. More than 600 future major-leaguers have played in the event. The stadium also displays historical information about the Congress—a fitting trib-ute to Hap Dumont, the sporting goods salesman with big baseball dreams.

The History of Lawrence-Dumont Stadium
City: Wichita
Location: Corners of Sycamore and Maple
316-267-3372

Lawrence-Dumont Stadium, built in 1934 as a Work Projects Administration assignment, is one of the 15 oldest baseball stadiums still in use in professional baseball. The stadium has under-gone renovations in 1972, '89 and 2001, result-ing in the current facility. Lawrence-Dumont is the second oldest stadium in the Texas League. Only Ray Winder Field in Little Rock, Arkansas, is older (built in 1932). From 1935, the NBC tour-nament has drawn huge crowds and hundreds of future major-league players to Wichita. Since Du-mont's death, the NBC has had five different own-erships, including the current owner, Rich Prod-ucts Corporation. The Wichita Wranglers, a Class AA team of the Kansas City Royals, have captured three Texas League championships since moving to Lawrence-Dumont Stadium in 1987.

Lawrence-Dumont Stadium is one of the 15 oldest facilities still in use in professional baseball.

Hall of Famers Buried in Kansas

Fred Clarke
St. Mary's Cemetery
East 12th Street, between
Wheat Road and Alexander Avenue
Winfield

Fred Clarke

Michigan

T-Ball
City: Albion

The precise origins of t-ball are a bit murky, and several independent parties—unbeknownst to each other—may have in fact originated the game. In the early 1970s, a trademark was registered with the United States government by Dr. Dayton Hobbs, but t-ball's origins date back to at least the 1940s and '50s, with several people claiming to be the actual inventor of the game. Claude Lewis, director of the Warner Robins, Georgia Recreation Department, formed a t-ball league in March 1958. Twenty children played the first year. Lewis designed rules for the new game and mailed the rulebooks out to recreation departments all over the country and overseas.

Albion, Michigan, also claims to be the place of invention for the sport in 1956, though Starkville, Mississippi, makes a nearly identical claim that t-ball was invented in their town in 1961. In fact, according to the Starkville Rotary Club's Web site: "In 1961, when it was apparent that younger children needed some way to participate in the program, Rotarians Clyde Muse and W. W. Littlejohn devised the game of T-Ball and added it to the summer baseball program." Dr. Hobbs has given credit to no less than the United States Navy with spreading the game overseas. United States presidents since Ronald Reagan have all hosted t-ball games on the South

Lawn of the White House with children getting a chance to play on the famous yard. Regardless of the exact origin, t-ball today is still a popular way
for youngsters to develop baseball skills while having a good time (as the
hundreds of leagues around the country attest). Incidentally, the name "Tee
Ball" is a registered trademark, while "t-ball" is the generic name.

House of David Museum
City: Benton Harbor
Location: 2251 Riverside Road
269-325-0039

As the House of David Museum
has documented:

> The House of David was
> a religious commune
> founded in 1903 by Ben-
> jamin and Mary Purnell.
> Based in and around
> Benton Harbor, Michi-
> gan, and High Island,

**The House of David Museum in Benton Har-
bor celebrates the fabled bearded players.**

the commune required its members to refrain from sex,
haircuts, shaving, and the eating of meat. Starting around
1907, the community ran the Springs of Eden Park, which
became a popular Michigan vacation spot in the 1930s.
The House of David operated a famous barnstorming baseball team, which toured rural America from the 1920s to
the 1950s, playing amateur and semipro teams in exhibition games. The organization also fielded nationally known
musical bands between 1906 and 1927. During that period,
these bands toured the country almost nonstop, primarily on the three top vaudeville circuits: the Pantages, the
Keith and the Orpheum. The House of David also operated
a world-famous amusement park and zoo. The commune
reached the peak of its operations from 1907 to 1927. Dif-
ficulties arose in the 1920s, as the *Detroit Free Press* and
other newspapers began running articles attacking Benjamin Purnell, who was accused of violating the commune's
oath of celibacy. Purnell was tried in Berrien County,
Michigan, for "public immorality," and 13 young women,
placed under oath, confessed to having had sex with the
patriarch. The trial led to Purnell's expulsion from the commune in 1927, and the former leader died in 1929; his body

was mummified and kept in a glass coffin in the commune. The group suffered further splintering after his death and ultimately split into two groups. One group, run by Purnell's wife, Mary, remained successful until her death at 91 in 1953. The group has since declined, but still has a few dozen members.

Today, visitors to this interesting museum will find artifacts related to the team and rare photos of legends such as Babe Ruth, Grover Cleveland Alexander and Satchel Paige, who all put on fake beards at various times in their careers to play with or against the House of David. Some information directly from the museum:

The House of David Museum was established in April 1997 in the little town of Riverside, Michigan. Feeling the need to save this wonderful history that was slowly slipping away, Chris Siriano made a decision to do whatever he could to save the story of the House of David by compiling artifacts, baseball memorabilia, posters, photos, wooden souvenirs, and artwork from the House of David times, and place them on exhibit for all others to see and learn about.

Siriano met with several House of David members day after day, for sometimes hours at a time, trying to learn their story directly from their mouths, listening to their memories of the amusement park, baseball teams, the faith, their personal lives, and so on. After over a year of meetings, and lots of enthusiasm, Siriano set out to devote his time to securing this great piece of history for future generations here in S.W. Michigan.

Upon asking the House of David members if they approved of this "Museum" idea, they at first had reservations, simply because they had so many times been taken advantage of, lied to, or ridiculed, they were basically untrusting of the general public to represent them in a museum. So at first, the answer was "You can set up a building and put House of David items in it, but only on the inside of the building can you put the name "House of David," similar to what the Benton Harbor Library has called "The House of David Room."

And so it started in a room of an old antique shop, calling the room the "House of David Room," and slowly more and more artifacts were acquired, more and more guests came to learn, and slowly the House of David people themselves came out to see what was going on.

The museum has grown and grown, forcing several moves to larger facilities, and eventually in 2004 a brand new facility was built to house the largest House of David collection in the world. The building is over 4000 sq. ft. and houses one of the first House of David Steam Engine Trains, hundreds of pieces of their famous pearlized ivory artwork, thousands of original photographs, baseball and basketball uniforms, posters, broadsides, and literally thousands of pieces of their wonderful history.

Recreation Park
City: Detroit
Location: Brush Street Mall behind Harper Hospital

Recreation Park, home of the National League's Detroit Wolverines from 1881–88, was built on this site in 1879. The park extended from Brady Street to Willis Avenue. It was here on May 2, 1881, that the first Major League Baseball game in Detroit was played—the first of more than 800 over its eight-season big-league association. Hall of Famers Dan Brouthers and Sam Thompson played for the Wolverines at Recreation Park, but the team went out of existence after the 1888 season. That's when the Wolverines moved to Cleveland and the park was used sporadically by other teams until being closed in 1894, at which point it was torn down. The historical marker that stands here now is located where left field used to be.

Lou Gehrig Bows Out
City: Detroit
Location: Westin Book Cadillac Detroit
1114 Washington Boulevard
313-442-1600

When this grand hotel opened in 1924, it was the largest in the world, with 1,200 rooms and 33 stories. On May 2, 1939, it became the scene of a dramatic baseball moment—a simple meeting that took place in its lobby. New York Yankees first baseman Lou Gehrig, hitting an anemic .143 after eight games in the new season, met with manager Joe McCarthy. Gehrig said to his boss, "I'm taking myself out, Joe." McCarthy asked why. "For the good of the team," Gehrig said. "Nobody has to tell me how bad I've been and how much of a drawback I've been to the club." This was the beginning of the end to Gehrig's incredible 2,130 consecutive-games streak. That afternoon at Detroit's Briggs Stadium, Gehrig was not in the starting lineup. The crowd, sensing the weight of the event, applauded for two minutes. Without the Iron Horse, the Yankees posted an inspired 22–2 victory over the Tigers with Gehrig replacement Babe Dahlgren collecting a home run and a double. The Baseball Hall of Fame in Cooperstown has a letter written by Gehrig on Book-Cadillac Hotel (now the Westin Book Cadillac Detroit) stationery to his wife Eleanor, recounting his conversation with McCarthy and his decision to take himself out of the lineup. Though it isn't dated, researchers believe it was most likely written on May 3, the day after the meeting.

Ernie Harwell Sports Collection

City: Detroit
Location: Detroit Public Library
5201 Woodward Avenue
313-833-1480

Part of the Burton Historical Collection at the Detroit Library is the Harwell Collection, donated by legendary sportscaster Ernie Harwell in 1967. It consists primarily of baseball books, team annuals, scorecards, clippings and photographs that were amassed by Harwell throughout his broadcasting career. The immensely popular broadcaster was working for the Atlanta Crackers when Dodgers owner Branch Rickey took notice of him. So impressed was Rickey that he brought Harwell to Brooklyn to broadcast Dodgers games in 1948. Harwell later had stints with the Giants and Orioles before arriving in Detroit in 1960. Harwell retired following the 2002 season, after 55 years in broadcasting.

Detroit Tiger Statues and Walk of Fame

City: Detroit
Location: Comerica Park
2100 Woodward Avenue
313-962-4000

The main concourse at Comerica Park is like a tour through baseball history. Divided into 20th century eras, the concourse lets fans progress through different time frames of baseball lore. "Decade Monuments" covering two 10-year periods each are

Six former Tigers greats are honored with life-size statues, just beyond the center field fence at Comerica Park.

placed throughout the concourse, towering from floor to ceiling and featuring artifacts and memorabilia. In center field (just beyond the General Motors Fountain), the Tigers have honored some of the franchise's greatest players with larger-than-life statues. Al Kaline, Hank Greenberg, Willie Horton, Ty Cobb, Charlie Gehringer and Hal Newhauser are the players immortalized.

Tiger Stadium
City: Detroit
Location: Corner of Michigan and Trumbull

This is one of the few former major-league ballparks to be honored by a state historical marker—and with good reason. From 1912 to 1999, Tiger Stadium was a baseball Mecca for fans throughout Michigan. Three generations witnessed the magical play of such stars as Ty Cobb, Hal Newhauser, Mickey Cochrane, Hank Greenberg, George Kell, Al Kaline, Denny McLain, Mickey Lolich, Alan Trammel, Jack Morris, Lou Whitaker, Kirk Gibson and Willie Horton. Baseball was actually played at the Michigan and Trumbull site as early as 1896, when 10,000-seat Bennett Park was built. From 1901 to 1912, Bennett was home to the American League Tigers. The stadium opened as Navin Field in 1912 and also existed through its 87-year run as Briggs Stadium and Tiger Stadium—the home of four World Series championship teams. The final game was played at Tiger Stadium on September 27, 1999, and many former players returned to pay tribute. They shared in the "transfer of power" to new Comerica Park, a ceremony in which home plate was dug up (for use at Comerica) and the Tiger Stadium flag was passed from player to player. Detroit won its last game at the old park, 8-2, over Kansas City—a win accentuated by an eighth-inning grand slam from Rob Fick. Tiger Stadium remains partially in place today, a crumbling, sel-

Tiger Stadium has not hosted a major-league game since 1999, but the venerable old ballpark is still standing today.

Some Memorable Moments at Tiger Stadium

★ OCTOBER 7, 1935: In Game 6 of the World Series, Tigers catcher/manager Mickey Cochrane scored the winning run in the bottom of the ninth inning, beating the Cubs and giving the Tigers their first World Series championship.

★ JULY 8, 1941: Ted Williams hit a three-run, ninth-inning home run to give the American League a 7–5 All-Star Game victory.

★ SEPTEMBER 14, 1968: Denny McLain, thanks to a ninth-inning Tigers rally, posted a victory over Oakland and became baseball's first 30-game winner since 1934.

★ JULY 13, 1971: Reggie Jackson's All-Star Game blast off Pittsburgh pitcher Doc Ellis hit the light standard positioned atop the right field bleachers—one of the stadium's most memorable home runs.

★ OCTOBER 14, 1984: In Game 5 of the 1984 World Series, Kirk Gibson's dramatic eighth-inning, three-run homer off Padres pitcher Goose Gossage sealed the team's fourth championship.

dom-used relic awaiting its final fate. In 2008, a portion of the stadium was demolished. Efforts continue to save the remaining portion of the structure, stretching approximately from dugout to dugout.

Michigan Sports Hall of Fame
City: Detroit
Location: 1 North Washington Blvd
Cobo Conference Center
248-540-6248

Started in 1955, this is one of the oldest "state" sports halls of fame. Located within a hallway at the Cobo Conference Center, hundreds of plaques are displayed along the walls honoring athletes and other notable figures from Detroit professional teams. Among the baseball players included in this "Hall of Heroes" are Charlie Gehringer, Sam Crawford, Hank Greenberg, Ty Cobb, Al Kaline, Lance Parrish, Jack Morris, Alan Trammel and Norm Cash. Honorees are voted in each year by living Hall of Fame members and local sports media. Admission is free (whenever Cobo Conference Center is open).

Ring Lardner House Marker

City: Niles
Location: Bond Street

An inscription on a marker here reads:

> Sportswriter, humorist, sardonic observer of the American scene, Ring Lardner was born in the house across the street on March 6, 1885. Possibly the best-known American author in the 1920s, he began his career writing sketches of sporting events for the Niles *Sun* and later worked for papers in Chicago and New York, where he wrote a popular syndicated column. Beginning in 1914 the *Saturday Evening Post* began publication of a series of articles that were to become his best-known work. Later entitled *You Know Me Al*, the articles were letters from an ignorant bush league baseball player to his friend and were among the first literary uses of American common speech. His death occurred in New York on September 25, 1933. Lardner's achievements were favorably compared to those of Mark Twain.

Interestingly, the great sportswriter influenced Ernest Hemingway, who sometimes wrote articles for his high school newspaper under the pseudonym Ring Lardner Jr.

National Polish-American Sports Hall of Fame and Museum

City: Orchard Lake
Location: 3535 Indian Trail (intersection of Commerce Road and Orchard Lake Road)
248-683-0401
Open by appointment, call for information.

The National Polish-American Sports Hall of Fame and Museum was founded in 1973 to honor and recognize outstanding American athletes, both amateur and professional, of Polish descent. A Hall of Fame Room and Museum was established in the Dombrowski Fieldhouse on the campus of St. Mary's College, Orchard Lake, 25 miles northwest of Detroit. The organization has inducted many baseball players, including Stan Musial, Ted Kluszewski, Carl Yastrzemski, Tony Kubek and Bill Mazeroski. When inducted, each member is asked to provide a piece or two of related memorabilia, an idea that has resulted in a sizable and impressive collection. A special display honors charter inductee Musial, the former St. Louis great who has been extremely generous in his involvement with the museum.

Tomb of Frank Navin
City: Southfield
Location: Holy Sepulchre Cemetery
25800 West 10 Mile Road
248-350-1900

The former Detroit owner loved his team so much that his gravesite is "guard-ed" by two very realistic looking, life-size bronze tigers. Navin died sud-denly while horseback riding in November of 1935. Ironically, it was just five weeks after his beloved Tigers won their first World Series championship, beating the Cubs in six games.

Hall of Famers Buried in Michigan

Larry MacPhail
Elkland Township Cemetery
6897 Cass City Road
Cass City
517-872-1112

DETROIT METROPOLITAN AREA

Norman "Turkey" Stearnes
Lincoln Memorial Park Cemetery
21661 East 14 Mile Road
Clinton Township
810-791-3486

Charlie Gehringer

Sam Thompson
Elmwood Cemetery
1200 Elmwood Street
Detroit
313-567-3453

Hal Newhouser
Oakland Hills Memorial Gardens
43300 West 12 Mile Road
Novi
248-349-2784

Harry Heilmann

Charlie Gehringer and Harry Heilmann
Holy Sepulchre Cemetery
25800 West 10 Mile Road
Southfield

Minnesota

Metropolitan Stadium

City: Bloomington
Location: Mall of America
Crossroads of Interstate 494 and Highway 77 (look for Camp Snoopy in the mall)

Metropolitan Stadium was built on a farm in 1956 for the American Association's Minneapolis Millers, who had just abandoned Nicollet Park. The Class AAA Millers played there five years, giving way in 1961 to the relocated Washington Senators, who gave the city its first taste of Major League Baseball. The Senators began their first Metropolitan Stadium season as the Twins and were joined by a National Football League expansion team, the Minnesota Vikings, who helped finance the building of a double-deck grandstand in left field. The renovation brought capacity to 45,919, where it stayed until the park closed after the 1981 season when the Twins and Vikings moved to the new Metrodome. Three years after shutting down operations, Metropolitan Stadium was demolished to make way for the Mall of America. The former site of home plate is marked by a plaque in the Camp Snoopy area of the mall. There is also a Metropolitan Stadium seat bolted to a wall, marking the landing spot for Harmon Killebrew's mammoth 520-foot home run in 1967.

Some Memorable Moments at Metropolitan Stadium

★ JULY 13, 1965: Twins star Harmon Killebrew homered, but the AL lost 6–5 in the stadium's only All-Star Game.

★ OCTOBER 7, 1965: Twins pitcher Jim Kaat gave Minnesota a two-games-to-none World Series lead over the Dodgers, driving in two runs and outpitching Sandy Koufax, 5–1.

★ AUGUST 10, 1971: Killebrew hit his 500th home run in a game against the Orioles.

★ Rod Carew won seven AL batting titles here.

Metropolitan Stadium, former home of the Twins, was located on property now occupied by the Mall of America.

Keep Your Eyes Peeled for . . .

★ Harmon Killebrew Drive (83rd Street, Bloomington) near the site of old Metropolitan Stadium

Original Baseball Hall of Fame Museum of Minnesota

City: Minneapolis
Location: 910 South Third Street

The Original Baseball Hall of Fame and Museum, discreetly hidden behind a Third Street sportswear store, is a treasure-trove of autographed baseball memorabilia, including jerseys, bats, balls, cards and much more. This small but packed baseball museum is the brainchild of Ray Crump, a man dedicated to Minnesota baseball history.

The Baseball Hall of Fame Museum of Minnesota may be small, but it has an impressive collection of memorabilia and artifacts.

Nicollet Park

City: Minneapolis

Location: Nicollet Avenue South and 31st Street

Fabled Nicollet Park, home to Minor League Baseball from 1896-1955, was the stomping grounds of the Class AAA American Association's Minneapolis Millers for 54 years. The Millers compiled the association's best won-lost record over that span and also won nine pennants, tying the total of their cross-river neighbors, the St. Paul Saints. The Millers provided a proving ground for 15 players who eventually ended up in the Hall of Fame, including Philadelphia lefty Rube Waddell, Boston's Ted Williams, Giants center fielder Willie Mays and Red Sox star Carl Yastrzemski. Nicollet Park was also 1944 home to the Minneapolis Millerettes of the All-American Girls Professional Baseball League, the wartime circuit that inspired the 1992 movie, *A League of Their Own*. Babe Ruth played several memorable exhibition games at Nicollet, one during the 1924 Ruth/Walter Johnson barnstorming tour.

In 1955, the year before it was torn down, Nicollet Park played host to the Junior World Series, in which the Millers beat the Rochester Red Wings to win their first and only Series title. The games in that Series were the final ones played at Nicollet. In 1983, a historic marker was erected on the former site of the ballpark, paid for in large part by donations from former players and fans whose fondness for the cozy, slightly decrepit, but always loved, ballpark stretched on for years after it was gone.

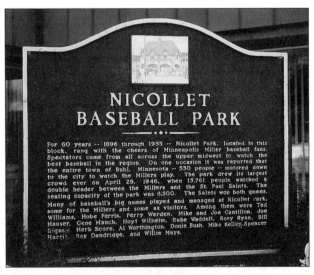

All that remains of once-proud Nicollet Park is this historic marker.

Some Memorable Moments at Nicollet Park

★ On a 1933 billboard posted on an outfield wall, Wheaties first used its slogan, "Breakfast of Champions." According to the The Wheaties Franchise, an American Sports icon since 1933: "General Mills' broadcast deal with the minor-league Minneapolis Millers on radio station WCCO included the large signboard that Wheaties would use to introduce its new advertising slogan. The late Knox Reeves (of the Minneapolis-based advertising agency) was asked what should be printed on the signboard for his client. He took out a pad and pencil, it is said, sketched a Wheaties package, thought for a minute, and then printed 'Wheaties—The Breakfast of Champions.'"

★ In 1938, a brash-but-brilliant Millers outfielder named Ted Williams took the league batting title with a .366 average.

★ JULY 4, 1940: Millers outfielder Ab Wright hit four home runs and a triple in five at bats for 19 total bases.

★ In 1951, the New York Giants assigned Willie Mays to Minneapolis. In 35 games, Mays collected 71 hits, 8 home runs and 30 RBI. This prompted a recall from Giants manager Leo Durocher.

Lexington Baseball Park

City: St. Paul
Location: Lexington Parkway and University Avenue

The Lexington Baseball Park was opened by Charles Comiskey in 1897. Comiskey, a former player and new team owner, had purchased a team in Sioux City, Iowa, and moved it here to St. Paul. The St. Paul Saints played at this site from 1897 to 1956, at which point the team moved to nearby Midway Stadium. Lexington Baseball Park was demol-

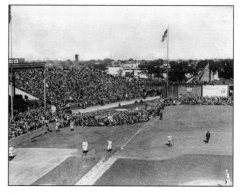

A vintage shot of St. Paul's Lexington Baseball Park.

ished in the 1950s, but today at the site,
on the wall of a bank, a plaque commemorates the stadium.

Midway Stadium
City: St. Paul
Location: 1000 North Snelling Avenue

After playing at Lexington Baseball Park,
the Saints moved here to Midway Stadium
and played here between 1957 and 1960.
The name "Midway Stadium" comes from

**A marker for the Lexington Base-
ball Park, St. Paul, Minnesota.**

the fact that the stadium had been located in St. Paul's Midway area, which
is called that because it is roughly halfway between downtown Minneapolis
and downtown St. Paul. After being abandoned by the Saints, the Minnesota
Vikings football team used Midway as a practice field, and then in 1982, the
park was demolished. No sign of it remains today, and currently the Saints
play at a new Midway Stadium located about a mile away from this site.

Missouri

Jake Beckley Monument
City: Hannibal
Location: 300 block of North Main Street

This recently restored memorial to Jake Beckley was originally unveiled on August 11, 1971.
Beckley was born in Hannibal on August 4,
1867, and played first base in the major leagues
for 20 years. Over that tenure, he played more
games (2,386), made more putouts (23,696) and
handled more chances (25,000) than any other
player at his position. Beckley retired with a .308
average, 87 home runs and 1,575 RBI. Beckley
had the bizarre habit of screaming the nonsen-
sical word "Chickazoola" at pitchers while ap-
proaching the plate, presumably to rattle them.
Beckley, who was inducted into the Hall of Fame

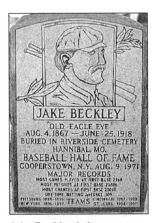

**Jake Beckley is long gone,
but not forgotten in
Hannibal.**

in 1971, just a few days before the dedication of his memorial, died in 1918
and is buried at Riverside Cemetery, State Route 79, Hannibal.

Historic Joe Becker Stadium

City: Joplin
Location: 1301 East Third Street

Joplin's historic Joe Becker Stadium, built in 1918, is where Mickey Mantle played in 1950, his second professional season. Mantle batted .383 with 26 home runs, 30 doubles, 12 triples and 136 RBI for the Western Association Class C team. That performance earned him an invitation to 1951 spring training with the Yankees. The venerable little park has survived two fires, countless storms and thousands of games from Little League to semipro. In addition to Mantle, such other stars as Stan Musial, Joe Garagiola and Ken Boyer played here. Today's Joe Becker Stadium is home to Missouri Southern State College, Joplin High School, American Legion Post 13 and several regional tournaments. The stadium is named for Joe Becker, a professional baseball umpire and scout who also served as business manager for the Joplin Miners minor-league team from 1936 to 1942.

Gabby Street Park

City: Joplin
Location: Gabby Street Boulevard (26th Street) between Main Street and Maiden Lane

Gabby Street, a one-time battery mate of Washington Senators great Walter Johnson and the manager who led the St. Louis Cardinals to National League pennants in 1930 and '31, first visited Joplin in 1923 as a minor-league player/manager. He met and married a local girl, then became a full-time Joplin resident until he died in 1951. The city held a day in Street's honor on January 19, 1950, dedicating the park and a street to his name. On hand to celebrate the affair were longtime friends Stan Musial, Joe Garagiola, Red Schoendienst and Enos Slaughter. Also present was Harry Caray, whose career Street influenced as a Cardinals radio broadcaster in the 1940s. The park today is mostly used for youth baseball.

Satchel Paige Memorial Stadium

City: Kansas City
Location: 51st Street and Swope Parkway

This stadium, used by amateur baseball organizations and for special events, is named for pitching legend Satchel Paige, who played

Satchel Paige Memorial Stadium serves amateur baseball leagues in the Swope Park district of Kansas City.

for the Kansas City Monarchs in the old Negro National League. Originally called the Catholic Youth Council Athletic Field, the 5,000-seat stadium was renamed in Paige's honor in 1982. Three days after the ceremony, Paige died, a tragedy that galvanized the community to renovate the then-deteriorating stadium

Satchel Paige Comprehensive Community School

City: Kansas City
Location: 3301 East 75th Street

Satchel Paige Elementary School was opened originally as a kindergarten through fifth grade magnet school with the unlikely name Satchel Paige Classical Greek Academy. The name referred to the school's focus on sports from the original Olympic Games. In 1998, the school was renamed Satchel Paige Comprehensive Community School. A statue of Paige stands inside the building, as well as a display case featuring an autographed baseball, a uniform, a pair of cleats and some other personal items.

Lou Gehrig's Last Game

City: Kansas City
Location: Municipal Stadium
A mile and a half southeast of downtown Kansas City at the intersection of 22nd Street and Brooklyn Avenue.

Home to four different teams from 1923 to 1972, Kansas City's Municipal Stadium, once called Muehlebach Field, was originally built as a home base for the Negro League's Kansas City Monarchs and the Kansas City Blues minor-league team of the American Association. The stadium was the early stomping grounds for such black baseball greats as Satchel Paige and John Henry Lloyd, as well as many of the great players it developed as a longtime farm team for the New York Yankees. In 1938, the stadium was re-christened Ruppert Stadium, in honor of Yankees owner Jacob Ruppert, and a few years later it was renamed Blues Stadium. From 1955 to 1966, now called Municipal Stadium, the Brooklyn Avenue ballpark was strictly big league—home of the Kansas City Athletics, relocated from Philadelphia. The ballpark was rebuilt with a double deck to accommodate more fans.

      Many Kansas Citians will remember the 1960s primarily as the era of flamboyant Charles O. Finley, the innovative, always-controversial owner who kept things stirred up with his contrary personality and futuristic ideas. Finley made ballpark changes that incurred the wrath of commissioner Bowie Kuhn; paraded his mascot, Charlie O. the Mule, around the city and stadium; installed a small zoo and picnic area down the right field line; and installed a mechanical rabbit (Harvey) that would rise from the ground be-hind home plate to supply balls to the umpire. He also pulled off Bill Veeck-like stunts that kept everyone shaking their head. Finley's final "stunt" was to make the A's disappear. He moved his club to Oakland in 1968, at which point the expansion Kansas City Royals were formed and Municipal Sta-dium took on yet another tenant—a relationship that lasted until Royals Sta-dium (now Kauffman Stadium) was opened in 1973.

Few fans know that Municipal Stadium played an emotional role in the tragic career-ending story of Lou Gehrig. It was in Detroit that the Iron Horse pulled himself out of the Yankees' lineup, ending his 2,130-game streak on May 2, 1939. But it is widely believed he never played again. He did, more than a month later on June 12, when the New Yorkers played an exhibition game at Blues Stadium against their top farm club. A frail, weak-ened Gehrig, whose illness had yet to be diagnosed, played three innings, batted once (eighth in the order) and grounded out to second base in his final professional at bat. He cleanly handled four putouts while playing first base. Gehrig was still traveling with the team at that point and had not yet been diagnosed as terminal. Teammate Tommy Heinrich was quoted as say-ing, "He actually didn't want to do that in Kansas City. But Gehrig, for the sake of those fans, went up to home plate." The 23,864 fans who watched that game were part of the largest crowd ever to attend an exhibition game in the history of the American Association.

The day after the game, the Yankees returned to New York while Gehrig took a train to the Mayo Clinic in Minnesota, where he would learn the details of his fa-tal disease. The next month, in a stirring Fourth of July cer-emony at Yankee Sta-dium, Gehrig made his famous "Luckiest Man Alive" speech. Two years later, he was dead.

Municipal Stadium was demol-ished in 1976 and the site is now a communi-ty garden. A marker at the site documents the history of Municipal Stadium.

Municipal Stadium, formerly called Blues Stadium, was the home of two major-league teams.

Some Memorable Moments at Municipal Stadium

★ AUGUST 9, 1930: Smokey Joe Williams of the Negro League Homestead Grays struck out 27 Kansas City Monarchs and allowed just one hit in 12 innings. The losing pitcher, Chet Brewer, struck out 19 and allowed four hits.

★ SEPTEMBER 8, 1965: Kansas City A's shortstop Bert Campaneris became the first man in modern baseball to play all nine positions in one game. (The A's lost 5-3 to the California Angels.)

★ SEPTEMBER 25, 1965: Satchel Paige, at age 59, pitched three scoreless innings against the Boston Red Sox in another of Finley's many Kansas City promotions.

Negro Leagues Baseball Museum

City: Kansas City
Location: 1616 East 18th Street

Negro League legend and baseball goodwill ambassador Buck O'Neil serves as board chairman at the Negro Leagues Baseball Museum, which was opened in January of 1991. The museum, originally located in the historic Lincoln Building, recounts in great detail the formation and history of the

The Negro Leagues Baseball Museum features a display honoring the greatest players at each position.

Negro Baseball League. Displays include rare Negro League pennants, autographed baseballs, photographs and an eight-minute videotape about the league's history—narrated by newsman Bernard Shaw. From old photos, contracts, scorecards and equipment, to a room honoring the nine best (one at each position) Negro League ballplayers, this museum does an excellent job of documenting a special group of athletes who excelled in the face of great adversity. When you visit, you might even bump into O'Neil, one of the more charismatic heroes baseball has produced.

Birthplace of the Negro League

City: Kansas City
Location: Paseo YMCA
1800 Paseo Boulevard between
18th and 19th Streets

In 1920, team owner (and former Negro League pitcher) Andrew "Rube" Foster met here with other independent team owners to brainstorm a plan to create a stable league for black baseball.

The Paseo YMCA, birthplace of the Negro League.

This summit resulted in the formation of the Negro National League (NNL). In addition to Foster's American Giants, charter members included the Chicago Giants, the Dayton Marcos, the Detroit Stars, the Indianapolis ABCs, the St. Louis Giants and the Kansas City Monarchs. Before this historic session, Negro League teams were primarily rudderless barnstormers. After the NNL was formed, however, black baseball grew into a popular, nationally recognized association. Over the next 40 years, Negro League baseball expanded to include more than 2,600 athletes and dozens of teams.

Missouri Sports Hall of Fame

City: Springfield
Location: 3861 East Stan Musial Drive
417-889-3100

This museum/hall of fame features a great second-floor display devoted to baseball, complete with a Mark McGwire area and Heavy Hitters area that includes memorabilia from many Missouri teams and players, including autographed jerseys, helmets, gloves and more. Some of baseball's most historic names—Babe Ruth, Willie Mays, Mike Schmidt, Reggie Jackson—are represented. Interactive displays include a broadcast booth and a pitching cage where visitors can stand behind home plate and witness, up close and personal, a major-league pitch traveling 100 mph.

Robison Field

City: St. Louis
Location: Near the corner of Natural Bridge Road and Vandeventer Avenue

Originally called New Sportsman's Park, Robison Field (the most popular name the park ever bore) was the home to several clubs: the National League

St. Louis Browns from 1893 to 1898, the St. Louis Browns of the American League from 1900 to 1908, the National League St. Louis Perfectos in 1899 and, finally, the National League St. Louis Cardinals from 1900 to 1920.

A marker at the site of Robison Field, St. Louis, Missouri.

The name of the ballpark officially became Robison Field in 1911, when Helene Hatheway Britton paid tribute to her father, Frank, and uncle, Emmet Stanley Robison, who ran the St. Louis Browns.

During the stadium's last couple of seasons, after the Robison family was no longer associated with the team, the park was often referred to as "Cardinal Field." Beaumont High School, opened in 1926, was built on the site. A marker can be found at the site today, thanks to the efforts of some dedicated ballpark fans. According to the writer, Joan M. Thomas, "Barbara Sheinbein, who is a board member of the Bob Broeg Chapter of SABR, conceived the idea of marking the locations of old ballparks when she went on a tour at a SABR convention in Cincinnati. None of the locations were marked, and she realized that the same was true of St. Louis. At the time she brought it up at a chapter meeting, I was there, and my book *St. Louis' Big League Ballparks* had just been released. As the parks are a pet subject of mine, I was more than happy to help." Together, along with several SABR members, the group has placed markers at several other ballpark sites (the others of which are documented in this book).

St. Louis Cardinals Hall of Fame Museum

City: St. Louis
Location: 111 Stadium Plaza

The St. Louis Cardinals Hall of Fame was the official repository for more than 100 years of St. Louis baseball history. Through photographs and memorabilia, visitors experienced the evolution of the game as witnessed by St. Louisans from the 1880s to the present. The museum, located inside the International Bowling Museum, included artifacts from the Cardinals' 15 World Series and nine championships, complete with the 1967 and '82 trophies, championship rings, scorebooks, programs, autographed balls and bats. An impressive Stan "The Man" Musial exhibit covered his amazing major-league career. Ozzie Smith, Bob Gibson, Lou Brock, Dizzy Dean, Rogers Hornsby, Joe Medwick and many other Cardinals greats were showcased as well. Mark McGwire's 1962 Corvette, which was presented to him

Stan Musial, a member of the St. Louis Cardinals Hall of Fame.

by the Cardinals in 1998 when he broke Roger Maris's single-season home run record, was on display. There was also a Mark McGwire "Bat Bench"—a sitting area made from bats, balls and bases. The St. Louis Browns were well-represented, too, as are the St. Louis Stars, the Negro National League team of St. Louis and James "Cool Papa" Bell. The museum, which was strategically located across from old Busch Stadium, was a great stopover for fans heading to a game. With admission you got the Cardinals Hall of Fame, the International Bowling Museum and four free frames of bowling. As of November 2008, the Cardinals Hall of Fame Museum closed as it entered a transitional period, during which the museum is designing a new facility that will be constructed in Ballpark Village, across the street from the new Busch Stadium.

St. Louis Stars Park

City: St. Louis
Location: Harris-Stowe State University
Southeast corner of Compton and Laclede

From 1922 to 1931, the St. Louis Stars existed as a Negro League baseball team that competed in the Negro National League. Founded after Dick Kent and Dr. Sam Sheppard took over the St. Louis Giants franchise from white promoter Charlie Mills, the Stars would go on to become one of the leading dynasties in Negro League history. They won three pennants in four years from 1928 to 1931, and played in Stars Park, which was completed in 1922 as one of the few ballparks built expressly for the Negro Leagues. The park became renowned for its 269-foot left

The Stars Park marker placed by SABR.

field wall, built to accommodate a trolley car barn. Even though there were special rules that in some years counted home runs hit over the car barn as ground-rule doubles, the park accommodated power hitters over the years. In 2007, a Stars Park marker was unveiled at the site where the ballpark once stood, today Harris-Stowe State University, SABR representatives Bob Broeg Chapter president Norm Richards and Ballpark Marker Committee members Barb Sheinbein and Joan Thomas were there to host the event.

Cool Papa Bell Avenue

City: St. Louis
Location: James "Cool Papa" Bell Avenue runs between Dr. Martin
Luther King Jr. Drive and Jefferson Avenue on what used to be called
Dixon Street.

It's named for the lightning-fast Bell, the legendary Negro League center
fielder who played from 1922 to 1950.

Cool Papa Bell Memorial

City: St. Louis
Location: St. Peters Cemetery
2101 Lucas and Hunt Road
Northwest of downtown St. Louis

The 10-foot-high memorial is located at the gravesite of Cool Papa Bell.
Made of African granite, it honors "A Universal Legend" and commemorates
Bell's 1974 induction into the Hall of Fame. The monument was designed by
Connie Bell Brooks, Cool Papa's only child, and was dedicated on July 20,
1996—a day the state of Missouri proclaimed James "Cool Papa" Bell Day.

Handlan's Park

City: St. Louis
Location: St. Louis University

The former site of Handlan's Park, where
the St. Louis Terriers once played.

In 1914-1915, the St. Louis Terriers
played in the short-lived Federal
League at this site where Handlan's
Park used to stand. Ice magnate
Phil Ball, who later would become
owner of the St. Louis Browns,
owned the team. In their first season, the Terriers posted a 62-89
record (.411) and finished in last
place, 25 games behind the league
champion Indianapolis Hoosiers. The Terriers improved by a great deal the
next year, as they were pennant contenders up until the last game of the season. The Terriers had an 87-67 mark (.565), ending up in second place 1/10th
of a percentage point behind the champion Chicago Whales, who finished
86-66 (.566).

Among the better known St. Louis Terriers players who played in
the major leagues were Al Bridwell, Mordecai Brown, Bob Groom, Fielder
Jones, Eddie Plank, Jack Tobin and Ed Willett. On October 17, 2007, the St.

Louis Chapter of SABR placed a marker at the site of Handlan's Park, now on the campus of St. Louis University.

Pujols 5 Westport Grill
City: St. Louis
Location: 342 Westport Plaza
314-439-0505

In Albert Pujols's first six seasons, he's been the only player in Major League Baseball history to start his career with six 30+ home run seasons. Now the St. Louis Cardinals superstar runs a restaurant in town, a place that takes its name from the No. 5 jersey that Albert Pujols has worn for the St. Louis Cardinals since his rookie season in 2000. The theme is clear as the space features numerous well-placed plasma TV screens. Images of Cardinals baseball and all other high-profile sports are represented throughout. The menu includes many meal-sized salads, stone-fire pizzas and a gourmet touch on the appetizers. The highlights are the variety of chicken dishes. Steaks, sandwiches and pasta round out the menu, which has plenty of vegetarian options.

Red Stocking Base-Ball Park
City: St. Louis
Location: 3750 South Compton

Red Stocking Base-Ball Park was a baseball grounds that served as home to the St. Louis Red Stockings of the National Association during the 1875 season. (It was also known as Compton Avenue Baseball Park or just Compton Park, as it was bounded by Compton Avenue, Gratiot Street, railroad tracks, Theresa Avenue and Scott Street.) Baseball was played here off and on until the late 1890s when the ballpark was demolished. On September 13, 2008, a marker dedicating the site location was unveiled and presented by the Bob Broeg Chapter of the SABR, with permission of the Bi-State

The former site of the park where the St. Louis Red Stockings played.

Development Agency. It was financed with funds by the SABR Chapter Ballpark Marker Committee, which continues to do exceptional work in helping to place these significant markers.

Sportsman's Park

City: St. Louis
Location: Herbert Hoover Boys & Girls Club
2910 North Grand Avenue

Baseball at the intersection of Grand and Dodier dates all the way back to 1875, but the 20th century brand that St. Louis fans can still remember began in 1902, when the American League's Browns moved into the modern-era Sportsman's Park. The Browns were the lone inhabitants of Sportsman's for 18 years while the Cardinals played their games at Robison Field. Neither team enjoyed a lot of success over that period and in 1920, the Browns accepted their cross-league rivals as tenants, a Sportsman's Park relationship that would last for 34 years.

While the Browns continued to flounder for most of their St. Louis existence, the Cardinals suddenly jumped into the spotlight with their first National League pennant and World Series championship in 1926. It was the first of 10 pennants and seven fall classic wins they would bring to the the ballpark. The Browns, who would move to Baltimore in 1953 and become the Orioles, managed only one AL pennant—and lost to their co-tenant Cardinals in an all-St. Louis World Series in 1944. When the Browns moved in 1953, Anheuser-Busch, the new owner of the

The former site of Sportsman's Park, the once-proud home of the St. Louis Browns and Cardinals, now belongs to a youth club.

Cardinals, renamed the park Busch Stadium. It remained home to the Cardinals until May 8, 1966, when they moved into new Busch Memorial Stadium in downtown St. Louis. After the move, August A. Busch Jr. donated the property for use as a private recreational facility that eventually became the Herbert Hoover Boys & Girls Club. Several signs and a plaque still commemorate the decades of baseball that was played there, and there's even a youth baseball field with home plate located in what was the right field area of Sportsman's Park. It's still possible for diehard fans to play on the exact spot where almost 100 years of St. Louis baseball history took place.

Some Memorable Moments at Sportsman's Park

★ MAY 5, 1925: Detroit player-manager Ty Cobb hit three homers, a double and two singles, driving in five runs in a game against the Browns.

★ OCTOBER 9, 1944: The Cardinals won Game 6 of the all-St. Louis World Series, 3-1, over the Browns.

★ OCTOBER 15, 1946: Enos Slaughter's "Mad Dash" around the bases gave the Cardinals a stirring Game 7 victory over Boston in a dramatic World Series.

★ AUGUST 19, 1951: Midget Eddie Gaedel drew a walk in a pinch-hitting appearance for the Browns, another wild promotion by owner Bill Veeck.

★ MAY 2, 1954: Stan Musial homered five times in a doubleheader split with the New York Giants.

Keep Your Eyes Peeled for . . .

★ McGwire Highway (Interstate 70). When Cardinals first baseman Mark McGwire hit his 70th homer of the 1998 season, his adopted state of Missouri named a section of I-70 in his honor. The six-mile stretch runs just past Busch Stadium and is marked in both directions.

★ St. Louis Walk of Fame on the sidewalk of Delmar Boulevard in the Loop District of University City. Brass stars are laid into the sidewalk honoring actors, writers, musicians, teachers and, of course, baseball players. Look for Cool Papa Bell, Yogi Berra, Lou Brock, Dizzy Dean, Bob Gibson, Rogers Hornsby, Stan Musial, Branch Rickey, Red Schoendienst, Jack Buck, Harry Caray, Bob Costas and Joe Garagiola.

Hall of Famers Buried in Missouri

Bullet Joe Rogan
Blue Ridge Lawn Memorial Gardens
2640 South Blue Ridge Boulevard
Kansas City

Zack Wheat and Satchel Paige
Forest Hill & Calvary Cemetery
6901 Troost Avenue
Kansas City

**Charles "Kid" Nichols and
Hilton Smith**
Mount Moriah & Freeman Cemetery
10507 Holmes Street
Kansas City

Zack Wheat

Cal Hubbard
Oakwood Cemetery
Cherry Street
Milan

ST. LOUIS METROPOLITAN AREA

George Sisler
Old Meeting House Presbyterian
Church Cemetery
2250 North Geyer Road
Frontenac

Satchel Paige

Jim Bottomley
I. O. O. F. Community Cemetery
North Church Street
Sullivan

Joe Medwick
St. Lucas Cemetery
11735 Denny Road
Sunset Hills

Sunny Jim Bottomley

Nebraska

Johnny Rosenblatt Stadium

City: Omaha
Location: 1202 Bert Murphy Avenue

Johnny Rosenblatt Stadium holds the distinction of being the largest non-MLB professional baseball stadium. Home to both the minor-league Omaha Royals and the annual NCAA Division I College World Series, it's a fan-favorite park that dates back to 1947, and it hosted the Single-A Omaha Cardinals in the 1948 season. The first professional baseball team to call Omaha its home was the St. Louis Cardinals' farm team. During the next few years, Rosenblatt saw a few other teams play there. In 1969, the Kansas City Royals moved their Triple-A team here, and it is still here at Rosenblatt. In 1964, the stadium was rechristened in honor of the former Omaha mayor, Johnny Rosenblatt, who played a huge part in helping to bring professional baseball and the College World Series to Omaha. On April 30, 2008, the city and the NCAA agreed to keep the College World Series in Omaha for another 25 years through 2035, but with the acknowledgment that the series be moved to the new

Johnny Rosenblatt Stadium was at one time the largest non-MLB professional baseball stadium.

downtown stadium. And that's where things stand today for Rosenblatt Stadium. As of this writing, a new stadium has been ordered for the 2011 College World Series and the land on which Rosenblatt Stadium currently sits is to be sold to pay off the debt remaining from its own multimillion-dollar renovations. The adjacent Henry Doorly Zoo is set to take control of the land and demolish Rosenblatt once the new downtown stadium is completed. The stadium land itself is slated to be used for parking.

Museum of Nebraska Major League Baseball

City: St. Paul
Location: 619 Howard Avenue

Nebraska has produced more than 100 major-leaguers, and this wonderful little museum, located in Grover Cleveland Alexander's hometown, focuses primarily on the five local legends who made it to the Hall of Fame: Alexander, Dazzy Vance, Sam Crawford, Bob Gibson and Richie Ashburn. There are also displays for many other former major-leaguers who have roots in the state. Opened in 1991 and moved to its current location in 2000, the exhibits include balls, jerseys, autographs, books, programs, scrapbooks and more.

Grover Cleveland Alexander Historical Marker

City: St. Paul

Location: Alexander Avenue, which runs north of the North Loup River through Howard County

The marker dedicated to Alexander is near an American Legion field that is also named for him. Alexander, the outstanding right-handed pitcher who won 373 major-league games over his 20-year career, died here on November 4, 1950, and he is buried at Elmwood Cemetery in St. Paul.

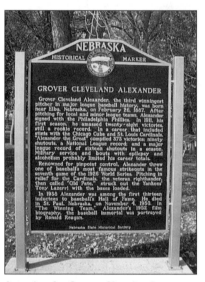

A marker for Grover Cleveland Alexander near St. Paul, Nebraska.

Richie Ashburn Field

City: Tilden

Location: 100 Center Street

Richie Ashburn, born in Tilden on March 19, 1927, was one of the most popular players of his era. The speedy former Philadelphia Philles center fielder topped the .300 plateau nine times, collected 2,574 hits and won batting titles in 1955 and '58. Ashburn, a career .308 hitter, was a member of the young, energetic 1950 Whiz Kids, who won the National League pennant on the last day of the season before losing to the Yankees in the World Series. After retiring as a player, Ashburn worked as a Phillies broadcaster for 35 years, many in the booth alongside legendary Harry Kalas. Ashburn was inducted into the Hall of Fame in 1995—the same day later Phillies great Mike Schmidt went in—and he died in New York in 1997. The municipal ballpark was renamed Ashburn Field in his honor and a display of Ashburn memorabilia, once located at a Tilden pharmacy, can be found at the Madison County Historical Society Museum, 210 West 3rd Street, Madison.

The museum is open weekdays from 2:00–5:00 PM and other times by special appointment.

Sam Crawford Field

City: Wahoo
Location: 5th and Elm Street

"Wahoo" Sam Crawford, born here on April 18, 1880, was a Cincinnati and Detroit star from baseball's dead-ball era. "Wahoo Sam" was one of the game's early sluggers, a long-ball threat and longtime outfield mate of Ty Cobb. Crawford is best remembered for the all-time record 312 triples he posted over a 19-year career. The one-two punch of Crawford and Cobb led Detroit to three consecutive American League pennants (1907-09), but the Tigers lost each year in the World Series. He wound up with 2,961 hits and a career batting average of .309. Crawford was elected to the Hall of Fame in 1957 and died in Southern California on June 15, 1968. The field named for him is used for youth baseball.

Sam Crawford was one of more than 100 former players with Nebraska roots.

North Dakota

Roger Maris Museum

City: Fargo
Location: West Acres Shopping Center
I-29 and 13th Avenue South

This hometown tribute to Maris—accessible to all and free at Maris's request—is a freestanding exhibit along the wall of one of the mall's corridors. Curator James R. McLaughlin has done an outstanding job paying tribute to Fargo's famous son, who died in 1985. Maris, who was born in Hibbing, Minnesota, on September 10, 1934, landed in Fargo when his father, a railroad worker, moved there in 1942. Both Roger and older brother Rudy became local legends, multi-sport athletes

The "Roger Maris wall" sits outside Lindenwood Park, where the Roger Maris Baseball League plays.

who starred at Fargo's Shanley High School. But Roger ended up stealing the spotlight. He returned four kickoffs for touchdowns in one high school football game and led the local American Legion baseball team to a state championship. The legend grew when Maris went on to major-league success with the Cleveland Indians, Kansas City Athletics, New York Yankees and St. Louis Cardinals—most notably as a two-time American League MVP with the Yankees and the man who broke Babe Ruth's single-season home run record. When Maris hit 61 homers in 1961, he became one of the most celebrated athletes in baseball history. The mall exhibit celebrates his 12-year career through videos, photos, bats, balls, trophies and many other Maris-related artifacts.

Roger Maris's grave in Fargo, North Dakota.

There are Maris reminders throughout Fargo. He played American Legion baseball at Barnett Field in north Fargo, where North High School now sits. There is Roger Maris Field and Roger Maris Drive in Lindenwood Park, where the Roger Maris Baseball League now plays. There is the Roger Maris Cancer Center and Roger Maris Gardens, a shrine for the modest, underappreciated baseball hero at Fargo's Jack Williams Stadium.

Roger Maris is buried at Holy Cross Cemetery in Fargo.

Ohio

Blue Ash Sports Center
City: Blue Ash
Location: 11540 Grooms Road

Within this multi-field sports complex, the spirit of old Crosley Field lives on. That's because the fan-friendly Cincinnati ballpark has been "reconstructed." Using original Crosley blueprints, the Crosley Field Restoration Project was dedicated to the "Youth of Baseball" in July 1988. The field includes the same dimensions, a grass infield, the infamous outfield terrace and an outfield wall with the same distances, heights and angles that were found at original Crosley. The reconstructed scoreboard is five stories high and has the same look that was found at Crosley when the last pitch was thrown there on June 24, 1970. Many original Crosley Field items have been acquired through donation and acquisition (including more than 400 original seats) and other artifacts were salvaged from a similar Crosley Field restoration project that had taken place in Kentucky. There are several plaques, an original ticket booth and handprints in cement, left by former Cincinnati stars. This new "Crosley Field" is home for many leagues as well as high school games (Moeller High), college games and other events and activities. It has also played host to several Old-Timers games.

Thurman Munson Memorial Stadium
City: Canton
Location: 2501 Allen Avenue SE

Thurman Munson Memorial Stadium (home to the Canton Coyotes in the Frontier League) was completed in 1989, named after the late Yankees catcher who was a graduate of Canton Lehman High School. Munson, a six-time All-Star, played 11 years with the New York Yankees and was named the American League Rookie of the Year in 1970 and AL MVP in 1976. Over his career, Thurman hit 113 home runs, drove in 701 runs and posted a career batting average of .292. Munson died tragically in a 1979 plane crash and his uniform, No. 15, is displayed on the center field wall at Munson Stadium.

Riverfront Stadium
City: Cincinnati
Location: Main Street

Riverfront Stadium was one of the circular "cookie-cutter" stadiums constructed in the United States in the late 1960s and early 1970s. These generic-looking stadiums were built as a means to help communities save money by having both their football and baseball teams play at the same place (called "multi-use stadiums"). In addition to Riverfront, Busch Stadium in St. Louis, Atlanta-Fulton County Stadium in Atlanta, Three Rivers Stadium in Pittsburgh, Shea Stadium in New York, RFK Stadium in Washington DC, Jack Murphy Stadium in San Diego and Veterans Stadium in Philadelphia were all built within a few years of each other (and today, only the parks in San Diego and Washington are still standing). Riverfront was often confused with Three Rivers Stadium in Pittsburgh by sportscasters because of the two stadiums' similar names and layouts. Interestingly, the exact site where Riverfront Stadium sat included the footprint of the 2nd Street tenement birthplace and boyhood home of famed cowboy singer and actor Roy Rogers. In fact, Rogers used to joke that he was born "somewhere between second base and center field."

Today, the ballpark is gone, of course, and the former site of the stadium is partially taken up by the Cincinnati Reds Hall of Fame and Museum. It was created by the Reds franchise and it pays homage to the team's past through displays, photographs and multimedia. Currently, the Hall of Fame section includes 71 inductees, encompassing players, managers, announcers, executives, and other contributors to the Reds franchise, dating back to 1869. In fact, the Reds are Major League Baseball's oldest team. The Hall of Fame existed only in the abstract from 1958 to 2002, despite several attempts to create a physical place. However, with the opening of Great American Ball Park in 2003, a physical facility finally became real. It's located on the west side of the park on Main Street and includes two floors. And again, it's partially located on the site of the Reds' former home, Riverfront Stadium, which makes for a nice "Remember when we used to see ball games here?" observation when you visit.

The hall also pays homage to Pete Rose, despite the controversial nature of his career. The exhibit dedicated to "Charlie Hustle" covers his career as baseball's all-time hits leader, even though he is currently under a lifetime ban from baseball. Artifacts of Rose's include: the bat and ball from hit 4,192; balls from hits leading up to 4,192; artifacts from the Crosley and Riverfront/Cinergy years; gloves that he used playing outfield, second base, third base, and first base; a uniform shirt from Pete's high school (Western Hills—also the alma mater of major-leaguers Don Zimmer, Eddie Brinkman, Russ Nixon and others); baseball cards; *Sports Illustrated* covers of Pete; and the "wall of balls" representing all 4,256 of Pete's hits.

Crosley Field
City: Cincinnati
Location: Findlay Street and Western Avenue

Cincinnati baseball was played at this site from 1884–1970, 59 of those years in cozy, fan-friendly Redland Field/Crosley Field. League Park sat at Findlay and Western from 1884–1901 before burning down. The ornate Palace of the Fans served as home of the Reds until the more modern, steel-and-concrete Redland opened in 1912. It remained Redland Field until 1934, when the name was officially changed to Crosley Field in in honor of new owner Powel Crosley Jr. Crosley Field was known for its irregular contours and simple, intimate atmosphere. Left fielders had to negotiate a terrace that began sloping upward about 20 feet from the wall, reaching a four-foot grade. Fans in right field enjoyed the Sun Deck and those bleachers intersected at a point with the center field wall, necessitating a white line with a hand-painted ground rule that read, "Batted Ball Hitting Concrete Wall on Fly to Right of White Line—Home Run." For many years, the tin roof of a laundry, the Superior Towel & Linen Service, provided an inviting target for home run hitters over the left field wall. Players had to walk through the third base stands to get to the field from their clubhouses. In January of 1937, Crosley Field virtually disappeared when a massive flood covered it with more than

20 feet of water. Seizing the moment, Reds pitchers Lee Grissom and Gene Schott posed for a now-famous photo rowing a boat over the center field fence. The last game at Crosley was played in 1970, when the Reds moved to Riverfront Stadium. Today, in an industrial park, a historic marker identifies the site of home plate (and some Crosley Field chairs are also on display).

Baseball Heritage Museum

City: Cleveland
Location: Located inside Cleveland's Historic Colonial Marketplace
530 Euclid Avenue
216-978-5068

The Baseball Heritage Museum is a museum in Cleveland devoted primarily to exploring the history of baseball leagues other than the major leagues.

Some Memorable Moments at Crosley Field

★ OCTOBER 1, 1919: The Reds won Game 1 of the World Series here, 9-1. Cincinnati's first World Series is also remembered as the "Black Sox" classic, in which eight members of the White Sox conspired with gamblers to lose. Chicago starter Eddie Cicotte reportedly signaled that the fix was on when he hit the first Reds batter, Morrie Rath, with a pitch.

★ MAY 24, 1935: The first night game in major-league history was played here, with President Franklin Delano Roosevelt throwing a switch from the White House to turn on the lights. The Reds beat the Philadelphia Phillies, 2-1.

★ MAY 27, 1937: Giants pitcher Carl Hubbell shut down the Reds in a rare relief appearance and received credit for his 24th straight win—a still-standing major-league record.

★ JUNE 11, 1938: Johnny Vander Meer pitched the first of two consecutive no-hitters, beating Boston 3-0. He came back on June 15 to no-hit the Dodgers at Ebbets Field.

★ JUNE 10, 1944: The youngest player in major-league history, 15-year-old Reds left-hander Joe Nuxhall, pitched two-thirds of an inning, giving up five runs on five walks, two singles and a wild pitch.

The museum grew out of Robert Zimmer's famed collection, focusing primarily on the Negro Leagues, women's leagues, Caribbean leagues, and industrial and barnstorming leagues. Former Cleveland Indians infielder Vern Fuller is the executive director. The museum includes many rare photos, jerseys, programs, letters, autographs and a wonderful gift shop detailing the important contributions from the Negro, Latin, Caribbean, Women's, and Industrial and Barnstormer leagues. A very interesting, unique collection that sheds light on many of baseball's lesser-known stars and leagues.

League Park

City: Cleveland
Location: East 66th Street and Lexington Avenue

Baseball was played at East 66th and Lexington as far back as 1891. But the steel-and-concrete League Park that entertained Cleveland fans with its quirky dimensions and odd rectangular shape was erected in 1910 and remained in use through 1946. League Park, which was called Dunn Field from 1920 to 1927, measured a whopping 375 feet down the left field line and an inviting 290 to the right, where drooling hitters were frustrated by a 40-foot combination con-

A youth center now occupies the building that once housed League Park's ticket booth and team offices.

crete-and-wire fence that knocked down potential home runs and created erratic bounces. Life was never dull in Cleveland. League Park never had a seating capacity over 22,000 and its final 14 seasons were shared with massive Municipal Stadium—home games at League during the week, at Municipal on weekends. The Indians finally moved into Municipal Stadium for good after the 1946 season. The ballpark was demolished in 1951, but remnants of the stadium remain. The two-story ticket booth, which also housed team offices, is now a youth center; a crumbling piece of the first-base grandstand still stands. The stripped-down diamond still exists at its original location. There is also a historic marker as well as rumblings about a plan to renovate the park as part of a neighborhood revitalization plan.

Some Memorable Moments at League Park

★ OCTOBER 10, 1920: Indians second baseman Bill Wambsganss made World Series history by completing an unassisted triple play in Game 5 against Brooklyn. In the same game, Elmer Smith hit the first World Series grand slam and Jim Bagby hit the first World Series homer by a pitcher.

★ AUGUST 11, 1929: Babe Ruth hit his 500th home run against the Indians.

★ SEPTEMBER 13, 1936: A 17-year-old Bob Feller struck out 17 Athletics in a two-hit victory.

★ JULY 16, 1941: Yankees center fielder Joe DiMaggio stretched his hitting streak to 56 games.

Municipal Stadium
City: Cleveland
Location: On the shore of Lake Erie between the lake and downtown Cleveland

Built in 1931 and opened in 1932 for baseball and other events, Municipal Stadium (also called Cleveland Stadium) was a ballpark for the ages. It was cavernous, an 80,000-seat steel-and-concrete monster built with hopes of landing the 1932 Olympics, which were ultimately held at the Los Angeles Coliseum. The Indians did not move to Municipal Stadium full-time until 1947, choosing to play 14 years at smaller League Park on weekdays and at Municipal Stadium on weekends and holidays. The center field bleachers at Cleveland Stadium were 470 feet from home plate and no batted ball ever reached them. On September 12, 1954, the Indians and Yankees played in front of 86,563 fans, the largest crowd in baseball history until the Dodgers moved into the Los Angeles Coliseum. Municipal was also home to the

Municipal Stadium, the massive home for Cleveland baseball and football, began its tenure as a weekend and holiday facility while weekday games were played at smaller League Park.

National Football League's Cleveland Browns and hosted college football, boxing, track and every other imaginable event. There was nothing glitzy about Municipal Stadium, which was dubbed by visitors as "The Mistake by the Lake." But the stadium was never lacking for excitement, thanks to such players as Bob Feller, Lou Boudreau, Larry Doby, Early Wynn, Rocky Colavito and Satchel Paige. The site of the stadium, which was demolished in 1996, is now occupied by the Browns' new football stadium. But the remains of the stadium still draw crowds—of fish. The rubble from the stadium was used to construct two 600-foot artificial reefs along the Lake Erie waterfront.

Some Memorable Moments at Municipal Stadium

★ The All-Star Games of 1935, '54, '63 and '81.

★ JULY 17, 1941: Joe DiMaggio's consecutive-game hitting streak ended at 56 in a 4–3 Yankees' win. Indians third baseman Ken Keltner twice robbed DiMaggio of hits.

★ JULY 17, 1960: Boston's Ted Williams hit his 500th career home run against Indians pitcher Wynn Hawkins.

★ MAY 15, 1981: Indians right-hander Len Barker pitched a perfect game, retiring all 27 Blue Jays he faced in a 3–0 victory.

★ APRIL 12, 1992: Boston left-hander Matt Young tossed a no-hitter—and lost to the Indians, 2–1.

Historic Cooper Stadium
City: Columbus
Location: 1155 West Mound Street

"The Coop" is home to the Columbus Clippers. It was built in 1931, when Branch Rickey purchased the Columbus Red Birds. Needing a new park, Rickey bought what was then farmland for $450,000 and had Red Bird Stadium built. The Red Birds left after the 1954 season and were replaced by the Columbus Jets, who played at Jets Stadium for 15 years. By 1970, the stadium had fallen into disrepair and the Jets departed. In 1977, Franklin County commissioner Harold Cooper, who had led the drive to lure the Jets in 1955, pushed for a stadium renovation and another professional team.

He got both. Columbus got the Clippers and the park, now called Franklin County Stadium, received a multimillion-dollar renovation. In 1984, the stadium was renamed to honor Cooper and plaques throughout the park document its historic past. Currently, there are plans afoot for the Clippers to move from Cooper Stadium at the conclusion of the 2008 season. The new ballpark, known as Huntington Park, will be located in the Arena District near Nationwide Arena. On September 1, 2008, the final game was played here as the Toledo Mud Hens bested the Columbus Clippers in front of a sell-out crowd of 16,770 fans, the third largest crowd in stadium history. As of May 1, 2008, a proposal to turn the site of Cooper Stadium into an auto racing facility was still in the discussion phase.

Stephan Field

City: Indian Hill
Location: Southeastern corner of Drake and Shawnee Run

A plaque marks Stephan Field, a place of the heart that was never home to Hall of Famers, but that still very much affects the lives of the people who live here. It is named for Paul Stephan, a man whose enthusiastic promotion of "knothole baseball" earned praise and whose leadership inspired hundreds of boys in the 1950s and '60s.

In 1953, Paul Jr. asked his father to manage his baseball team. Paul agreed, thus starting his legendary commitment to area baseball. Although he had never played the game, Stephan was a loyal Reds

Local hero Paul Stephan is honored for his undying commitment to the game.

fan and he coached and managed teams here for two of his sons. He didn't stop there, dedicating his time to many other teams and players for more than 20 years. The 1950s "knothole teams" practiced wherever they could get a field and Paul was a one-man operation, doing everything from lining and dragging the fields, carpooling, scheduling, and finding umpires, sponsors, uniforms and equipment, etc. His wife, Alice, helped with storing and mending uniforms as her husband preached the gospel of baseball to hundreds of youngsters—teaching them to love the game.

From one team in 1953 to three in 1955 to 12 in 1962, the homegrown league was designed to help kids have a good time playing while learning about values and sportsmanship. In recognition of Paul's volunteer labor, Stephan Field was dedicated in August of 1964. The ceremony included speeches by the mayor and council members, and three Cincinnati players delivered a letter of commendation from the Reds. Today's Stephan Field is used for baseball, soccer, picnics and other family-related activities. And the plaque honors the man who helped teach baseball's magical lessons to many children.

Jimmie Foxx Memorial Field

City: Lakewood
Location: Kauffman Park
Arthur Avenue (north end)

On August 8, 2000, the city of Lakewood dedicated this field to Jimmie Foxx, who made Lakewood his home after playing baseball. He raised his family here and became an integral part of the community,

Hall of Famer Jimmie Foxx made Lakewood his home after retiring.

volunteering many hours on the town's sandlot baseball fields. Members of his family unveiled the plaque at the ceremony and several former players, including Herb Score and Mel Harder, took part in the event.

Cy Young Park

City: Newcomerstown
Location: 591 North College Street

A park, monument and museum exhibit honor the great Cy Young.

Cy Young's career numbers defy logic. He won 511 games—94 more than any other pitcher—over a 22-year career that straddled the turn of the century. He also pitched 749 complete games, compiled a career 2.63 ERA and posted 15 20-win seasons, five of 30 or more. Born in this area in 1867, Young made his major-league debut in 1890 with Cleveland in the National League, subsequently pitched for the St. Louis Nationals and spent the final 11 seasons of his career in the American League for Boston and Cleveland. Young was a two-game winner for the Red Sox in the first World Series in 1903 and he made history on May 5, 1904, when he pitched the first perfect game of the 20th century, stopping the Philadelphia Athletics, 3-0. Young, who also threw no-hitters in 1897 and 1908, is the namesake for the annual awards handed out to the AL and NL top pitchers. Young finished his career with the Boston Braves in 1911 and was voted into the Hall of Fame in 1937. He died in Newcomerstown on November 4, 1955. Young's namesake ballpark hosts youth baseball and a monument honors his memory. Exhibits and artifacts at the Newcomerstown Historical Society Museum also honor Young , as well as the town's other local sports legend, former Ohio State football coach Woody Hayes.

Wesley Branch Rickey Boyhood Home
City: Rushtown
Location: 770 Duck Run

Branch Rickey helped break baseball's color barrier by signing up Jackie Robinson with the Brooklyn Dodgers, who became the modern major league's first African-American player in 1947. In honor of him, a marker here reads:

Branch Rickey

"Boyhood Home of Wesley Branch Rickey, Baseball Pioneer, Innovator, Executive" Branch Rickey, a pivotal figure in the history of baseball, was raised in this house with his brothers, Orla and Frank. Rickey started baseball's farm team system while he was president, vice president, and manager of the St. Louis Cardinals from 1917-1942. As president of the Brooklyn Dodgers from 1942-1950, he signed Jackie Robinson to a major league contract, which resulted in the desegregation of baseball. "The Mahatma," as Rickey was known, also ran the Pittsburgh Pirates from 1950-1955. Rickey's career in major league baseball began in 1904 as a Cincinnati Red. Later he played with the St. Louis Browns and the New York Highlanders (now known as the Yankees). Branch

A boyhood home marker honors the memory of Branch Rickey, the pioneer and innovator who grew up in Rushtown.

Rickey was born in 1881 and died in 1965. He was posthumously inducted into the Baseball Hall of Fame in 1967. His grave is located approximately one mile southeast of this marker on the eastern edge of Rush Township Cemetery.

Note that the property is privately owned. The maple trees Branch Rickey supposedly planted on both sides of the rural road are now mature and have grown into a lovely archway.

Swayne Field

City: Toledo
Location: Monroe Street and Detroit Avenue

Swayne Field, which opened in 1909, was home to the legendary Toledo Mud Hens until it was torn down in 1956. It was named for Noah Swayne, a prominent Toledo lawyer and baseball fan. From 1926 to 1931, Casey Stengel managed the Hens, which all but guaranteed huge crowds. Other Mud Hens stars included Bill Terry, Hack Wilson and Roger Bresnahan, a local hero. The area today is the site of the Swayne Field Shopping Center.

Wakeman Red Cap Field

City: Wakeman
Location: Intersection of US 20 and Cooper Street in Fletcher Park

A marker near the site of Wakeman Red Cap Field.

A marker honors the former site of Wakeman's Red Cap Field, home of one of this area's best semipro teams during the 1930s and '40s. Lights were installed at Wakeman Field on July 24, 1935, making it possible for night baseball to be played here just two months after Cincinnati's Crosley Field hosted the first night game in major-league history. The Red Caps were part of the Wakeman Baseball Club, which existed to encourage aspiring ballplayers. Wakeman Field was visited annually by Harlem Globetrotters founder Abe Saperstein's Ethiopian Clowns, a traveling African-American team. Appearances were made by such legends as Satchel Paige, Josh Gibson, Al Schacht and Jesse Owens.

"Sad" Sam Jones/Mary Weddle-Hines Historical Marker
City: Woodsfield
Location: Creamery Street

A two-sided historic marker commemorates two local sports legends. Sam Jones, dubbed "Sad Sam" by a New York sportswriter who thought he always looked downcast, pitched for 22 seasons in the American League. Jones's signature season was 1923, when he finished 21–8 for the New York Yankees and threw a no-hitter against the Philadelphia Athletics. The Yankees won their first World Series that year (beating the Giants) and Jones's relief effort helped the Yanks secure their Game 6 clincher. Despite his nickname, the 229-game career winner was actually a whimsical and humorous man.

Mary Weddle-Hines played for the Fort Wayne Daisies of the All-American Girls Professional Baseball League in 1954. A trailblazer for women athletes, Weddle-Hines originally played professional softball before joining the Daisies. She was one of about 600 women to play in the league.

Keep Your Eyes Peeled for . . .

★ The Westville Sign at the edge of town reading "Hometown of Harvey Haddix."

★ The Bob Feller statue positioned outside of Cleveland's Jacobs Field.

Hall of Famers Buried in Ohio

William "Buck" Ewing
Mount Washington Cemetery
Mount Washington

Waite Hoyt and Miller Huggins
Spring Grove Cemetery
4521 Spring Grove Avenue
Cincinnati

Waite Hoyt

Walter Alston
Darrtown Cemetery
Shollenbarger Road
Darrtown

Eppa Rixey
Green Lawn Cemetery
687 US Highway 50
Milford

Cy Young
Peoli Cemetery (in yard
of United Methodist Church)
State Route 258
Peoli

Miller Huggins

CLEVELAND METRO AREA

Red Ruffing
Hillcrest Memorial Park
26700 Aurora Road
Bedford Heights

Ed Delahanty
Calvary Cemetery
10000 Miles Avenue
Cleveland

Eppa Rixey

Billy Evans
Knollwood Cemetery
1678 Som Center Road
Mayfield Heights

Elmer Flick
Crown Hill Cemetery
8592 Darrow Road
Twinsburg

Jesse Haines
Bethel Cemetery
Phillipsburg Road
Phillipsburg

Jesse Haines

Roger Bresnahan
Calvary Cemetery
2224 Dorr Street
Toledo

Addie Joss
Woodlawn Cemetery
1502 West Central Avenue
Toledo

Oklahoma

Shrine to Mickey Mantle

City: Grove
Location: Hollywood at Home Video Store
536 West 3rd Street, Suite 7

Terry and Valerie Hembree were close friends of "The Mick." For 12 years, they helped coordinate his marketing and charity efforts and over the years acquired numerous artifacts from their pal. Today, this dedicated husband and wife make it possible for everyone to enjoy their one-of-a-kind collection of Mickey Mantle memorabilia at the video store they run in Grove. This exhibit features thousands of items dedicated to the memory of Mantle, including memorabilia from his younger days in Commerce and his pre-profession-

A video store in Grove celebrates the career of Mickey Mantle, who hailed from Commerce.

al days with the Baxter Springs Whiz Kids. Also highlighted are details of his New York Yankees career, numerous statues and figurines, balls, bats, gloves, jerseys, collector's items, autographed items and a variety of baseball cards from every era. TV monitors play Mantle game highlights, with interviews and stories told by Mick himself. And keep your eyes open when you visit—you might see an old ballplayer or two, both former teammates and opponents who have been known to drop in unexpectedly.

Other Mickey Mantle-Related Sites in Oklahoma

★ Mickey Mantle's boyhood home, 316 South Quincy Street, Commerce.

★ Commerce High School at 420 D Street in Commerce. This is where Mantle attended high school. In 2000, a ceremony was held to name the baseball field "Mickey Mantle Field."

★ Mickey Mantle Boulevard. This road, which passes within a few blocks of Mantle's boyhood home, is a renamed section of US 69.

★ Portrait of Mickey Mantle at the State Capitol Building in Oklahoma City. Several years ago, a portrait of Mickey Mantle was unveiled at the capitol on the fourth-floor rotunda of the building.

Oklahoma Sports Museum
City: Guthrie
Location: 315 West Oklahoma Avenue
405-260-1342

Opened in 1996, this 30,000-square-foot museum has a remarkable number of items staked in the rich heritage of Oklahoma baseball. Tributes are paid to all Oklahoma-related Hall of Famers, including Mickey Mantle, Ferguson Jenkins, Paul and Lloyd Waner, Carl Hubbell, Willie Stargell and Warren Spahn. The museum gives out the "Warren Spahn Award" to the major leagues' most dominant left-handed pitcher. Throughout the museum are historic baseball items, including Pepper Martin's 1931 World Series jacket and Bobby Murcer's rocking chair, which used to sit beside his locker at Yankee Stadium. Hundreds of jerseys, bats and balls are also on display.

The Oklahoma Sports Museum in Guthrie honors Oklahoma baseball legends, including Mickey Mantle, Carl Hubbell and Warren Spahn.

Waner Park

City: Harrah
Location: Right off 23rd Street and Peebly Road

Lloyd and Paul Waner, both Hall of Famers, hail from Harrah. It's no surprise that the Little League field, the same area where they played as kids, is named for them. Their combined total of 5,611 hits are a record for major-league brothers—Paul with 3,152, Lloyd with 2,459. For a good part of their careers in the 1920s and '30s, the brothers formed two-thirds of the Pittsburgh Pirates outfield.

Lloyd Waner is buried at Rose Hill Burial Park, 6001 NW Grand Boulevard, Oklahoma City.

Carl Hubbell Exhibit

City: Meeker
Location: Meeker City Hall
West Main Street

In addition to the sign that welcomes visitors to Hubbell's hometown, there is also an exhibit for him at the local city hall. Hubbell, the Hall of Fame left-hander known for his devastating screwball, played 16 seasons for the New York Giants (1928–43), winning 253 games. Visitors to city hall can see many Hubbell artifacts, including his personal scrapbook and a collection of baseballs autographed by such contemporaries as Babe Ruth and Lou Gehrig.

Meeker, the birthplace of Carl Hubbell, honors the pitching great with a welcome sign and an exhibit at city hall.

Carl Hubbell is buried at Meeker New Hope, State Highway 18 (one mile south of US Highway 62), Meeker.

Mickey Mantle and Johnny Bench Statues

City: Oklahoma City
Location: Bricktown Ballpark
2 South Mickey Mantle Drive

"The Brick," as Southwestern Bell Bricktown Ballpark is informally known, opened in 1998 and is home to the Pacific Coast League's Oklahoma Redhawks. The Brick is a gorgeous retro park where fans can get close to the ac-

tion. Oklahoma legends Mantle
and Bench are honored by statues
outside the park. The Mantle display also includes his handprints
in cement.

National Softball Hall of Fame and Museum

City: Oklahoma City
Location: 2801 NE 50th Street
405-424-5266

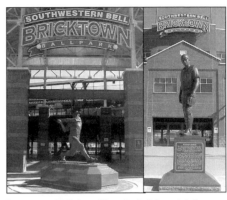

Statues of Mickey Mantle (left) and Johnny
Bench (right) greet visitors at "The Brick" in
Oklahoma City.

The museum here, dedicated to
the history of softball, is located
at the ballpark. Established in
1957, it honors hundreds of players from the amateur game of softball and
features many artifacts. As for the ASA Hall of Fame Stadium, it is widely
regarded as the finest softball facility in the nation and has played host to
the best softball competition in the world, including USA teams that represent the nation in international competitions. Among the most recent USA
Softball National Teams to play in ASA Hall of Fame Stadium were the 2007
USA Women's and Men's National Teams, which brought home the gold
in the World Cup of Softball 3 and the first American Challenge Series.
Annually, ASA Hall of Fame Stadium plays host to a wide variety of softball
events, including the nation's number one collegiate contest, the NCAA
Women's College World Series (WCWS), which
annually draws more than 63,000 spectators from
around the nation. ASA Hall of Fame Stadium has
hosted the event 15 times and is scheduled as the
home of the WCWS through 2008.

Jim Thorpe Birthplace

City: Prague
Location: South on Highway 99 to Moccasin Trail,
five miles west and one mile south.
(Note: turn south one mile, then turn west after
you pass the Pleasant Home Baptist Church.)

A historic marker identifies where the great Thorpe
was born on May 28, 1887. The short "Jim Thorpe
Road" is about a half mile from the marker, just south
of Prague near State Highway 99.

Jim Thorpe's former
Yale home is near his
hometown of Prague.

Jim Thorpe Monument

City: Prague
Location: Prague Historical Museum
Junction of Highway 62 and Highway 99

Outside this museum, which also sells Thorpe-related books, postcards, etc., is a historic marker identifying the area as Jim Thorpe's hometown.

Jim Thorpe Home

City: Yale
Location: 706 East Boston

The legendary Olympian, baseball and football star lived in this house from 1917 to 1923. Thorpe, who is better known for his ties to college and professional football, played six years of Major League Baseball for the Giants, Reds and Braves. Many sports awards and family items are on display. The home, which he purchased for his family, is located near his birthplace in Prague. About 100 yards away from the home is State Highway 51, also called the "Jim Thorpe Memorial Highway."

Keep Your Eyes Peeled for . . .

★ A sign in Binger announcing it as hometown of Johnny Bench.

★ A sign in Meeker announcing it as hometown of Carl Hubbell.

★ Joe Carter Avenue in Oklahoma City.

Hall of Famers Buried in Oklahoma

Joe McGinnity
Oak Hill Cemetery
1311 East Washington
McAlester

Joe McGinnity won 20 or more games seven times.

South Dakota

Babe Ruth Stayed Here
City: Deadwood
Location: Historic Franklin Hotel
700 Main Street

Built in 1903, the Historic Franklin Hotel has played host to thousands of famous and infamous people. It was during a 1921 barnstorming tour that Babe Ruth first stayed at the Franklin, which is located in one of the oldest active gold-mining towns in the country. Ruth played at the nearby First Ward Rodeo Grounds, where a baseball diamond still exists. To honor some of its many famous guests, the Franklin Hotel has a number of "historic" rooms that are themed after the celebrities, both sports and otherwise, who slept there. Room 209 is the Babe Ruth room, and it comes complete with photos and other Ruth-related items. Rooms are also named after boxers Jack Dempsey and John L. Sullivan.

South Dakota Amateur Baseball Hall of Fame
City: Lake Norden
Location: 519 Main Street
605-785-3553

This small museum offers a pictorial history of the amateur game in South Dakota. It also has artifacts from about half of the 24 big leaguers who were born in the state. There is also archival material and memorabilia relating to the history of amateur baseball in South Dakota since 1900.

The Birth of American Legion Baseball
City: Milbank
Location: Next to the Unity Square Athletic Complex
904 4th Avenue East (Highway 12)

American Legion Baseball was born here in 1925 and a historical marker commemorates the event near the community baseball field. A portion of the inscription reads, "In this city on July 17, 1925, by action of the South Dakota Department of the American Legion, the nationwide organization of Legion Junior Baseball was first proposed as a program of service to the youth of America." Since 1926, the league's first official year, millions of teenagers have played in the renowned national youth league, including such Hall of Famers as George Brett, Richie Ashburn, Reggie Jackson, Joe

Morgan, Johnny Bench, Don Drysdale, Brooks Robinson, Ted Williams and Stan Musial.

Sioux Falls Stadium

City: Sioux Falls
Location: 1001 North West Avenue

Built in 1941, Sioux Falls Stadium is nicknamed "The Birdcage" in honor of the Northern League's Canaries who play there. Baseball in Sioux Falls dates back to 1885, with the "Canaries" making their first appearance in 1889. The Sioux Falls team of that era wore bright yellow uniforms and were called the "Yellow Kids," in honor of the well-known "Yellow Kid" promoted by the William Randolph Hearst newspapers (and whose comic appeared in the *Sioux Falls Press*). When a local sportswriter suggested the team change its name to Canaries, the moniker stuck. This park was home to the Northern League Canaries in 1942 and again from 1946 to 1953. The city went without a franchise until 1966, when the Sioux Falls Packers began play. The Packers ceased operations after the 1971 campaign and the park was used sparingly until 1993, when the independent Northern League was formed. Extensive renovations to the park began in 1999 and were completed two years later. Today, the stadium is a testament to the proper blending of modern conveniences within a classic, throwback structure. Photographs throughout the park document its long and colorful history.

Renovated Sioux Falls Stadium is an ideal place to go on a warm summer evening to watch the local Canaries.

Wisconsin

Davy Jones Marker

City: Cambria
Location: Cambria-Friesland Historical Society
Wagoner House
112 North Madison Street

David Jefferson "Davy" Jones played 15 seasons with a number of teams, including the Milwaukee Brewers, St. Louis Browns, Chicago Cubs, Detroit Tigers, Chicago White Sox, and Pittsburgh Rebels. He also played alongside some of the early legends of the game, including Ty Cobb, Sam Crawford, Frank Chance, Three Finger Brown, Hugh Duffy and Jesse Burkett. Also, Jones played part of one season with the Chicago White Sox, where several of his teammates would later be implicated in the 1919 "Black Sox" scandal. Lawrence S. Ritter immortalized Jones in the classic baseball book *The Glory of Their Times*, interviewing him along many of the other players of the Deadball Era. Rather than being a full-time player, Jones was more of a platoon player who was an average hitter and a fast runner. He played in the major leagues from 1901 to 1918, compiling a .270 career batting average with over 1,000 hits.

Born in Cambria as David Jefferson, he later changed his last name to Jones. Jones attended college at Northern Illinois University, and learned to be a druggist before becoming a ballplayer while living in Portage and Mauston, Wisconsin. Because of this, Davy Jones would go on to purchase a drugstore in Detroit in 1910 during his playing days where he'd work in the off-season. Jones was 21 years old when he broke into the big leagues on September 15, 1901, with the Milwaukee Brewers. The marker here was placed by David Stalker, a tireless, dedicated fan from Watertown, Wisconsin. In the last six years or so, he has been on a campaign to have markers placed in honor of Deadball Era players (and now some others) and to date, he has researched, created and placed seven markers, with four more in the works).

Burleigh Grimes Exhibit

City: Clear Lake
Location: One floor of the Clear Lake Area Historical Museum
450 Fifth Avenue

Open from Memorial Day through Labor Day, the Burleigh Grimes exhibit has been on display in his hometown for three decades. When he retired in 1934, Grimes was the last of the legal spitballers, a fiery and competitive pitcher for seven different teams. Over his 19 big-league seasons, Grimes topped the 20-win plateau five times and posted a 270–212 record. He was just 26 when the spitter, his money pitch, was banned in 1920. But he was one of 17 pitchers who were exempted from the ban because of their veteran status. Grimes relied on the pitch for the rest of his career. The museum exhibit, lovingly maintained by several of Grimes's old friends, is loaded with memorabilia. Grimes was inducted into the Hall of Fame in 1964 and died in Clear Lake on December 6, 1985, at the age of 92. He is buried at Clear Lake Cemetery, 5th Street and South Avenue West (Veterans Memorial Drive), Clear Lake.

The Burleigh Grimes exhibit at the Clear Lake museum commemorates the 19-year career of one of baseball's last legal spitballers.

Baseball great Hank Aaron was on hand for the dedication of his statue in 1994, where he made his pro debut.

The Professional Debut of Hank Aaron

City: Eau Claire
Location: Carson Park Stadium
Carson Park (A 130.6-acre park located on Half Moon Lake with access from Lake Street or Menomonie Street.)

Carson Park Stadium is where Hank Aaron began his career for minor-league Eau Claire in 1952. A statue of Aaron outside the stadium commemorates this, as well as the first professional home run he hit here. Before coming to Eau Claire, Aaron played for the Negro League's Indianapolis Clowns. But he signed with the Boston Braves in June of 1952 and was assigned to Eau Claire. In his one season for Eau Claire, Aaron batted .336 and hit nine home runs in 87 games. The future Hall of Famer was also chosen to play for the Northern League's All-Star team and earned rookie of the year honors. Fittingly, Aaron returned in 1994 for the dedication of his statue. The stadium dates back to 1937 when it served the Northern League's Eau Claire Bears and, later, the Eau Claire Braves. Carson Park Stadium today hosts the amateur Eau Claire Cavaliers, American Legion Baseball, Little League and several high school teams.

Billy Sullivan Marker

City: Fort Atkinson
Location: Jones Park
615 Janesville Avenue

William Joseph Sullivan Sr. was a catcher for the Boston Beaneaters (1899–1900), Chicago White Sox (1901–1914) and Detroit Tigers (1916). Sullivan was a subpar hitter, but an excellent defensive catcher. His son, Billy Jr., also became a major-league catcher. Born in this area, the marker here was placed by the aforementioned David Stalker.

The Billy Sullivan marker placed by David Stalker of Watertown, Wisconsin.

Addie Joss Exhibit

City: Juneau
Location: Juneau City Park
Lincoln Drive near Mill Street

At the community center in this quaint city park is a display dedicated to local legend Addie Joss, who pitched for the Cleveland Indians from 1902 to 1911. Joss, acknowledged as one of the greatest pitchers of his era, was cut down in the prime of his career. He pitched nine seasons before dying suddenly, at age 31, of tubercular meningitis. His trademark pinwheel, side-arm delivery baffled hitters and helped Joss post four straight 20-win seasons. Included among his 160 career victories was the second perfect game of the century in 1908, another no-hitter in 1910 and 45 shutouts. Joss, who was elected to the Hall of Fame in 1978, is honored by a historic marker and a baseball field that bears his name.

Simmons Field

City: Kenosha
Location: Sheridan Road at 78th Street

Simmons Field has an unusual history. It was created as a result of the Simmons Bedding Company being headquartered in Kenosha—because the factory's baseball team was in need of a field! As a result of that need, Simmons Field opened in Kenosha in 1920 with a seating capacity of 7,000. But it wasn't just used by the company team.

　　　The 1919 Chicago White Sox—the team later known infamously as the "Black Sox" after fixing the 1919 World Series—had arranged to play against the Simmons team during the summer of 1920. However, a suspicious fire destroyed the wood grandstand in its inaugural season, and rumors persist to this day that supporters of the Nash Motor Company team started the Simmons fire. The existing concrete grandstand was built in 1930. In 1947, the Simmons Company sold the ball field and the city re-dedicated the field to the Kenosha Comets the next year. The Comets, of the All-American Girls Professional Baseball League (AAGPBL), had played in Kenosha at Lakefront Stadium since the league was founded in 1943. The team played at Simmons Field from 1948 until their final season in 1951.

Over the years, Simmons Field has been used by Little Leagues and amateur leagues and for exhibition games. Many well-known players, including Warren Spahn, Bob Feller and Satchel Paige, all pitched here over the years. Today, Simmons Field continues to be called home by various high schools, recreational and amateur baseball teams. Despite its remodels through the years, Simmons Field still maintains a "classic" baseball ambiance. The historic grandstand behind home plate looks much like it did during the days of the AAGPBL and it still evokes memories of the baseball greats who played here. Interestingly, Simmons Field is considered to be the last remaining field in its original configuration from the glory days of the AAGPBL (All-American Girls Professional Baseball League).

The "American League" Is Born
City: Milwaukee
Location: Republican House Hotel
Corner of 3rd and Kilbourn

The grand Republican House Hotel stood at this location from 1885-1961. On March 5, 1900 (in room 185), it was the location for an important meeting that altered the course of baseball history. Five representatives of the former Western League (including Ban Johnson and White Sox owner Charles Comiskey) met here and finalized plans to change the name of their eight-team alignment to the "American League." After the 1900 season, the new "major league" was ready to challenge the longstanding National League for players and prestige. A historic marker was dedicated here in July 2001, to coincide with the centennial of the AL.

County Stadium
City: Milwaukee
Location: 1 Brewers Way
Helfaer Field

County Stadium opened in 1953—the first ballpark built with lights and the first built entirely with public funds. Three days after opening to the public,

County became a ma-
jor-league park when
the Braves announced
they would relocate
there from Boston; in
1970, five years after
the Braves had moved
to Atlanta, the Ameri-
can League's Brewers
relocated to Milwau-
kee from Seattle and
played at County Sta-
dium through 2000, at
which time the aging
structure was demol-
ished.

The former County Stadium, now the site of Helfaer Field, has become a haven for youth baseball and softball in the shadow of Miller Park.

Baseball is still played on the grounds where County Stadium once stood. Helfaer Field, a beautiful youth baseball and softball facility built in the shadow of new Miller Park, provides a nostalgic reminder of days gone by. Just off the concourse down the third-base line, fans can visit a memorial to the 192 men who played for the Milwaukee Braves from 1953 to 1965. A few steps away, the exact site of home plate at County Stadium is marked. And over the outfield wall sits a monument to the Miller Park workers who died in a construction accident as well as bronze statues of Hall of Famers Hank Aaron and Robin Yount and a series of tributes to other Brewers stars. Helfaer Field has 502 bleacher seats and additional concourse seating of 220. It has quickly become the premier location for youth baseball and girls softball in Milwaukee.

Some Memorable Moments at County Stadium

★ SEPTEMBER 23, 1957: Hank Aaron gave Milwaukee its first pennant with an 11th-inning home run against St. Louis.

★ MAY 26, 1959: Twelve innings of perfection were for naught when Pittsburgh's Harvey Haddix lost to the Braves in the 13th.

★ APRIL 30, 1961: Giants center fielder Willie Mays hit four home runs in a 14-4 win over the Braves.

★ SEPTEMBER 9, 1992: Robin Yount collected his 3,000th career hit in a 5-4 loss to Cleveland.

Horlick Field

City: Racine
Location: 1648 North Memorial Drive, on the corner of High Street and North Memorial Drive.

Although football was played here as early as 1922 (as the home field for the Racine Horlick Legion) and is still played by several high schools, there is some great baseball history, too. In 1943, the year the All-American Girls Professional Baseball League was formed, the Racine Belles moved in. One of four charter franchises (along with the Rockford Peaches, Kenosha Comets and South Bend Blue Sox), the legendary Belles played here until 1950. Today, though the field has been modified to accommodate football, baseball is still played by various amateur leagues. If you poke around, you'll find the original left-center field distance

Horlick Field in Racine was home to the Racine Belles of the All-American Girls Professional Baseball League.

marker still standing in the southeast corner of the park, hidden beyond the east football grandstand. A bronze plaque at the original entrance commemorates the Belles' history in the park.

Addie Joss Marker

City: Watertown
Location: Washington Park
635 South 12th Street

A marker here dedicated to famed pitcher Addie Joss reads:

> Born in Woodland, WI, April
> 12, 1880. Addie played baseball
> for Watertown and Watertown's
> Sacred Heart Team in 1899.
> Along with his future major
> league catcher Red Kleinow,
> they played before large crowds
> here at Washington Park. On
> April 26, 1902 Addie pitched a

**A marker in Watertown celebrates
the life and legacy of Addie Joss.**

one hitter for Cleveland in his
major league debut, the team
he played for through 1910. As a pitcher, he won twenty or
more games for four straight years, and had a lifetime 1.89
ERA. Addie is credited for pitching two no-hitters, including a perfect game on Oct. 2, 1908. Considered one of the
greatest pitchers in baseball history he was elected into the
National Baseball Hall of fame in 1978, and into the Wisconsin Athletic Hall of Fame in 1951.

David Stalker placed the marker here, one of the seven he has
placed around the country, with several more to come.

Fred Merkle Marker

City: Watertown
Location: Watertown Historical Society
Octagon House Grounds
919 Charles Street

In 2005, a SABR member named David Stalker who lives in Watertown
(and is a Fred Merkle aficionado) collaborated with members of the Merkle
family to purchase a granite memorial marker for Merkle, who was born in
Watertown. The plaque deliberately avoids any mention of the infamous
"Merkle Blunder" from 1908 that typically defines the player. In SABR's
Deadball Era Committee Newsletter (February 2006), Stalker wrote, "The
person who has heard the bonehead story, and reads it, will see that there is
so much more than just the 9-23-08 play. For these reasons I feel as though

I am granting him his wish, in helping forget, or at least look past the infamous play." The monument is about two blocks west of Washington Park, where Fred Merkle Field is located. Stalker's dedication has resulted in a series of other markers dedicated to Deadball Era players. As he wrote on the Web site seamheads.com,

> I consider the Deadball Era the most exciting time of our National Pastime. We are all familiar with the names of Ty Cobb, Honus Wagner, Shoeless Joe Jackson, and Cy Young playing during this time, and Babe Ruth starting his career in this era. My goal with this monument project is to teach the public about the lesser known stars and players as well. Starting in the communities where, or near, the player was born, or where he played prior to his major league career. Eliminate numbers, and all the players from this era are equal. They all played with, and against each other. Each one has an interesting life and story, worth recording and remembering.

> I could not agree more, and David and his team continued do amazing work, creating baseball landmarks where they deserve to be.

The Fred Merkle marker placed by David Stalker.

A marker for Red Kleinow placed by Watertown's David Stalker.

Red Kleinow Marker

City: Watertown
Location: Washington Park
635 South 12th Street

John Peter "Red" Kleinow was a reserve catcher who played in the Major Leagues from 1904 through 1911. He was a member of the New York Highlanders from 1904 to 1910, the Boston Red Sox from 1910 to 1911 and the Philadelphia Phillies in 1911. In an eight-season career, Kleinow was a .213 hitter (354-for-1,665) with three home runs and 135 RBI in 584 games, including 146 runs, 45 doubles, 20 triples and 42 stolen bases.

Kleinow died in New York at age 42. The marker here is part of the David Stalker series.

Hall of Famers Buried in Wisconsin

Al Simmons
St. Adalbert's Cemetery
3801 South 6th Street
Milwaukee

Dave "Beauty" Bancroft
Greenwood Cemetery
8402 Tower Avenue
Superior

Al Simmons had a lifetime batting average of .334.

Dave Bancroft led the league in putouts by a shortstop four straight years.

ROADSIDE BASEBALL

THE WEST

Arizona

Warren Ballpark

City: Bisbee
Location: Ruppe Avenue between Bisbee Road and Arizona Street
(About 10 miles north of the US-Mexico border in Southeast Arizona)

The first professional ballpark in Arizona is still in use today. Warren Ballpark is actually one of the oldest professional parks in the United States, dating back to June 27, 1909, when a local Bisbee team beat a team from El Paso, 8-3. In 1913, the New York Giants and Chicago White Sox stopped there as part of their world barnstorming tour, and from 1928 to 1955, Class C and D minor-league teams played there. In 1930, the original wooden grandstand was replaced with concrete and steel. A historic plaque was placed at the ballpark in 1994 by the city of Bisbee and high school teams play there today. Interestingly, Warren Ballpark holds a place in American labor history as it was the location where 1,300 kidnapped miners were held during the Bisbee Deportation in 1917.

Francisco Grande
Baseball Complex

City: Casa Grande
Location: 26000 Gila Bend Highway

The Giants trained at Casa Grande for 23 years before moving to Scottsdale in 1984. The complex included a cloverleaf of baseball diamonds, which are still there—often covered with golf balls from a nearby driving range. The big field where Willie Mays and Willie McCovey once played is now covered with weeds. The bleachers are gone, but two concrete ramps that once led to the seating area still remain—ruins that provide a small hint of what once was. The golf resort that occupies the nearby property keeps an autographed photo of Mays hanging in the bar, as well as a few other baseball momentos from the Francisco Grande Baseball Complex.

Willie Mays, Willie McCovey and Orlando Cepeda once graced the fields at Francisco Grande.

Rendezvous Park
City: Mesa
Location: 3rd Street and Center

The Chicago Cubs left California's Catalina Island to train in the desert back in 1952. Ernie Banks played many games here before the Cubs left in 1966. The park sat vacant until Charlie Finley moved the Oakland A's spring base to Mesa in 1969. But the A's have been gone since 1976 and the former Rendezvous Park is now the site of the Mesa Convention and Visitors Bureau.

Don & Charlie's
City: Scottsdale
Location: 7501 East Camelback Road
480-990-0900

Chicago native Don Carson opened his eatery here in 1981 and it has grown into a tourist attraction—for its great food as well as its sports memorabilia, particularly items having to do with baseball. Adorning the walls in every room of the spacious restaurant are hundreds of signed baseballs, jerseys, bats, mitts and more. There's a seat from old Comiskey Park right by the front door, signed photographs and artwork—it's as much a sports museum as a restaurant and well worth a visit after a Cactus League game. During spring training, the restaurant is a favorite haunt of players, coaches, managers and umpires. Don and Charlie's is open daily from 5-10 PM.

Don & Charlie's memorabilia collection includes a Comiskey seat.

Sun City Stadium
City: Sun City
Location: 111th and Grand Avenue

The Milwaukee Brewers trained here from 1973 to 1985. Rookies Robin Yount and Paul Molitor started out here; Hank Aaron spent his last spring training here (1976). Torn down in 1996, it is now the location for an apartment complex.

Gene Autry Statue

City: Tempe
Location: Tempe Diablo Stadium
2200 West Alameda Drive

Just inside the main entrance to the spring training home of the Anaheim Angels, appropriately, is
a bronze bust of longtime owner Gene Autry. The
popular cowboy singer and actor, who made 95
movies and recorded several hit songs, owned the
Anaheim franchise for 38 years after retiring from
Hollywood and he watched his Angels win three
pennants, but never a World Series. Autry is also

The Cowboy still watch-
es over spring activities
in Tempe.

saluted at Edison
International Field
in Anaheim (where

the Angels play their regular-season games)
with a retired No. 26, symbolic of his honorary status as the team's 26th player. Next to
the bronze bust in Tempe is a wall that displays the Gene Autry "Courage Awards."

Hi Corbett Field

City: Tucson
Location: 3400 East Camino Campestre
Randolph Park
602-327-9467

Historic Hi Corbett Field has served as a spring training facility since 1945.
Named in honor of prominent Tucson resident Hi Corbett, who was instrumental in bringing major-league spring training games to Tucson and Phoenix, the park was spring home for the Cleveland Indians from 1945 to 1992
(Corbett was a close friend of former Indians owner Bill Veeck) and the current Cactus League home of the Colorado Rockies, who moved into the complex as a 1993 expansion team. The Class AAA Tucson Toros of the Pacific
Coast League played at Hi Corbett Field from 1969 to 1998, but now play
(as the Tucson Sidewinders) at new Tucson Electric Park, which is shared
by the Arizona Diamondbacks and Chicago White Sox as a spring training
facility. Despite significant renovations over the years, Hi Corbett Field still
maintains its "old time" flavor.

The Cactus League has been operating in Arizona long enough to
have produced some of its own "Lost Ballpark" sites—places where legends
of the game once roamed.

Keep Your Eyes Peeled for ...

★ The statue outside Phoenix's Bank One Ballpark on Seventh Street, the one of the Arizona ballplayer signing an autograph for a young fan. Around the corner, near the ballpark's main rotunda, are showcases displaying memorabilia from the 2001 World Series, Arizona's dramatic seven-game victory over the New York Yankees.

★ "Diamonds Back" Youth Fields are sponsored by the Arizona Diamondbacks. There are currently seven youth ball fields in the Phoenix area that have been created as part of this charitable program:

An autograph-signing player serves as a constant reminder and mission statement outside Bank One Ballpark in Phoenix.

Curt Schilling Field
Indian Bend Elementary School
Phoenix
This is where the Diamondbacks' star pitcher attended school as a child.

Brian Anderson Field
Lions Park
Guadalupe

Jay Bell Field
Gateway Elementary School
Phoenix

Matt Williams Field
Simpson Elementary School
Phoenix

Randy Johnson Field of Dreams
East Lake Park
Phoenix

Steve Finley Field
Smith Park (southeast corner of 41st Avenue and Grant Street)
Phoenix

Todd Stottlemyre Field
Guadalupe

Hall of Famers Buried in Arizona

Jocko Conlan
Green Acres Cemetery
401 North Hayden Road
Scottsdale
480-945-2654

Jocko Conlan

California

Site Where Famous Japanese-American Baseball Team Played
City: Alameda
Location: 2179 Clement Avenue

From 1916 to 1938, this was the location of the Alameda Japanese-American ATK baseball field. Games were played on weekends against other Japanese-American and semipro teams, and the park served both as a recreational and social gathering place for the Japanese community. Today it's the site of the AAAAA Storage facility and the historic plaque that's here, dedicated in 1992, marks the approximate location of home plate.

 **Gene Autry Statue**
City: Anaheim
Location: Edison International Field
2000 Gene Autry Way
714-634-2000

At the stadium's Gate 2 entrance, former Angels owner Gene Autry is immortalized with a life-size bronze statue and plaque. In front of the stadium, under the giant helmets, are the handprints of six former Angels players cemented in the stadium courtyard: Bobby Grich, Bob Boone, Reggie Jackson, Rod Carew, Don Sutton and Jim Fregosi. Just inside Gate 4 is a beautiful statue honoring Michelle Carew, Rod Carew's daughter, who died in 1996.

Jack Norworth Grave
City: Anaheim
Location: Melrose Abbey Memorial Park
2303 South Manchester Avenue
Plot: North Patio Crypt, 46GG

This is where Jack Norworth, the man who wrote "Take Me Out to the Ballgame" is buried. The 1908 classic was written on some scrap paper on a train ride to Manhattan, New York. Norworth then provided those paper scrap lyrics to Albert Von Tilzer who composed the music, which in turn was published by the York Music Company, and before the year was over, a hit song was born. Born in Philadelphia, Pennsylvania, Norworth was the cowriter of many popular Tin Pan Alley hits. Although "Take Me Out to the Ball Game" is his most famous song, it wasn't until 1940 that he actually witnessed a baseball game. The number he penned called "Shine On, Harvest Moon" was an even bigger hit at the time. Other popular tunes credited to Norworth include "Back to My Old Home Town"; "Come Along, My Mandy"; "Dear Dolly"; "Good Evening, Caroline"; "Holding Hands"; "Honey Boy"; "I'm Glad I'm a Boy/I'm Glad I'm a Girl"; "I'm Glad I'm Married"; "Kitty"; "Meet Me in Apple Blossom Time"; "Over on the Jersey Side"; "Since My Mother Was a Girl"; "Sing an Irish Song" and "Smarty." "Turn out Your Light, Mr. Moon Man" is a sequel to "Shine on, Harvest Moon." He retired to Southern California, and was living in Laguna Beach at the time of his death.

La Palma Park
City: Anaheim
Location: Harbor Boulevard

La Palma Park in Anaheim is where Joe DiMaggio played while in the Army.

Built in 1939, La Palma Park (known today as Glover Stadium/Dee Fee Field) hosted the Seattle Rainiers (of the Pacific Coast League) for spring training in that year. The St. Louis Browns trained here in 1946, and Connie Mack brought his Philadelphia A's here in the springs of 1940,

1941 and 1943 for their training season. During World War II, Joe DiMaggio played several games here as a member of his airbase team (the Yankee Clipper was stationed at the nearby Santa Ana Army Air Base). Today the field is used for local leagues, including high school and college games.

Pearson Park Grandstands
City: Anaheim
Location: Lincoln and Harbor Boulevards

Since the early 1920s, locals have gathered in this park to watch amateur and semipro baseball over the years. (Connie Mack's A's would also travel down the street from La Palma Park and play here during their spring training trips in the 1940s.) Though the grandstand has had some work done to it over the years, it remains a beautifully maintained example of an old-time baseball structure.

Pearson Park in Anaheim has a long, storied history.

Babe Ruth in Brea, October 31, 1924.

Babe Ruth and Walter Johnson Game
City: Brea
Location: Brea Bowl
St. Crispen Avenue and Napoli Drive

On October 31, 1924, Babe Ruth and Walter Johnson played a barnstorming game here that has become a solid part of the area's folklore. Sponsored by the Anaheim Elks Club, it was a homecoming for Johnson of sorts in that he grew up in the neighboring oil town of Olinda. Nearly 5,000 people turned out for the event at the Brea Bowl field, incredible given that nearby

A rare shot of Walter Johnson at the Brea Bowl in 1924.

It's hard to see, but that's Babe Ruth at bat against Walter Johnson at Brea Bowl in 1924.

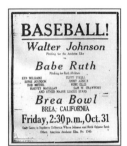

Anaheim's total population back then was just 2,000. Ruth's team won, 12-1, and the day was capped by two Ruth home runs (one of which supposedly traveled 550 feet). Remarkably, this game was documented by an 18-year-old named George E. Outland, who over the years carried on his hobby of photographing baseball players (and eventually getting may of his shots signed by the players). A poster promoting the event (left) touts it as the "only game in Southern California where Johnson and Ruth oppose each other."

Today, the site of the old Brea Bowl is a quiet neighborhood. Just two blocks away, at 227 North Brea Boulevard, there's an auto repair company. The old garage that still stands at the site is where all of the players got dressed for the game after getting off the nearby train. From here, they marched down to the nearby field.

Olive Memorial Stadium

City: Burbank
Location: George Izay Park
West Olive Avenue and
Mariposa Street
818-238-5300

This field was the former spring training home of the St. Louis Browns from 1949 to 1952. During that time, many celebrities such as Bob Hope and Nat King Cole would come out to watch the ball games, which featured other visit-

The former site of Olive Memorial Stadium in Burbank.

ing major league stars. Satchel Paige, Luke Appling, Nellie Fox, Ralph Kiner and Willie Mays all played here. After enduring years of structural damage from earthquakes, the ballpark was razed in 1994, but the diamond still remains. The war memorial plaques that once adorned the outside stadium have been remounted near where the grandstand once stood.

Big League Dreams Sports Parks
City: Cathedral City
    Location: 33700 Date Palm Drive
    760-324-5600
City: Mira Loma (Riverside area)
    Location: 10550 Galena Street
    909-685-6900
City: Chino Hills
    Location: 16333 Fairfield Ranch
    909-287-6900

These recreational facilities offer playing fields for many sports, from volleyball to flag football, but they are best known for their baseball/softball fields that are designed and built as replicas of famous historic major-league stadiums. Youth and adults can play on a replica of Chicago's Wrigley Field, New York's Yankee Stadium, Boston's Fenway Park, the Polo Grounds, Forbes Field,

Fans, and players, can re-create the experience of playing at many fields, including the Polo Grounds.

Ebbets Field, Tiger Stadium and Crosley Field. The dream of brothers Rick and Jeff Odekirk, both former baseball players, their goal was to create an environment that would give the average youth or adult player the chance to play on a "Field of Dreams." Judging from how popular these places have become, they have succeeded.

Babe Ruth Marker
City: Dunsmuir
Location: Dunsmuir City Field
Dunsmuir Avenue, toward the northern end of town

On October 22, 1924, Babe Ruth played an exhibition game here in Dunsmuir, a logging town located about 98 miles south of the Oregon border.

It was part of his nationwide barnstorming tour and Babe was joined
by Yankee teammate Bob Meusel
and manager Christy Walsh. The
game was sponsored by the Dunsmuir Lions Club and drew about
900 fans. Following his appearance, Babe wrote the town the following letter:

Dunsmuir, where Babe Ruth came to play
on a barnstorming trip back in the 1920s.

        "To everybody (and that
means everybody) in Dunsmuir, Ca-
lif. We don't know yet how to tell you what a wonderful time we had in Dunsmuir. . . . When it comes to beautiful girls, wonderfully fine fellows, and the
real two-fisted spirit of California—little Dunsmuir gave us more laughs, more
hospitality, more thrills, and more things
to remember than any place between
Broadway & Shasta." (Quote excerpted
from the Dunsmuir Centennial Book.)

        The original field where the
game took place still stands and today
is used by the Dunsmuir High School
Tigers. A commemorative marker in hon-
or of Ruth was also placed at the field.
(And there's plenty of other Ruth lore in
town, from the movie theater where he
appeared to present some local sports
awards to the nearby woods where he returned to hunt on occasion.)

The marker at the Dunsmuir field
where Babe Ruth once played.

George Brett Field

City: El Segundo
Location: Recreation Park
Corner of Pine and Eucalyptus
Streets

Located a couple of blocks from
where the Royals slugger went to
high school, this field was dedicated
to Brett on April 24, 1999 (Brett was
on hand for the ceremony). George
Brett's three brothers, who all played
professional baseball, also attended
El Segundo High.

George Brett Field in El Segundo is near
where the slugger grew up.

Oaks Park

City: Emeryville (between Oakland and Berkeley)
Location: 1120 Park Avenue

From 1913 to 1957, this was the site of Oaks Park, also called Emeryville Park, the home of the Pacific Coast League Oakland Oaks. It was torn down in 1957 to clear the way for a Pepsi-Cola bottling plant, which in time would also be torn down to make way for a Pixar animation studio.

Walter Johnson's Alma Mater

City: Fullerton
Location: Fullerton Union High School
201 East Chapman Avenue
714-626-3801

Walter Johnson attended high school here, graduating in 1905, and is represented on the school's "Wall of Fame." Other ballplayers who attended the school and also made it to the wall are Hall of Fame Pirate shortstop Joseph Floyd "Arky" Vaughan (Class of 1930) and former player/manager Del Crandell (Class of 1947). Other notable school graduates and Wall of Fame members include Richard Nixon (Class of 1927–28) and guitar legend Leo Fender (Class of 1932.)

Walter Johnson Athletic Field

City: Fullerton
Location: Ted Craig Regional Park
3300 State College Boulevard
714-990-0271

Near the site of where the Brea Bowl used to be is this baseball complex named for Walter Johnson, who spent a portion of his youth in the nearby oil town of Olinda. (There's also a street called Walter Johnson Lane nearby.)

Dedeaux Field

City: Los Angeles
Location: USC
1021 Childs Way

Located directly on the USC campus and named after legendary coach Rod Dedeaux, the home of the baseball Trojans opened on March 30, 1974.

Russ McQueen pitched a no-hitter as 'SC swept a doubleheader from California. The Trojans went on that year to win an unprecedented fifth straight national championship, and Dedeaux Field has been their home ever since. Rod Dedeaux is of the winningest baseball coaches in NCAA history, serving as the Trojans' head coach from 1943 to 1945 and 1951 to 1986, racking up 41 winning seasons in 45 years. Significant improvements to the facility have been made in the 2000s, including a Hall of Fame on the first base side of the park. Dedeaux Field is toward the northwestern end of the USC University Park campus between Vermont Avenue (west) and McLintock Avenue (east). Dedeaux Field seats more than 1,800 spectators and features a natural grass field, 10-foot outfield fences, a spacious press box, a state-of-the-art scoreboard/messaging center and lighting comparable to most professional baseball facilities. It also offers modern locker rooms and practice facilities as well as an enclosed Pavilion Club and the USC Baseball Hall of Fame.

More Dedeaux: Mater Dei High School in Santa Ana also boasts a baseball stadium and outdoor athletic complex named the Rod Dedeaux Baseball Stadium in honor of the man considered "the game's true master coach." Dedeaux, in addition to the impact he made on collegiate and international baseball, was also very influential in the Mater Dei program.

Jackie Robinson Plaque
City: Los Angeles
Location: Los Angeles Memorial Coliseum
3911 South Figueroa Street
213-747-7111

In 2005, Jackie Robinson, UCLA's only four-sport athlete and the legend who shattered Major League Baseball's color barrier, was honored with a plaque at the Los Angeles Memorial Coliseum. The event was in commemoration of his historic breakthrough in Major League Baseball, almost 58 years ago to the day (April 15, 1947). On hand that day were UCLA chancellor Albert Carnesale and athletic director Dan Guerrero, along with several other famed members of the Los Angeles sports community. Vin Scully, the legendary broadcast voice of the Los Angeles Dodgers since 1950, emceed the festivities, which featured a welcome by Coliseum Commission president William Chadwick along with poignant speeches from Carnesale, Coliseum commissioner Zev Yaroslavsky, Guerrero, Dodgers' vice chairman Jamie Mc-Court, former Dodger player and Robinson teammate Don Newcombe and Jackie Robinson's widow, Mrs. Rachel Robinson.

Jackie Robinson Stadium

City: Los Angeles
Location: UCLA
Constitution Avenue
From 405 South: Exit Wilshire Boulevard. East. Turn left onto Sepulveda
       Boulevard. Turn left onto Constitution Avenue. The
       stadium is on the right.
From 405 North: Exit Montana Avenue. Turn right onto Sepulveda
       Boulevard. Turn right onto Constitution Avenue.

The UCLA Bruin baseball stadium is named for alumnus Jackie Robinson, who broke the color barrier when he joined the Brooklyn Dodgers in 1947. Robinson was a four-sport letterman at UCLA, competing in football, basketball, track, and baseball. Elected to baseball's Hall of Fame in 1962, Robinson had a .311 lifetime batting average and played in six All-Star Games. He was the National League Rookie of the Year in 1947. His best season was in 1949, when he led the NL with a .342 batting average and 37 stolen bases, and was named NL MVP. A bronze statue of Robinson is now located near the concession stand on the concourse level. The statue was dedicated on April 27, 1985, before the UCLA-Arizona State game.

Jackie Robinson is honored in Los Angeles at UCLA, where a stadium bears his name.

Wrigley Field

City: Los Angeles
Location: 42nd Street and Avalon Boulevard

On April 27, 1925, Wrigley Field opened at the corner of Avalon Boulevard and 42nd Street in South Central Los Angeles. Owned by chewing gum magnate William Wrigley, it was partially modeled after the other Wrigley Field in Chicago. Interestingly, this park was called Wrigley Field first (Chicago's park got the name in 1926). Wrigley owned the Los Angeles Angels, who played here, sharing the park with the Hollywood Stars at various times (Wrigley Field was the home of the Angels from 1925 until 1957; the Stars played here from 1926 until 1935, and also played here in 1938). Given its proximity to Hollywood, Wrigley Field was regularly used for movies such as *Pride of the Yankees*, *The Kid from Left Field*, *Damn Yankees*, *It Happens Every Spring*, *The Geisha Boy* and many more. An episode of *The Munsters* was filmed here, and millions of fans saw Wrigley on TV regularly as it was the park

A public park now occupies what was once Wrigley Field's center field.

used for the 1960s TV show Home Run Derby. In the only season that Major League Baseball was played at Wrigley Field (1961), 248 home runs were hit there, more than in any other ballpark in major-league history during a single season. The last game was played at Wrigley Field on October 1, 1961, and the stadium was demolished in 1966. Today, the former site of Wrigley Field is occupied by a public park and recreation center, a community mental health center, and a senior citizens center. Though there is no plaque or marker, most of the houses beyond the left field wall, the ones so visible during *Home Run Derby*, still remain.

Gilmore Field
City: Los Angeles
Location: CBS Television City
7800 Beverly Boulevard

Gilmore Field was constructed in 1938 to accommodate the Hollywood Stars, a Minor League Baseball team owned by Bing Crosby, Barbara Stanwyck, and Cecil B. DeMille. Maybe the most intimate baseball venue ever designed (home plate was a scant 34 feet from

The former site of Gilmore Field in Los Angeles.

the seats, first and third bases only 24 feet away), Gilmore Field was as much a place to watch the stars come out as to watch baseball. When it opened on May 2, 1939, Jack Benny, Al Jolson, Gary Cooper, Robert Taylor and Bing Crosby hosted pre-game festivities, and starlet and coowner Gail Patrick (also the wife of Bob Cobb) threw out the first pitch to movie comedian Joe E. Brown. A special VIP room under the stands made it easy for celebrities to socialize in private. Gilmore Field was torn down in 1958 and all that remains from back then are a row of palm trees tracing the line beyond where the left field wall once stood. (The field lights were sold to the Dodgers'

AAA farm team and are still
being used at Avista Stadium
in Spokane, Washington.) A
historical marker with some
photos of the park is displayed near where Gilmore's
front entrance used to be, on
the wall of Studio 46.

A plaque was unveiled at the site of Gilmore Field in the mid-1990s.

Los Angeles Coliseum
City: Los Angeles
Location: 3911 South Figueroa Street

Though famous for hosting two Olympics (1932 and 1984), college and pro
football and many other notable events, the Los Angeles Coliseum was also
the home of the Los Angeles Dodgers from 1958 to 1961. After moving out
from Brooklyn, the Dodgers played here while Dodger Stadium was being
built. Due to the huge capacity and demand for pro baseball, the team drew
over two million in both 1959
and 1960. An awkward place
for baseball, the left field line
was just 250 feet, and to com-
pensate, a 40-foot screen was
erected where Wally Moon hit
his famous "Moonshots." The
1959 All-Star Game was played
here and the American League
beat the National League, 5–3.
A plaque mounted on the famous Coliseum peristyle arch-
es commemorates the Dodg-
ers' victory over the Chicago

The Los Angeles Coliseum has played host to the Olympics and football, and also baseball.

White Sox in the 1959 World Series. Game 5's attendance was 92,706, still
an all-time record. Another baseball attendance record was set here at the
Coliseum. Four months before the Dodgers opened in Los Angeles, beloved
catcher Roy Campanella was paralyzed in a car accident. A year later, on
May 7, 1959, the Dodgers and Yankees (in an exhibition game) drew 93,103
people to the Los Angeles Coliseum to honor Campanella. It still ranks as
the largest crowd ever for a major-league game. In a pre-game ceremony,
Campanella was wheeled out to second base by his longtime teammate,
shortstop Pee Wee Reese. The lights in the Coliseum were turned off, and
the fans lit matches to greet him. Today, college football is the main sport
played at this venerable Los Angeles landmark.

Washington Park
City: Los Angeles
Location: Washington and Hill Streets

Washington Park was
mainly used for base-
ball and was the home
of the Los Angeles An-
gels from 1912 until
they moved to Wrigley
Field late in the 1925
season. (Babe Ruth
fronted a team here
that played against
a team led by Walter

Washington Park was once located in downtown Los Angeles.

Johnson as part of a 1924 barnstorming tour). Prior to 1912, the Angels had
played at a ball field next to Chutes Park, a city amusement park. The new
Washington Park, located at Washington and Hill Streets, was just a short
distance from Chutes. The Venice Pacific Coast League team in 1913-14 also
played home games at Washington Park, except for Sunday morning and special holiday games. There are some sources suggesting that William Wrigley
Jr., owner of the Angels, wanted to build an underground parking garage
beneath the ballpark but was not allowed to. Apparently, he then decided to
build a new ballpark, Wrigley Field, which opened in 1925 nearby at 42nd
Street and Avalon Boulevard. There is no marker identifying this site as the
former location of the ballpark, which today is near downtown Los Angeles.

Joe DiMaggio's Boat
City: Martinez
Location: Martinez Marina Park
North of downtown Martinez at the foot of Ferry Street, near Amtrak's
Martinez train station

Joe DiMaggio was born here in Martinez on November 25, 1914. Today, you
can see DiMaggio's Chris Craft, the *Joltin' Joe*, on display at the Martinez
Marina park. The boat was a gift to DiMaggio from the Yankees, presented
to him at the end of the 1949 season, during Joe DiMaggio Day at Yankee
Stadium. (That day, despite being ill, DiMaggio got two hits to help beat
Boston and thus set up the next day's last game of the season, a pennant-
clinching victory.) After retiring to the Bay Area following his baseball career, DiMaggio often used this boat for short trips with his then-wife Marilyn
Monroe. Years afterward, he donated the boat to the town. (There's a plaque
on the boat today, describing some of its history.)

Joe DiMaggio Exhibit
City: Martinez
Location: Martinez Museum
1005 Excobar Street
925-228-8160

Also in DiMaggio's hometown, at the Martinez Museum, there is a small display of DiMaggio items, including his 1914 birth certificate.

Newport Sports Museum
City: Newport Beach
Location: 100 Newport Center Drive, Suite 100
949-721-9333

The Newport Sports Museum boasts perhaps the greatest collection of baseball Hall of Fame memorabilia outside of Cooperstown. This collection includes not only the greatest players the game has ever seen, but also the greatest teams. The Hall of Fame Room contains every team-signed World Series Champion ball dating back to 1940, plus, a collection of balls signed by every Cy Young winner since the award's inception in 1956. They also have over 110 baseballs signed by members of the Hall of Fame, including Hank Aaron, Yogi Berra, Ty Cobb, Joe DiMaggio, Catfish Hunter, Babe Ruth, Willie Mays, Mike Schmidt, Duke Snider and Jackie Robinson. Right next to these Hall of Fame baseballs are uniforms worn in competition by several baseball greats, including George Brett, Mickey Mantle, Carlton Fisk, Carl Yastrzemski, Hank Aaron and Brooks Robinson. Whether it was Bobby Thomson's famous "shot heard round the world" or Jackie Robinson stealing home, these 47 stadium seats have seen it all. The Stadium Room at the Newport Sports Museum contains a collection of seats from famous baseball stadiums from both the past and present, including Ebbets Field, the Polo Grounds, Comiskey Park, Braves Field, Yankee Stadium, Fenway Park and more. In front of all of these seats you can see a mural of Nolan Ryan's last no-hitter thrown as an Angel on June 1, 1975, autographed by Nolan himself, as well as Bobby Grich and Brooks Robinson. Other sports are represented at this excellent Southern California museum, but the collection of baseball artifacts is truly jaw-dropping, making this place must visit for any fan.

Hans Lobert Races a Horse
City: Oxnard
Location: E Street and Wooley Road, near Driffill Elementary School

On November 11, 1913, the New York Giants and the Chicago White Sox played a game here in this small coastal town as part of their famous 1913 barnstorming tour. Giants outfielder Fred Snodgrass was from Oxnard, and it was due to this connection that Oxnard was placed on the schedule. Players and managers including John McGraw, Chris-ty Mathewson, Tris

A famous All-Star Game was once played on this field in Oxnard.

Speaker, Hal Chase, Fred Merkle, Sam Crawford and Hans Lobert were all treated like royalty upon their arrival by train the day of the big game. After a huge ceremonial barbecue, the teams made their way to the newly built grandstand, where thousands of people from all over Southern California had gathered. The Giants ended up winning the game, 3-2, but it was an event that happened after the game that made the most news. Hans Lobert, the Giants' speedy third baseman, had agreed to race a horse around the diamond at the game's conclusion, which he did. Umpire Bill Klem signaled the start and the race was on. Though Lobert led rounding second, the horse bumped him near shortstop to take the lead and win the race by a nose. The event was capture by newsreel cameras and shown all over the country. The field where the game and the race took place still exists, as part of the Drif-fill Elementary School in Oxnard.

Jackie Robinson Memorial Field
City: Pasadena
Location: Brookside Park
360 North Arroyo Boulevard

At the north end of Brookside Park, a ballpark was named for Jackie Robin-son on January 30, 1988. Pasadena City College baseball team plays their home games on this field. The plaque reads: "Jackie Robinson Memorial Field—A scholar, an athlete, a trailblazer. Dedicated January 30, 1988." Rob-inson starred as an All-Southern California infielder at Pasadena Junior Col-lege (1937-38) before going on to break the color barrier in Major League Baseball in 1947. When his illustrious career with the Brooklyn Dodgers was over, Robinson was then inducted into the Major League Baseball Hall of Fame. Along with that, he was also honored by PCC with a bronze bust of his image located today in the Court of Champions on campus. Robinson is the only player in history to have his No. 42 retired by all of MLB's teams. In fact, no player in any other professional sport has ever been honored in such a way.

Robinson Memorial

City: Pasadena
Location: Located on Garfield
Avenue, north of Union Street, across
the street from city hall.

Dedicated on November 6, 1997, these
two huge bronze sculptures commemorate the lives of brothers Jackie and Mack
Robinson, who grew up in Pasadena.
While we all know that Jackie Robinson

**Jackie and Mack Robinson grew up in
Pasadena and are memorialized there.**

broke the color barrier in baseball when
he joined the Brooklyn Dodgers in 1947, it's worth noting that Mack Robinson
won the silver medal in the 200-meter race in the 1936 Olympics.

Jackie Robinson's Home

City: Pasadena
Location: 121 Pepper Street

In 1920, an uncle in Pasadena invited
Mollie Robinson and her five children
to leave Cairo, Georgia, and come live
with him. (Mollie's husband had abandoned her.) So she packed up Edgar,
Frank, Mack, Jackie and Willa Mae
and headed west to this spot, where a
four-bedroom cottage once sat. For 24
years, the Robinson family lived at this
address. Jackie, who ran with the "Pepper Street Gang" for a time, went on to
graduate from Washington Junior and

**A sidewalk marker in Pasadena
marks where Jackie Robinson lived
with his family when they arrived
from Georgia.**

Muir Technical High School. He then attended two-year Pasadena Junior
College, where he starred in football, track and baseball. The next year he
entered UCLA. The marker sits on the sidewalk in front of where the house
once stood (now a vacant lot).

Jack Benny Statue

City: Rancho Cucamonga
Location: The Epicenter
Rochester Avenue off Foothill Boulevard

On the old Jack Benny show, audiences got used to a train conductor calling out the stops of "Anaheim, Azusa and . . . Cucamonga." So, in tribute to

the famed comedian, the Rancho Cucamonga Quakes erected a life-size bronze statue of Jack Benny at the main entrance to their park. (And named the ball-park's street "Rochester" after Benny's sidekick.) The Quakes are the California League affiliate of the Anaheim Angels and this impressive minor-league park opened in 1993.

The White Sox Redwood

City: Riverside
Location: Low Park near the corner of Arlington and Magnolia

On Arbor Day, 1914, members of the Chicago White Sox planted a tree in this park, a tree that has thrived ever since. "The White Sox Redwood," as it is known, was placed by first baseman Hal Chase and third baseman Harry Lord during a ceremony before the Sox played an exhibition game at Evans Park, located just a couple of blocks away. Near the base of the tree is a plaque commemorating the game that was played the same day the tree was planted. Also, a mere baseball toss form the tree stands, behind a gate, sits the very first orange tree planted in California.

The author's son, Charlie, posed near the White Sox Redwood marker in Riverside.

Jack Benny stands at the park of the Rancho Cucamonga Quakes.

Lefty Gomez Field

City: Rodeo
Location: 470 Parker Avenue

This is one of only three sports-related sites currently honored in California as a state point of historical interest. (The other two are the Los Angeles Coliseum and the Willow Springs International Raceway in Rosamond.) Vernon "Lefty" Gomez was born in Rodeo and first played for the nearby San Francisco Seals. In 1929, the New York Yankees picked him up for $35,000 and two years later, the lanky southpaw with the trademark high leg kick won 21 games for the Yankees with the support of teammates like Lou Gehrig and Joe DiMaggio. Along with right-hander Red Ruffing, this lefty-righty combination was the core of the pitching staff in the 1930s. Gomez's 6-0 World Series record gave him the most wins without a loss in major-league history. He also won the pitching version of the triple crown twice (1934, '37), leading the American League in victories, ERAs and strikeouts. Lefty Gomez was inducted into the Baseball Hall of Fame in 1972 and he died in Greenbrae, California, on February 17, 1989.

Tony Gwynn Stadium

City: San Diego
Location: San Diego State University
5500 Campanile Drive
619-594-5200

Tony Gwynn Stadium became the new home of the San Diego State baseball program during the 1997 season. The $4 million facility was made possible through the generosity of San Diego Padres owner John Moores and his wife, Becky, who donated the funds to build the park that's named for the school's most famous player. In 2002, Tony Gwynn became the coach of the Aztecs baseball team. In addition to Tony, his brother Chris was an All-American baseball player at San Diego State and a member of the 1984 US Olympic baseball team. He went on to play parts of 10 seasons in the major leagues for the Dodgers, Royals, and Padres, and today he is a Padres scout.

Stephen and Mary Birch Foundation Baseball Museum

City: San Diego
Location: San Diego State University
5500 Campanile Drive
619-594-5200

This museum is located on the concourse of Tony Gwynn Stadium behind the third base stands. Constructed thanks to a grant from the Stephen and Mary Birch Foundation, the free museum features displays and exhibits honoring past Aztec players and teams who have contributed to the tradition of San Diego State baseball. Among the high points are lockers highlighting the careers of former Aztecs Tony Gwynn of the San Diego Padres and SDSU's Golden Spikes Award winner, Travis Lee. Along with photos, scrapbooks, trophies and other memorabilia, the museum also features a big-screen television for viewing Aztec highlights.

THE WEST • California

Albert Spalding Residence

City: San Diego
Location: Point Loma Nazarene University
3900 Lomaland Drive
619-849-2200

Today this ornate building is part of a college campus. But from 1899 to 1915, it's where legendary baseball pioneer (and star player) A.G. Spalding lived until his death. Spalding had retired from baseball and, after being introduced to esoteric school of thought known as "theosophy" by his wife, he moved his family here to what was then the Utopian community of the Theosophical Society. In the 1950s, the order left this building.

"America's Most Scenic Ballpark"

City: San Diego
Location: Carroll B. Land Stadium
Point Loma Nazarene University
3900 Lomaland Drive
619-849-2200

Nestled on the seaside cliffs of San Diego overlooking the Pacific Ocean, no other collegiate baseball park, or perhaps any baseball park, can match the picturesque views of Carroll C. Land Stadium. In 1998, the Crusaders' home field was designated "America's Most Scenic Baseball Park" by Baseball America. The park was re-named in 1998 for Carroll Land, who coached collegiate ball at the school for 39 seasons.

The Pacific Ocean lies behind the outfield fence at Carroll B. Land Stadium.

San Diego Hall of Champions

City: San Diego
Location: 2131 Pan American Plaza, in Balboa Park
619-234-2544

Located in beautiful Balboa Park, this renowned museum and hall of fame features a permanent baseball exhibit, which occupies a large gallery on the first level of this 70,000-square-foot facility. It features many exhibits commemorating San Diego baseball sports history, including hundreds of pieces of memorabilia, and also provides opportunities for interactive, hands-on experiences for both kids and adults. There is also a permanent exhibit dedicated to San Diego legend, Ted Williams.

Lane Field

City: San Diego
Location: West Broadway
and Pacific Coast Highway

Built right alongside the Pacific Ocean in 1936, Lane Field was home to the Pacific Coast League San Diego Padres from 1936 to 1957. Hoover High School's Ted Williams played here in 1936–37 and it was here where Red Sox general manager Eddie Collins came to scout Williams in 1936. The next season, the Red Sox purchased him for $25,000. Lane Field was torn down in the late 1950s and the site is currently a parking lot. Plans are underway as of this writing to erect a historic marker.

A vintage shot of Lane Field in San Diego.

The site of Lane Field today (a marker can also be found here).

Lefty O'Doul Bridge

City: San Francisco
Location: Third Street, China Basin, leading into Pac Bell Park

This bridge is named in honor of one of the Bay Area's most beloved players, who still holds the National League record for hits in a season—254. So influential were his ambassadorial efforts that today he is called "The Father of Baseball in Japan." During his best season in 1929, he hit .398 with 32 home runs for the Philadelphia Phillies. He also struck out just 19 times in 638 at bats, which is still a record low.

McCovey's Cove

City: San Francisco
Location: Pac Bell Park
24 Willie Mays Plaza

This is where the kayaks, canoes and other small vessels gather to await the next home run by Barry Bonds and other left-handed sluggers—located just over the right field wall.

McCovey's Cove has provided the landing spot for many Barry Bonds home runs.

Willie Mays Statue

City: San Francisco
Location: Pac Bell Park
24 Willie Mays Plaza

At the stadium's main entrance, surrounded by 24 palm trees, is a nine-foot sculpture of the Giants legend.

Lefty O'Doul's

City: San Francisco
Location: 333 Geary Street
415-982-8900

This San Francisco landmark was opened in 1958 by Francis "Lefty" O'Doul, who was born in San Francisco in 1897. A pitcher and later manager for the Pacific Coast League's San Francisco Seals (O'Doul also pitched in the majors and then played outfield for the Giants and

Willie Mays stands at Pac Bell Park.

Phillies), O'Doul was a beloved local figure and perennial fan favorite. After spending the 1934 season with the New York Giants, at age 37 he came back to manage the San Francisco Seals from 1935 to 1951 (and other PCL teams through 1957), pitching and pinch hitting, as well as becoming a renowned teacher of young players, including Joe DiMaggio. He had started making annual visits to Japan in the 1930s as a baseball ambassador and fans adore him there to this day. The memorabilia in O'Doul's is plentiful and authentic, and the restaurant also features one of the last Hofbrau menus in San Francisco.

Seals Stadium

City: San Francisco
Location: 16th and Bryant

From 1931 to 1957, this quaint, single-level neighborhood ballpark served as the home to the Pacific Coast League San Francisco Seals. Joe DiMaggio played his minor-league ball here in the 1930s. In fact, his 61-game hitting streak was stopped here in 1933 when he went 0-5 against the Oakland Oaks' Ed Walsh. The Seals' last game at the stadium was on September 13,

The former site of Seals Stadium in San Francisco.

1957. Then the Giants took over, fresh from their move from New York's Polo Grounds. They played here during their first two years in San Francisco while Candlestick Park was being built, attracting over two million fans. The Giants' last game at Seals Stadium was on September 20, 1959, and Seals Stadium was demolished in November of 1959. If you were to try walking it off today, home plate is underneath an Old Navy clothing store. First base is where Petco is and center field, where Willie Mays once played, is now a parking lot. The building that was once the famous Hamm's brewery building still looms over the site from behind where home plate would have been. Also, a marker was recently placed here to commemorate the ballpark.

The Double Play Bar & Grill features a collection of memorabilia from Seals Stadium.

Double Play Bar & Grill

City: San Francisco
Location: 2401 16th Street (at Bryant)
415-621-9859

Located directly across the street from where old Seals Stadium used to be is the historic Double Play, a bar and grill that has been in business at this site since 1909. While it was a famous hangout before and after games at Seals Stadium, today it's become a shrine to the memory of the long-gone park. You'll find photos, caps, jerseys and mitts covering the walls, some Seals Stadium seats, and above the bar, next to a 1939 Seals jersey, is a round gold object—the top of the stadium flagpole. In the back dining room, all four walls are part of a Seals Stadium mural, painted in exquisite detail right down to the last fan.

Recreation Park

City: San Francisco
Location: 15th and Valencia

Pre-Seals Stadium, this was home to the Seals from 1906 to 1930; and home to the Mission Reds from 1926 to 1930. During their famous 1920s barnstorming tour, Babe Ruth's Bustin' Babes played Lou Gehrig's Larrupin' Lous here.

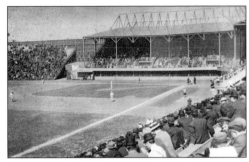

A vintage image of Recreation Park in San Francisco.

Ewing Field

City: San Francisco
Location: Turk and Masonic

This was home to the San Francisco Seals in 1914, before the dense fog forced the team to return to Recreation Park.

A vintage shot of Ewing Field in San Francisco.

The Ball Player Statue

City: San Francisco
Location: Golden Gate Park

This popular statue of a baseball player was created by Douglas Tilden. Tilden, who hailed from Chico, California, lost his hearing at age five from scarlet fever. He went on to study sculpture, eventually being granted a scholarship in Paris to study under the renowned sculptor, Paul Chopin, who was also deaf. This statue is Tilden's first work, and upon completion it was accepted by the Salon des Artistes Français on the Champs-Élysées in 1889.

Bay Area Sports Hall of Fame

City: San Francisco
Location: 201 Spear Street, 11th Floor
415-296-5610

This non-profit organization was conceived and founded by the San Francisco Chamber of Commerce in 1979. Annual contributions are made to aid in the development of Bay Area youth through The Youth Fund. Their noble work funds many projects in the city, and their inductees are visible throughout the Bay Area, presented as a series of plaques in public areas. These are the six locations where the baseball inductee plaques can be viewed:

Network Associates Coliseum
7000 Coliseum Way
Oakland
510-569-2121
Dick, Bartell, Rollie Fingers, Curt Flood, Catfish Hunter, Reggie Jackson, Ernie Lombardi, Billy Martin, Joe Morgan, Vada Pinson, Bill Rigney, Frank Robinson and Willie Stargell

Pac Bell Park
24 Willie Mays Plaza
San Francisco
Vida Blue, Orlando Cepeda, Juan Marichal, Willie Mays, Willie McCovey and Lefty O'Doul.

Sacred Heart Cathedral Prep School
Sacred Heart Cathedral Preparatory
1055 Ellis Street
San Francisco
415-775-6626
Dolph Camilli, Joe Cronin and Harry Heilmann

University of California, Berkeley
510-642-6000
Sam Chapman

San Francisco International Airport
(domestic terminal)
650-624-7200
Dominic DiMaggio—Gate 80
Joe DiMaggio—Gate 81
Dennis Eckersley—Gate 80
Lefty Gomez—Gate 90
Eddie Joost—Gate 83
Dave Stewart—Gate 87

Jackson Playground
Arkansas (between 17th and Mariposa Streets)
San Francisco
Tony Lazzeri

Historic Municipal Stadium
City: San Jose
Location: 588 East Alma Avenue
408-297-1435

Built as part of Franklin Roosevelt's Works Progress Administration (WPA), Municipal Stadium opened on March 8, 1942, when the San Francisco Seals defeated the Portland Beavers, 15–8. Now home for the San Francisco Giants' Class A minor-league

Municipal Stadium in San Jose dates back to 1942.

affiliate, the San Jose Giants, old-time Municipal Stadium celebrates local baseball history with a series of painted murals located around the entire stadium. Included is a timeline of baseball in San Jose, which is accompanied with every former San Jose alumnus to make it to the major leagues.

Chicago Cubs Spring Training Field
City: Santa Catalina Island
Location: Country Club Road in Avalon

From 1921 to 1951, this was the spring training facility for the Chicago Cubs. Cubs owner William Wrigley built a diamond and a practice field in Avalon, with the ball field's dimensions matching those of Wrigley Field in Chicago. Surrounded by eucalyptus trees, the field was located below Wrigley's mountainside country club, which housed the players' locker rooms. (Wrigley, in fact, owned the island.) Wrigley himself was a familiar face at the ball field, usually sitting in the bleachers to watch the workouts. Typically, the Cubs pitchers, catchers and rookies arrived in mid-February. The rest of the team followed a week later. By mid-March, the team would break camp and sail for Los Angeles for a couple of weeks of exhibition games in California. Then the Cubs would slowly work their way across the Southwest, playing a game each day in towns along the way.

Today at the site, where a ball field still sits, there are three plaques. The top plaque once sat on the tower of Wrigley Field in Los Angeles and was dedicated at that stadium's opening in 1926 by Judge Kenesaw Mountain Landis. It reads: "This tower was erected by Wm. Wrigley, Jr. in honor of the baseball players who gave or risked their lives

The plaque marks the Cubs' Catalina past.

in the defense of their country in the great World War. Jan. 15, 1926." The middle plaque was placed by the Avalon Men's Softball League in dedication of Wrigley and the plaque on the bottom reads as follows: "Los Angeles was the home of the Los Angeles Angels, Pacific Coast League AAA ball club. William Wrigley, Jr. bought the Angels in 1921. Ownership was transferred to the Santa Catalina Island Company in 1932. From 1941 to 1957 the club was owned by the Chicago National League ball club, the Chicago Cubs. For 26 years between 1921 and 1951, the Chicago Cubs held their annual spring training at this field in Catalina."

Lenny Dykstra's Carwash
City: Simi Valley
Location: 1144 Los Angeles Avenue
805-581-9300

Former Phillies and Mets star Lenny Dykstra has been "cleaning up" out here in the years since retiring from baseball in 1996 with a chain of successful car washes. (There's a second location in Corona at 465 North McKinley Street and a third location opening shortly.) "Nails" has made sure that his customers have lots to look at as their vehicles are scrubbed, installing an impressive showcase with lots of memorabilia from all sports.

Billy Hebert Field
City: Stockton

Billy Hebert Field is a stadium that's primarily used for baseball and was the home field of the Stockton Ports until the team moved to Banner Island Ballpark in 2005. The stadium is still used for high school baseball playoffs. It has a capacity of 6,000 people and opened up back in 1953. The field is named for William Herbert, the first resident of Stockton to die during World War II. Interestingly, Babe Ruth hit what is considered to be the longest home run at this park. Today there is a small plaque across the street to commemorate where the ball landed.

Historic Recreation Park
City: Visalia
Location: 440 North Giddings Street
559-625-0480

Recreation Park has been the home of professional baseball in Visalia since 1946. It is part of a city park named Recreation Park that includes a skate park, basketball courts and picnic areas. (The stadium itself does not have a name.) An all-wood structure stood on the current site before the existing stadium was built in 1967. The concrete exterior of the main grandstand covers soil removed from the trench used to build Highway 198 through central Visalia. With a capacity of 1,647, the stadium remains the second smallest in Minor League Baseball. The front row of seats behind the backstop is just 28 feet from home plate, providing perhaps the closest view of game action in all of professional baseball. Dozens of major-league All-Stars like Barry Zito, Mark McGwire, Ken Griffey Jr., Don Drysdale, and Kirby Puckett have played at the stadium through the first 50 seasons of professional baseball in Visalia. The park is currently the home of the Visalia Oaks, the Class A affiliate of the Colorado Rockies.

Keep Your Eyes Peeled for . . .

★ **Stengel Field**
Verdugo Park across the street from Glendale Community College
Glendale
This field, named for the "Old Professor" (and longtime Glendale resident) Casey Stengel serves as the home of the Crescenta Valley High School's Falcons.

★ **Ted Williams Parkway**
Poway
In 1992, a section of State Route 56 in North San Diego County was rechristened the Ted Williams Parkway in honor of its local baseball hero.

★ **Plaque at Dodger Stadium**
1000 Elysian Park Avenue
Los Angeles
213-224-1400
It remains one of the crown jewels in professional sports and a landmark. Opened in 1962, the stadium had a plaque unveiled when it opened and the plaque can be found on the upper level, just inside the gate near the gift shop.

★ **Fiscalini Field**
1103 East Highland Avenue
San Bernardino
The Pittsburgh Pirates spent spring training here back in the 1940s.

★ **Brookside Park**
Pasadena
The White Sox spent spring training here in the 1930s–'40s and it's
also now the location of the 4,500-seat Jackie Robinson Stadium.

★ **Johnny Berardino's Star on the Hollywood Walk of Fame**
Berardino started in the major leagues with the St. Louis Browns
in 1939 and went on to play for the Pirates and Indians (he was on
the 1948 World Champion Indians team). But he is probably best
known as *General Hospital's* Dr. Steve Hardy, a role he played for
33 years until his death in 1996.

Hall of Famers Buried in California

Harry Hooper

Arky Vaughan

Harry Hooper
Aptos Cemetery
7600 Soquel Drive
Aptos

Joseph "Arky" Vaughan
Eagleville Cemetery
West side of Main Street, north of
town
Eagleville

**LOS ANGELES METROPOLITAN
AREA**

Casey Stengel
Forest Lawn Cemetery
1712 South Glendale Avenue
Glendale
800-204-3131

Bobby Wallace and Sam Crawford
Inglewood Park Cemetery
3803 West Manchester Boulevard
Inglewood
310-412-6500

Leo Durocher
Forest Lawn Cemetery
Hollywood Hills
6300 Forest Lawn Drive
Los Angeles
323-254-7251

Hank Greenberg
Hillside Memorial Park & Mortuary
6001 West Centinela Avenue
Los Angeles
310-641-0707

Hank Greenberg

Frank Chance
Rosedale Cemetery
1831 West Washington Boulevard
Los Angeles
323-734-3155

Chick Hafey
Holy Cross Cemetery
2121 Spring Street
St. Helena
707-963-1703

Chick Hafey

Bid McPhee
Cypress View Mausoleum
3953 Imperial Avenue
San Diego
619-263-3151

SAN FRANCISCO-OAKLAND
METROPOLITAN AREA

George Kelly

George Kelly and Joe DiMaggio
Holy Cross Cemetery
1500 Old Mission Road
Colma
650-756-2060

Tony Lazzeri
Sunset View Cemetery
101 Colusa Avenue
El Cerrito
510-526-6212

Tony Lazzeri

Ernie Lombardi
Mountain View Cemetery
5000 Piedmont
Oakland
510-658-2588

Vernon "Lefty" Gomez
Mount Tamalpais Cemetery
2500 5th Avenue
San Rafael
415-459-2500

Eddie Mathews
Santa Barbara Cemetery
901 Channel Drive
Santa Barbara
805-969-3231

Ernie Lombardi

Lefty Gomez

Colorado

Coors Field is one of baseball's most scenic ballparks.

Coors Field
City: Denver
Location: 2001 Blake Street
(at 20th Street)
800-388-ROCK

As we all know, balls just seem to travel a little further here 5,280 feet above sea level. Here at the gorgeous home of the Colorado Rockies, just so you know where you are, the upper deck's 20th row is painted purple, signifying exactly one mile above sea level. (The rest of the seats at the park are green.)

Colorado Sports Hall of Fame

City: Denver
Location: INVESCO Field at Mile High
303-839-8735

The Colorado Sports Hall of Fame museum (presented by Coors Brewing Company) is located on the west side of INVESCO Field. Inductees to the Colorado Sports Hall of Fame are chosen by an independent selection committee composed of media representatives from throughout the state of Colorado. Baseball players and coaches who have been inducted since 1960 include Goose Gossage, Bill Fanning, L.C. Butler and Robert "Bus" Campbell, among others with ties to the Colorado area. Also, tours of INVESCO Field are offered through the museum, and part of the tour includes a view of the former site of Mile High Stadium (now the INVESCO Field parking lot). Mile High Stadium, built in 1948, was originally home to the Bears, Denver's minor-league baseball team. When the American Football League was launched in 1960, it began to serve a second sports team, the Denver Broncos, and continued as a baseball and football venue for almost 40 years. In 1985, a then-minor-league affiliate of the Cincinnati Reds arrived in Denver and finally, in 1993, the Colorado Rockies became Denver's first Major League Baseball team, playing their games at Mile High Stadium. The team moved into their brand new home, Coors Field, in 1995 and Mile High was demolished after the 2001 football season.

B's Ballpark Museum

City: Englewood
Location: 8611 East Otero Place
720-351-0665

It's located in the Denver suburb of Englewood, a small baseball paradise that's the result of Bruce Hellerstein's lifelong love of baseball parks. From the moment you enter and see the main stairway, lined with autographed classic ballpark lithographs, you'll know you've found ballpark heaven. As Bruce's sign on the wall says, it's the "sole place on earth where all the ballparks come together to capture the innocence of our national pastime."

In the "Paradise Park" room you'll see 18 unique wooden seats from America's all-time classic ballparks. The Polo Grounds, Yankee Stadium, Griffith Stadium—they're all here. There's a rare piece of Yankee Stadium's original copper façade, a home plate actually used in Fenway Park, bricks from now-demolished parks and more ballpark relics.

One of the museum's showpieces is a faithful re-creation of the grand entry rotunda of Brooklyn's Ebbets Field (which incorporates two actual lighting fixtures pulled from the original rotunda!). There's also a piece of original brick from Ebbets and a replica of the rotunda's tile floor to complete the reproduction.

Books, photos, research files, statues, and sculptures, even an actual on-deck circle from Tiger Stadium—it's a phenomenal place crafted by someone with a true love of ballparks.

Note that the exhibits are open to the public from 9:00 until 5:00 on Saturdays and 9:00 until 1:00 on Sundays. During other times, call for an appointment. (There is a nominal admission charge.)

Idaho

McDermott Field
City: Idaho Falls
Location: Elva Street at Blaine Avenue in Highland Park
208-522-8363

Idaho Falls has the longest continuous membership in the Pioneer League, going back to 1940, the year after its formation. Historic McDermott Field, opened in 1940 as Highland Park, has seen all of the action over the years. Most of the main grandstand was rebuilt in 1976 after young arsonists set fire to the park, and that's when the name changed, too (after E.F. McDermott, a local newspaper publisher). The park still has some nostalgic charm, though, and today is home to the Idaho Falls Padres.

Harmon Killebrew Field
City: Payette
Location: Payette High School
1500 6th Avenue South
208-642-3327

Hall of Fame slugger Harmon Killebrew was born here in Payette on June 29, 1936. This is the high school that "Killer" attended and today the school's sports field is named in honor of him. (There's also a Harmon Killebrew display inside the school.) Throughout the course of his career, Killebrew won six American League home run titles and ended his career with a total of 573 round trippers. He played with the Washington Senators and Minnesota Twins from 1954 through 1975, and hit over 40 home runs on eight occasions and 30-or-more 10 times while driving in 100-plus runs nine times. Harmon Killebrew was inducted into the Baseball Hall of Fame in 1984.

Walter Johnson Memorial Park
City: Weiser
Location: Corner of Hanthorn and
East 3rd Street

This small town played a big part in
the career of Walter Johnson, as it is
where he was first signed to play Major
League Baseball. Johnson, who
was born in Humboldt, Kansas, in
1887 and moved to California with his
family soon after birth, found himself
in Idaho in 1907. He was spending his
time pitching in a semipro league and

Walter Johnson Memorial Park
commemorates the pitching great.

digging holes for the Weiser Idaho Telephone Company when the Washington Senators signed him. Washington manager Joe Cantillon, who was already interested in a local outfielder named Clyde Milan, sent an injured catcher to Idaho to scout the pair of players. Both were signed; Johnson for a $100 bonus, train fare, and a salary of $350 a month. In addition to this baseball field named in honor of Johnson, another local landmark is the train station where The Big Train bid farewell to his Weiser teammates as he set off on his Hall of Fame career.

Walter Johnson Display
City: Weiser
Location: Snake River Heritage Center
2295 Paddock Avenue
208-549-0205

You'll find a Walter Johnson display at this small museum, including photos, artifacts and even one of Walter Johnson's uniforms.

Montana

Cobb Field
City: Billings
Location: 901 North 27th Street
406-252-1241

Cobb Field is not named for Ty Cobb, as one might assume. Rather, it's named in tribute of Robert Cobb, who back in the 1940s was owner of the

Pacific Coast League's Hollywood Stars. It was due to Cobb's successful efforts that organized professional baseball made it to Billings in the first place, which is why the field bears his name. Although he played a big role in the success of the PCL on the West Coast, Cobb is perhaps best remembered as the founder and owner of the legendary Brown Derby restaurant in Hollywood. In fact, the Cobb salad was named for him (a creation that came about as a result of Cobb asking that a salad be thrown together for him with whatever scraps were left lying around in the kitchen.) Home to minor-league baseball since 1948, Cobb Field hosts the Mustangs in the Rookie-Advanced Pioneer League, and they are affiliated with the Cincinnati Reds.

Denton Field
City: Miles City
Location: Main Street

Another WPA ballpark, Denton Field was built back in 1940 to the specifications of professional Minor League Baseball. Today, the ballpark is still up to code for the Pioneer League.

Nevada

Las Vegas Club
City: Las Vegas
Location: 18 East Fremont Street
702-385-1664

It started back in 1962, when this club's owner, the recently deceased "Marvelous" Mel Exber, asked Dodgers base-stealing sensation Maury Wills for an autograph just before a game in L.A. Wills signed for the Brooklynite and baseball lover, and the rest is history. After the '62 season, when Wills and his teammates, including Duke Snider, Sandy Koufax, Don Drysdale, and other rolled into Vegas for some extended R & R, Exber brought them to his club, which ended up becoming a memora-

The Las Vegas Club is filled with memorabilia from Dodgers greats such as Duke Snider.

bilia shrine for Dodgers fans. With its Ebbets Field façade, free sports museum and "Dugout Restaurant," the Las Vegas Club's classic sports theme remains unique in a town where pyramids, palaces and volcanoes dominate the strip.

The Nevada Griffons
City: West Highland
Location: Lyons Field
Jason Meisenheimer at 417-667-8308

The Nevada Griffons, a team of collegiate athletes, play here at the Lyons Stadium during June and July. In the 15 years that the Griffons have played in Nevada, many have gone on to play professional baseball. Games start at 7:00 PM.

Oregon

Historic Civic Stadium
City: Eugene
Location: 20th and Williamette

Built in 1938, Civic Stadium was originally designed as both a football and baseball facility. It was part of a Works Progress Administration project that was to develop much of the surrounding area as well, and today, the Depression-era wooden stadium is one of the oldest in the minors. Originally home to semipro baseball, in 1969 the Pacific Coast League Emeralds moved in and have been here ever since. (From 1950 to 1968, professional baseball was played at nearby Bethel Park, which has been torn down). Over the years, Civic Stadium has been used for everything from high school football and soccer to a rodeo in the mid-1980s. The girls' Little League Softball World Series is also held here each August.

Oregon Sports Hall of Fame
City: Portland
Location: 21 SW Salmon
503-227-7466

Since 1980, the Oregon Sports Hall of Fame has inducted the best of Oregon athletes, teams, and coaches, as well as those who have made a special, lifetime contribution to sports. The inductees at the Oregon Sports Hall of Fame currently include 27 baseball players. Johnny Pesky, Bobby Doerr,

Artie Wilson, Dale Murphy, Wally Bachman, Mickey Lolich and Rick Wise are but a few of them. The highlights of the baseball exhibit here include a "Dugout Display" and a virtual demonstration that lets you catch a simulated 90-mile-per-hour baseball. Players are inducted by members of the public (anyone can join for $25 a year to become a voting member) and artifacts include lots of Portland Beavers memorabilia and even a pair of seats from long-gone Vaughn Street Ballpark.

Sckavone Stadium

City: Portland
Location: SE McLoughlin
and Spokane (located in
Westmoreland Park)
503-823-PLAY

Built in 1940, this neighborhood stadium has been the
launching ground for several
professional careers and local
championship teams. Named
for Nick Sckavone, the man
who spearheaded the efforts
to get the park built in the first
place, it was rebuilt in 1992.

Sckavone Stadium in Portland is a local landmark whose history dates back to 1940.

PGE Park

City: Portland
Location: 1844 SW Morrison
503-553-5400

Today the home of the Pacific Coast League AAA Portland Beavers, PGE Park has a rich and storied history that dates back to 1926. Originally named Multnomah Stadium, on October 9, 1926, the stadium hosted its first event as the University of Washington's football team beat the University of Oregon, 23–9. Baseball arrived in 1956 when the Portland Beavers left the notori-ously fire-prone Vaughn Street Ballpark and moved into Multnomah. In 1967, Multnomah Stadium was purchased by the City of Portland and renamed Civic Stadium. In the '60s and '70s, teams like the Portland Beavers and the Portland Timbers played here and more recently, the stadium has hosted a wide array of speakers, performers and international sporting events, from the Billy Graham Crusade to the women's World Cup soccer events of 1998 and 1999. Other sports figures and entertainers who have appeared at the stadium over the years include Joe DiMaggio, Pete Rose, Norm Van Brocklin, Elvis Presley, Bob Hope, David Bowie, Tom Petty and Bob Dylan. (Pelé even played his last game here.) After a $38.5 million overhaul completed in April of 2001, Portland's PGE Park is now poised to attract a major league franchise to Portland, but PGE has been careful to maintain the historic charm of the park that dates back more than 75 years.

Vaughn Street Ballpark

City: Portland
Location: 2409 NW Vaughn Street

Built in 1901, Vaughn Street Ballpark (also called Lucky Beavers Stadium) was home to the Portland Beavers of the Pacific Coast League until 1955. They won four pennants between 1910 and 1914, and this is also where future Hall of Famer, Red Sox second baseman Bobby Doerr was signed. The rickety wooden park caught fire many times during its existence, and it was torn down a year after the Beavers moved to Multnomah Stadium in 1955. Today, a marker at the site (now occupied by industrial buildings) identifies that a stadium once stood there.

Utah

Franklin Covey Field

City: Salt Lake City
Location: 77 West 1300 South
801-485-3800

Opened in 1994, this stadium boasts something else besides top-notch Pacific Coast League baseball. What distinguishes Franklin Covey Field are the exquisite panoramic views of the jaw-dropping Wasatch Mountains out beyond the outfield wall. The stadium was specifically designed to reflect the natural beauty of the mountain range, and the architects at HOK hit this one out of the park. The Salt Lake Stingers (AAA affiliate of the Anaheim Angels) play here and they were the 2002 American Conference Champs. (For the park's first seven years, they were called the Salt Lake Buzz.) In the stadium's first year open, the Buzz set an all-time Pacific Coast League attendance record with more than 714,000. Salt Lake's Marty Cordova ate up the league that year with a .358 average and next season was the American League Rookie of the Year. Affordable, comfortable and aesthetically unique, this is a wonderful place to enjoy a ball game.

Washington

Sick's Stadium

City: Seattle
Location: Lowe's of Rainier
2700 Rainier Avenue South
206-760-0832

Sick's Stadium, opened in 1938, was the second ballpark built on this site. Before that, Dugdale Park had been built here in 1913 and was home to the Pacific Coast League Seattle Indians. However, on July 4, 1932, Dugdale completely burned down after a fireworks celebration. Sick's, a new steel-and-concrete structure, opened on June 15, 1938. Named for Rainiers team owner Emil Sick, the 12,000-seat park hosted Minor League Baseball until the early 1960s. Then, in 1967, a major-league franchise, the Seattle Pilots, was awarded to Seattle. To

Sick's Stadium was the home of the short-lived Seattle Pilots.

accommodate the Pilots, Sick's capacity was increased to 25,000. The Pilots played here for just one season and after 1969 the team was bought by Bud Selig and moved to Milwaukee, where they became the "Brewers." After the Pilots left, Sick's Stadium was used as a minor-league ballpark until 1976 and then it sat empty until 1979, at which point it was demolished. (By that time, the Mariners had been created and played at the Kingdome. The Kingdome was torn down in 2000 and was located where the current Seattle Seahawks stadium is at 201 South King Street.) At the former site of Sick's Stadium today is a Lowe's Home Improvement Warehouse. There is a glass display case inside the store that shows some memorabilia from the Rainiers and Pilots, and just outside the front door is a bronze home plate with a metal statue of a player holding a bat.

The inscription reads: "BATTER UP! You are standing on the former site of Sicks' Seattle Stadium, home of the Seattle Rainiers and Seattle Pilots. If the year were 1942, you'd be in perfect position to knock one out of the park."

Historic Cheney Stadium

City: Tacoma
Location: 2502 South Tyler
(Intersection of Tyler and 19th Street in Tacoma just off of Highway 16)
253-752-7707

Built in 1960, Cheney Stadium is now the oldest park in the Pacific Coast League. Home to the Mariners' AAA Tacoma Rainiers, Cheney Stadium has seen many All-Star major-leaguers, from Willie McCovey to A-Rod to Mark McGwire. But what makes the park really special is that it is partially made up of old pieces of Seals Stadium, from San Francisco. Look closely if you visit, because Cheney Stadium's light standards and blue reserved bleacher seats were once actually part of the famed Bay Area stadium. (They were moved up here once Seals was dismantled.) The origin of Cheney Stadium goes back to 1957, when local businessmen Ben Cheney (a statue of whom now sits in a box seat here at the ballpark) and Clay Huntington began working to bring Pacific Coast League baseball to Tacoma. In the fall of 1959, the San Francisco Giants met with Tacoma officials

Cheney Stadium's namesake, Ben Cheney, sits constant watch in the stadium.

to discuss moving their Triple-A Phoenix club to Tacoma. The Giants committed to the move, provided that Tacoma would construct a stadium in time for April 1960. The deal went through and in less than four months, the stadium was built, including the parts from Seals Stadium in San Francisco. The first scheduled game was rained out on April 14, 1960. When the game was rescheduled as part of a day/night doubleheader on April 16, the Tacoma Giants lost the inaugural Cheney Stadium game 7-2 to the Portland Beavers. Tacoma took the nightcap by a score of 11-0. The winning pitcher of Game 2 was future Hall of Famer Juan Marichal.

Hall of Famers Buried in Washington

Amos Rusie
Acacia Cemetery
14951 Bothell Way NE
Seattle
206-362-5525

Earl Averill
Grand Army of the Republic
Cemetery
8601 Riverview Road
Snohomish
360-568-4090

Amos Rusie had 246 career wins and 1,950 strikeouts.

Wyoming

Burial Site of Benjamin Franklin Hunt
City: Greybull
Location: Hillside Cemetery

Ben Hunt began his Major League Baseball career in 1910 with the Boston Red Sox after several years in the minors. The 22-year-old played for two seasons on two different teams and ended his big league playing career in 1913. He died in 1927.

ROADSIDE BASEBALL

OUTSIDE THE LINES

Alaska

The Midnight Sun Game
City: Fairbanks
Location: Growden Memorial Park
Located near the intersection of Wilbur and Airport Road

> "What began nearly 100 years ago on a bet between two lo-
> cal bars has evolved into one of baseball's unique natural
> events. The Midnight Sun Game, played in Fairbanks on
> the summer solstice every year since 1906, is played in the
> middle of the night with only natural light."
> —Baseball America's 12 'Must-See' Events

Growden Park is home to the Fairbanks Alaska Goldpanners, one
of six teams in the Alaska Baseball League, a premier wooden-bat collegiate
summer league. The Goldpanners have been the starting point for many
major-leaguers, including Barry Bonds, Jason Giambi, Dave Winfield, Graig
Nettles and dozens of others since forming in 1960. That same year, the
Goldpanners adopted the tradition of one of baseball's most unique events:
"The Midnight Sun Game." A Fairbanks landmark event since 1906, the
annual game takes place in June on the longest day of the year (June 21st),
where this area experiences almost a full 24 hours of daylight. It starts at

10:30 PM and often lasts until 2:00 AM or so. Since Fairbanks is only 160 miles south of the Arctic Circle, the sun is just beginning to set in the north as the game gets under way. At the conclusion of the game, the sun is beginning to rise again in the north; one of the world's rarest natural phenomenons. (The light fades towards the middle of the game, but usually returns fully by the end of the game.) Never once has artificial lighting been used for this unique event, and never has the game been postponed or delayed because of darkness. Also, as tradition dictates, the game is stopped at midnight for the singing of the Alaska Flag Song.

Through 1962, the Goldpanners played the North of the Range All-Stars in the Midnight Sun Game, but, since 1963, they've been matched up against a different opponent, usually a team from out of state. (Before the Goldpanners took over the game, various local and military teams played against each other.) The game is traditionally a celebration of the summer solstice and is treated as a holiday in Fairbanks, with shops and businesses closing early.

About Growden Park: Originally named Memorial Park, Growden was renamed in 1964 in honor of James Growden, who, along with his two sons, was killed in a tidal wave created by the Good Friday Earthquake of 1964. Growden had been heavily involved in Fairbanks youth activities for years. In 1964, it became the first outdoor lighted facility in Alaska, and though the seating capacity is about 3,500, in 1967, more than 5,000 fans jammed the park for the Midnight Sun Game, when the Goldpanners played Kumagai-Gumi of Japan.

Interestingly, there are box seats and grandstand benches from old Sick's Stadium in Seattle, which was home to the old Seattle Rainiers minor-league team and the 1969 Seattle Pilots major-league team.

Hawaii

The Babe Ruth Banyan Tree
City: Hilo
Location: In front of the Hilo Hawaiian Hotel
71 Banyan Drive
702-438-1166

Before Babe Ruth led a team of all-stars to Japan in 1934, he brought his wife and daughter to Hawaii in 1933. While here on the Big Island, he did what you might expect: played in two exhibition baseball games in Honolulu, played some golf, ate at all the best places and soaked up the local culture. But Babe (just after hitting two homers in one of the games) also ceremoniously planted a banyan tree on Banyan Drive, an idyllic piece of land facing beautiful Hilo Bay. Many celebrities did this while visitng. Several weeks before, Cecil B. DeMille (in Hilo to shoot the film *Four Frightened People*) had planted a banyan tree. Also, between the years of 1933 and 1972, FDR, Amelia Earhart, Richard Nixon and many other notables took part in tree planting along Banyan Drive. The Babe's tree has continued to thrive over the years in front of this popular hotel. It is surrounded by a swatch of red ginger and a plaque with "Babe Ruth" on it.

Honolulu Stadium

City: Honolulu
Location: Corners of King and Isenberg

The old Honolulu Stadium where Ruth played his exhibition games was torn down in 1976. Opened in 1926, the legendary stadium also hosted everything from Elvis Presley to Jesse Owens to dozens of other sports and entertainment events. On the two-acre site today is Stadium Park.

Hall of Famers Buried in Hawaii

Alexander Cartwright
Oahu Cemetery
2162 Nuuana Avenue
Honolulu
808-538-1538

Alexander Cartwright

Canada

The First Baseball Game in North America
City: Beachville, Ontario
Location: On King Street west of Zorraline behind Baptist Church, in the subdivided lots.

The first recorded ball game in North America was played in Beachville on June 4, 1838. Little did the men who gathered to play in this pasture know that they were making such history. (The game occurred one year prior to the famous Cooperstown game.) This claim of "first" is based upon a letter from Dr. Adam E. Ford's to *Sporting Life* magazine in which he detailed the rules of the game and recalled the names of various players. The letter, published May 5, 1886, was entitled "A Game of Long-ago Which Closely Resembled Our Present National Game." Ford had grown up in Beachville, and what sets his letter apart from other remembrances of baseball games was the amount of detail he provided on how the game was played, the players, the rules, the diagrams—clearly something organized had happened in this small Canadian town almost 50 years earlier. Ford's original letter is in the Hall of Fame in Cooperstown, New York, but officials there have never formally recognized the validity of his claim for Beachville. However, the town prides itself in the fact with signs at either end of town commemorating that first game.

Beachville District Museum
City: Beachville, Ontario
Location: 584371 Beachville Road
519-423-6497

A diorama of the historic game played here in Beachville is on view at this small museum, as is a plaque placed here in honor of the game.

The Oldest Active Baseball Facility in North America
City: London, Ontario
Location: Labatt Memorial Park
Riverside Drive and Wilson Avenue

This Canadian ball field is the world's oldest site continually in use for baseball. It opened in 1876 as Tecumseh Park, and after the original grandstand was destroyed by flood in 1937, the Labatt family (Labatt Beer) stepped in to refurbish the park, build new grandstands, and donate it to their home city.

It was most recently home to the
London Werewolves of the Frontier
League, who left in 2001, and today
it's home to the London Majors, a
member of the Intercounty Baseball
League in southwestern Ontario, as
well as several London-area minor-
league teams.

Labatt Memorial Park is believed to be
the oldest active baseball facility in
North America.

Delorimier Stadium

City: Montreal, Quebec
Location: De Lorimier Avenue and Ontario Street

Delorimier Stadium was home to the Montreal Royals International League
baseball team from 1928 to 1960, and from 1946 to 1953, it was home field
to the Montreal Alouettes of the Canadian Football League. Built by former
Major League Baseball manager George Stallings, Montreal lawyer and politi-
cian Athanase David, and businessman Ernest Savard, Delorimier Downs, as
it was originally called, opened in May 1928. In 1935, general manager Frank
Shaughnessy had a lighting system installed in the stadium for night games.

The stadium saw many careers start here. Gene Mauch, who later
came back to manage the Montreal Expos, played here early in his career,
along with future Hall of Fame members Sparky Anderson, Roberto Clemente and Jackie Robinson, the player who
broke pro baseball's color barrier as a
Royal in 1946.

After the Montreal Royals folded
in 1960, the stadium saw limited use. Pri-
or to the full destruction of the stadium,
the building was dismantled in bits, and
the interior was used to house makeshift
classrooms as the student population in
Quebec grew rapidly. A school now occupies the site and there is no marker.

Jackie Robinson Statue

City: Montreal, Quebec
Location: Olympic Stadium
4549 Pierre-de-Coubertin Avenue
514-8GO-EXPOS

The statue of Jackie Robinson here is in

Montreal honors Jackie Robinson
with this statue at Olympic
Stadium.

tribute to the fact that Robinson made his organized baseball debut as a member of the Montreal Royals in 1946.

Jarry Park
City: Montreal, Quebec
Location: 285 Faillon W
514-273-1234

Jarry Park was the site of the first major-league games played outside the United States when the Montreal Expos opened here on April 14, 1969. The Expos played here through the 1976 season, after which they moved into Olympic Stadium, built for the 1976 Games. The cozy park had a capacity of 28,000 and featured baseball's first bilingual public address announcements. Long home runs to right field had a good chance of landing in a public swimming pool. Jarry Park is still standing and is used regularly for social and civic events, professional tennis and other large outdoor gatherings.

Phil "Babe" Marchildon Plaque
City: Penetanguishene, Ontario
Location: Phil Marchildon Memorial Park

A plaque here honors local baseball hero Phil "Babe" Marchildon. In the 1940s, he pitched for the Philadelphia A's and the Boston Red Sox, and he was inducted into the Canadian Sports Hall of Fame in 1976. The plaque was dedicated in this park (which also bears Marchildon's name) by the Penetanguishene Sports Hall of Fame on April 26, 1997.

Canadian Baseball Hall of Fame and Museum
City: St. Marys, Ontario
Location: 386 Church Street S
519-284-1838

The original dream of a Canadian Baseball Hall of Fame and Museum began in 1983 in Toronto. From its inception, the Canadian Baseball Hall of Fame has preserved Canada's baseball heritage and helped promote the growth of baseball in Canada at every level. A decade later, business and community leaders from the small Southwestern

The Canadian Baseball Hall of Fame in St. Marys, Ontario.

Ontario town of St. Marys began a bid to establish a permanent home for the facility. On June 4, 1998, "The Stonetown" was unveiled. St. Marys is fast becoming Canada's Cooperstown, and beyond. In addition to building a new, state-of-the-art, interactive museum, the plan for the rest of the 32 acres resembles a typical spring training type of venue that presently can only be found in Florida or Arizona. This will consist of a small baseball stadium, three baseball diamonds, lodging, a conference services center, auditorium, walking trails, picnic grounds, and an amphitheater. The Stonetown will also soon become the permanent training center for Canada's Olympic Baseball Team and Canada's premier venue for camps, tournaments and championships for all ages. About 70 seats from old Exhibition Stadium are in use for watching games on the fields today, and many more will be used for the new stadium being built here. The historic building that the museum is located in was built in 1886.

Babe Ruth's First "Professional" Home Run

City: Toronto, Ontario
Location: Hanlan's Point
Take ferry from the mainland; ferry docks are located at the south end of Bay Street, on Queens Quay West.

Though he'd hit a homer in an exhibition game for Baltimore down in Fayetteville, North Carolina, Babe Ruth hit his first professional home run in a game while in Toronto. This happened shortly after he had been traded to the Boston Red Sox and they placed him on the Providence Grays of

Babe Ruth hit his first professional home run at Hanlan's Point in Toronto. The stadium was torn down in the 1930s.

the International League. Playing here, Ruth hit this, his only minor-league homer on September 5, 1914, at Toronto's old Hanlan's Point Stadium in a game against the Maple Leafs. The stadium was torn down back in the '30s but a plaque near the site commemorates Ruth's home run.

Maple Leaf Stadium

City: Toronto, Ontario
Location: Bathurst Street and Lakeshore Boulevard

Maple Leaf Stadium was erected in Toronto in 1926 by Lol Solman to serve

A vintage shot of Maple Leaf Stadium in Toronto.

his Toronto Maple Leafs baseball team of the International League. It remained the home stadium for the Leafs for 42 seasons, until they left town following the 1967 season. Before Maple Leaf Stadium existed, the team had played at Hanlan's Point Stadium (which is no longer standing but covered in this book). The opening game at Maple Leaf Stadium was held on April 29, 1926, and it saw the Leafs stage an exciting come-from-behind win over the Reading Keystones in extra innings before a rain-drenched crowd of 12,781. And it wasn't all baseball here. Back on November 8, 1926, Maple Leaf Stadium is where the first professional American football game to be played outside of the United States took place, a 28–0 victory of the New York Yankees over the Los Angeles Wildcats (both teams of the first American Football League). Lights for night games were installed here in 1934, and then in the early 1960s, Leafs owner Jack Kent Cooke tried to convince the Toronto city council that a new stadium was needed to attract a major-league team. However, his efforts failed to win the council over and after the Leafs left, the run-down stadium was considered to be a safety hazard. Demolition began within a few months and the stadium was completely demolished by 1968. Apartments shaped like the old ballpark currently occupy the site.

Nat Bailey Stadium

City: Vancouver, British Columbia
Location: 33rd and Ontario Street

Built in 1951, this is one of the oldest structures still in use by the minor leagues. Originally named Capilano Stadium after a local brewery, the park was renamed in 1978 when the Triple A Vancouver Canadians entered their inaugural season in the Pacific Coast League. The park was named for Nat Bailey, a longtime supporter of baseball in the Vancouver area and the first owner of the popular White Spot restaurant chain.

Also by Chris Epting

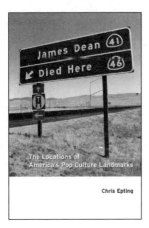

Takes you on a journey across North America to the exact locations where the most significant events in American popular culture took place. It's a road map for pop culture sites, from Patty Hearst's bank to the garage where Apple Computer was born.

This fully illustrated encyclopedic look at the most famous and infamous pop culture events includes historical information on over 600 landmarks—as well as their exact locations. An amazing portrait of the bizarre, shocking, weird and wonderful moments that have come to define American popular culture.

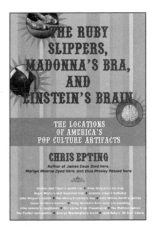

An entertaining and rollicking road map through the entire history of rock and roll! From beginnings (the site where Elvis got his first guitar), to endings (the hotel where Janis Joplin died), and everything in between. Includes sidebars on musical greats like Bob Dylan, The Beatles, The Rolling Stones, and U2.

Anyone who has ever wondered where Dorothy's ruby slippers, George Washington's teeth, or the world's largest olive are located will be thrilled to take this journey to find hundreds of the most important items from America's popular culture.

Toll Free 1.800.784.9553 • www.santamonicapress.com